EARLY HISTORY OF KAMARUPA

EARLY HISTORY OF KAMARUPA

FROM THE EARLIEST TIMES TO THE END OF THE SIXTEENTH CENTURY

K.L. BARUA

GYAN

Published by

Gyan Publishing House
5, Ansari Road
Daryaganj, New Delhi-110002
Phone: 011-47034999, 9811692060
E-mail: books@gyanbooks.com

Distribution Network
gyanbooks.com
India, USA, Canada, UK, Australia

ISBN: 978-93-7414-374-2 (PB)

First Published, 1933

2nd Impression 2025

Printed at: Gyan Press, Delhi.

EARLY HISTORY OF KAMARUPA
Author: K.L. BARUA

COPPER PLATE SEAL OF THE KAMARUPA KINGS

EARLY
HISTORY OF KĀMARUPA

FROM THE EARLIEST TIMES TO THE END OF THE SIXTEENTH CENTURY.

By

RAI K. L. BARUA BAHADUR, B.L.,

DEPUTY COMMISSIONER, ASSAM (Retired), PRESIDENT, KĀMARUPA ANUSANDHAN SAMITI, HONORARY SECRETARY, PROVINCIAL COIN COMMITTEE ASSAM, etc.

Published by the Author.

SHILLONG.

1933.

PREFACE.

This book aims at presenting, as far as possible, a connected history of the old kingdom known as Prāgjyotisha or Kāmarupa from the earliest times till the death of the Koch king Narnārāyan towards the end of the sixteenth century. It may therefore be called the history of Kāmarupa during the pre-Ahom period. The materials on which a full chronological record of this long period can be attempted are by no means ample but they are at least not less numerous than those now available for compiling a historical account of the neighbouring province of Bengal during the same early period. About 1000 years before the Christian era the greater part of lower Bengal was probably under the sea while the greater part of northern Bengal was included in Prāgjyotisha. Allusions to the, smaller kingdoms in Bengal, then above the sea, are therefore rare in the oldest Aryan records but Prāgjyotisha, which was then a powerful kingdom. is often mentioned in the epics and the Puranas, The Aryan wave extended to Kāmarupa directly from Videha and Magadha long before lower Bengal became either habitable or fit for Aryan occupation. Kāmarupa was therefore Aryanized long before central and lower Bengal. The Magadha empire was founded by Chandra Gupta in the fourth century B. C. About this time, or after, the whole of northern Bengal, to the south of the

Jalpaiguri district and west of the Trisrota, was absorbed in the Maurya empire together with the Tamralipti region in the south west. The Mourya empire of Asoka undoubtedly included northern Bengal between the Teesta (Karatoya) and the Kosi, for within this area *stupas* erected by Asoka were found by Yuan Chwang in the seventh century A. D. This area continued to be included in the Magadha empire at least till the sixth century A. D. During the rule of the Imperial Guptas this stretch was known as Pundravardhana. To the east and north of Pundravardhana Kāmarupa continued as an independant kingdom ruled over by an indigenous line of kings who traced descent from Naraka, Bhagadatta and Vajradatta who were heroes mentioned in the epics. From epigraphic records, so far brought to light, it is possible to trace an almost unbroken genealogy of these kings from about the middle of the fourth century A. D down to the twelfth century or a period of nearly nine hundred years. Very few of the old Hindu kingdoms in India can present such unique genealogical records covering such a long period. No less than twelve copper-plate inscriptions, inscribed seals and rock-inscriptions recorded by various kings of Kāmarupa during this period have been discovered and deciphered. Epigraphic records left by the famous Gupta emperor Samudra Gupta, Yasodharman, king of Malwa, who was a famous conqueror, Adityasena, who belonged to the line of "Later Guptas of Magadha", Jayadeva, a well-known king of Nepal and some of the Pāla kings and Sena kings of Bengal provide useful material for the history of Kāmarupa during this period. The Raghuvangsa of Kālidasa, the very valuable accounts of the Chinese writers, the Harsha-Charita of Bānabhatta, the Rāja-tarangini of Kahlan and the translations from Tibetan records, recently made available, also throw valuable light.

The local epigraphic records constitute, however the most important foundation on which a reliable frame-work of history can be based. These can be enumerated as follows in chronological order:-

(1) The Nidhanpur copper-plate inscription of Bhāskara-varma-Deva (*Circa* 610 A.D.) discovered and deciphered by Pandit Padmanath Bhattacharya Vidyavinod and published in Epigraphia Indica, Vols XII and XIX. One plate of this inscription is still missing.

(2) The Nalanda clay-seal of Bhāskaravarman, (*circa* 643 A. D.) deciphered by Mr. K. N. Dikshit and published in the Journal of the Bihar and Orissa Research Society, Vol. VI (1920).

(3) The Hāyungthal copper-plate inscription of Harjara-varma-Deva (*circa* 825 A. D.) discovered and deciphered by Pandit Padmanath Bhattacharya Vidyavinod and published by him in his "Kāmarupa Śāsanāvali". Only the middle plate of this inscription has been discovered.

(4) The rock-inscription of Harjara-varma-Deva near Tezpur (dated 510 Gupta era equivalent to 829 A. D.) deciphered by M. M. Pandit Haraprasad Śāstri and published in the Journal of the Bihar and Orissa Research Society, December 1917.

(5) The Tezpur copper-plate inscription of Vana-

māla-Varma-Deva (*circa* 854 A. D.) deciphered by Pandit Kamalakanta and published in the Journal of the Asiatic Society of Bengal Vol. IX, 1840.

(6) The Nowgong copper-plate inscription of Balavarma-Deva III (*circa* 883 A. D.) originally deciphered by the late M. M. Pandit Dhireswara Bhattacharya Kaviratna and published in the 'Assam". It was subsequently re-deciphered by Dr. Hoernle and published in the Journal of the Asiatic Society of Bengal (No. 1 of 1897).

(7) The Bargaon copper-plate inscription of Ratnapāla-varma-Deva (*circa* 1025 A. D.) deciphered by Dr. Hoernle and published in the Journal of the Asiatic Society of Bengal (Part I of 1898).

(8) The Sualkuchi copper-plate inscription of Ratnapāla-varma-Deva (*circa* 1026 A. D.) deciphered by Dr. Hoernle and published in the Journal of the Asiatic Society of Bengal, (part I of 1898).

(9) The Gauhati copper-plate inscription of Indrapāla-varma-Deva (*circa* 1038 A. D.) deciphered by Dr. Hoernle and published in the Journal of the Asiatic Society of Bengal (part I of 1897).

(10) The Guakuchi copper-plate inscription of Indrapāla-varma-Deva (*circa* 1051 A. D.) deciphered by Pandit Padmanath Bhattacharya Vidyavinod and published by him in his "Kāmarupa Śāsanavali".

(11) The first copper-plate inscription of Dharmapāla-varma-Deva (*circa* 1092 A. D.) collected by the late Hem Chandra Gosain, deciphered by

Pandit Padmanath Bhattacharya Vidyavinod and published in his "Kāmarupa Śāsanavali".

(12) The second or *Puspabhadrā* copper-plate inscription of Dharmapāla-varma-Deva (*circa* 1110 A. D.) deciphered by the late Hem Chandra Gossain and published by Pandit Vidyavinod in his "Kāmarupa Śāsanavali".

(13) The rock-inscription in North Gauhati dated 1127 Saka equivalent to 1205-06 A. D. relating to the defeat of Mahammad-i-Bukhityar in Kāmarupa. Col. Gurdon read a paper on this inscription in 1918. A photograph of this inscription also appears in Pandit Vidyavinod's "Kāmarupa Śāsanavali". This inscription was referred to by me in my paper on the "Earlier Muhammadan invasions of Kāmarupa" read in the anniversary meeting of the Kāmarupa Anusandhan Samiti during 1931.

General Jenkins collected and forwarded to the Asiatic Society of Bengal the inscription of Vanamāla and another said to have been recorded by Dharmapāla in the thirtysixth year of his reign. The Society published the text of the Vanamāla inscription but the one said to have been recorded by Dharmapāla was not published at all and it is not traceable now. Probably it was one of the Dharmapāla inscriptions now published by Pandit Vidyavinod. All the inscriptions deciphered by Dr. Hoernle were sent to him by Sir Edward Gait who was then Secretary to the Chief Commissioner of Assam and was collecting materials for his "History of Assam" which was actually published after he left Assam. Pandit Padmanath Bhattacharya Vidyavinod recovered the oldest and the most valuable of all the copper-plate inscriptions, viz, that of Bhāskaravarman as well as the stray-plate of Harjaravarman. He has also published for the first time the text of the Guakuchi grant of Indrapāla and of both the Dharmapāla grants. The perseverence with which he searched for and recovered nearly all the lost plates of Bhāskaravarman's grant is indeed beyond all praise. It was the late Pandit Hem Chandra Gossain who collected both the Dharmapāla inscriptions and deciphered one of them. For a decipherment of the rock-inscription of Harjaravarman, through the late Pandit Haraprasad Śāstri, we are indebted to the efforts of Col. P. R. Gurdon who also, for the first time published the translation of the text of the North-Gauhati (Kanai borosi) rock-inscription. The find of so many valuable epigraphic records, soon after the publication of the first edition of Gait's History of Assam, was in no small measure due to the interest in historical research created by the foundation of the Kāmarupa Anusandhan Samiti through the efforts mainly of the late Mahamahopadhyaya Pandit Dhireswara Kaviratna, Pandit Vidyavinod and Rai Bahadur Kali Charan Sen, all backed by the strong support of Col. Gurdon who was instrumental in securing for the Samiti official recognition and financial assistance.

While, therefore, there exist quite a good number of epigraphic records which enable us to piece together an almost uninterrupted chronicle of the Kāmarupa kings from the fourth down to the twelfth century A.D. it is rather surprising that we have not been able to find a single coin minted by any of the numerous kings prior to Narnārāyan, the Koch king ot the sixteenth century. It is not at all likely that the Kāmarupa kings did not strike coins. We have it on the authority of the Silimpur inscription deciphered by Mr. R. G. Basak that about the twelfth century the Kāmarupa king Jayapāla, who was probably the son of Dharmapāla, offered to make a *tulapurusha* gift of gold, including 900 gold coins, to a Brahman named Prahāsa. This proves that gold coins were actually minted by these kings and, as evidenced by the Nalanda seal of Bhāskaravarman, the art of impressing seals on clay or molten metal was known as early as the seventh century. Coins of the Kāmarupa kings, previous to the Koch rajas, buried as treasure, cannot be looked for in the surface. They must lie buried deep in the earth overlaid by layers of silt deposited, during centuries, by the innundations of the Brahmaputra. Only deep excavations at probable sites are likely to reveal such coins and other antiquities. Unfortunately no such exploration has yet been undertaken in Assam. Further the old Hindu kings of Kāmarupa were supplanted by the Koch kings and then by the Ahom kings who minted coins of their own. The old coins of the Kāmarupa kings, which were no longer used as coins, must have therefore been largely melted into bullion or used in ornaments. This is another reason why such coins are not now met with. The absence of numismatic evidence to corroborate the history of the early period can therefore be explained.

Although epigraphic records that have come down to us are by no means few in number, other memorials, besides coins, such as palaces and temples, apart from temple images and ruins scattered here and there, belonging to the pre-Ahom period, are almost non-existent. Sir Edward Gait, in his History of Assam, has assigned good reasons for the small number of the monuments of ancient Kāmarupa. He writes :–

"Some of the legends which have been mentioned suggest that in the distant past the inhabitants of the country which we now call Assam attained considerable power and a fair degree of civilisation; and this view is confirmed by the narrative of the Chinese pilgrim Hiuen Tsiang and by the copper-plate inscriptions which will be referred to in the next chapter. This being so, the question will doubtless be asked why so few memorials of their time have come down to us. The reason is that nature has vied with man in destroying them. The Brahmaputra valley is an alluvial country, and the impetuous, snow-fed rivers which debouch from the Himalayas find so little resistance in its friable soil that they are constantly carving out new channels and cutting away their banks; consequently no buildings erected in their neighbourhood can be expected to remain for more than a limited time, except at a few points like Gauhati, where rock pierces through the alluvium.

Though occurring at distant intervals, violent earthquakes are, in Assam, quite as great a cause of destruction as fluvial action; there are few masonry structures which could resist a shock like that of 1897, which not only laid in ruins the towns of Shillong, Gauhati and Sylhet, but also overthrew many of the monoliths, which are so marked a feature of the Khasi and Jaintia Hills, and broke down most of the piers of the Sil Sāko, an ancient stone bridge, not far from Hājo, which marks the bed of a river that has long since left it and taken another course. A less sudden, but almost equally potent, cause of damage is found in the luxuriant vegetation of the country. The *pipal* (ficus religiosa) in particular is a great enemy of masonry buidings; and once a seed of this tree has germinated in the interstices of such a building, its downfall is only a question of time. Owing to this cause, many neve of the more recent Ahom palaces and temples are already in a state of decay.

Of the damage done by man, it is necessary only to mention the way in which religious zeal led the early Musalman invaders to break down Hindu temples, and the widespread havoc wrought by the Burmese in a spirit of wanton mischief.

The ruins which still survive represent only an inconsiderable fragment of the buildings that were once in existence, but more will doubtless come to light when the jungle which now covers so vast an area in Assam comes to be removed to make way for the extension of cultivation".

I am afraid Sir Edwrad Gait has not fully enumerated the instances of damage done by man even within living memory. While a school-boy, I noticed the digging up of the foundations of an old fortification in the eastern part of Gauhati town and the breaking of the carved and chiselled stones for road-metal. Though a boy I then wondered why such nicely carved stones dug out were ruthlessly broken into fragments. I now realize that the remains of the fortification then exposed probably belonged to the citadel named "Sri Durjaya" or the "impregnable" by Ratnapāla in the eleventh century A. D. No one in authority then intervened to stop the destruction. Again when the great earthquake of 1897 destroyed the Silsāko "an ancient stone bridge" as recorded by Sir Edward Gait himself, no one in authority then raised his little finger to prevent the people of Barpeta and other places from taking away the stones of the piers and the platform, though, at that time, the Deputy Commissioner of Kamrup was Col. Gurdon, an officer having keen interest in historical research and preservation of ancient monuments and the Chief Secretary to the Government of Assam was Sir Edward Gait himself, the author of the History of Assam. Mr. N. K. Bhattasali in his recent paper on Mahammad Bukhtiyar's invasion referring to this stone bridge, makes the following observation:-

"It is very much to be regretted that the Government of Assam did not attempt to restore this priceless monument of antiquity soon after it was shaken by the earthquake. Attempts should even now be made to see if the monument can be restored and the Assam Council should vote the expenditure".

In any civilized country this would undoubtedly be done but in Assam it has not yet been possible to spend even ten thousand rupees to erect a house to stock the ancient relics already collected by the Kāmarupa Anusandhan Samiti.

What Sir Edward Gait anticipated in the last paragraph quoted above from his book has however materialized. Numerous remains of ancient sculpture and architecture have been discovered in Assam since he left the province.

Of the various epigraphic records enumerated above all, except the clay-seal of Bhāskaravarman, the stray-plate of Harjaravarman, the Guakuchi inscription of Indrapāla and the two inscriptions of Dharmapāla were available when the second edition of Gait's history of Assam was published, but only 14 pages have been devoted in that book for the history of the period from the fourth to the twelfth century A. D. On the other hand 23 pages have been devoted to the history of the rule of the Koch kings who flourished for a comparatively brief period during the sixteenth and the seventeenth centuries. Sir Edward Gait has however treated the Ahom period very fully and his book is really a connected history of Assam during the rule of the Ahom kings. The necessity of a book giving a fuller treatment to the history of the pre-Ahom period has always been stressed and the materials so far collected justify an attempt in this direction. When I set myself to this task, however, I had no idea that Pandit Vidyavinod was engaged in a work more or less of similar scope in Bengali. His Kāmarupa Śāsanavali publishes the text and Bengali translations of all the inscriptions with copious notes and he has also given a chronology of the Kāmarupa kings in his introduction entitled

Kāmarupa Rājavali. He has not, however, attempted to present a detailed history of the period which is actually covered by the inscriptions published in his book. Students of history must, however, be indebted to him for publication, in one volume, of all the old inscriptions. He has also taken great pains to correct the readings of most of these inscriptions.

The early history of Kamarupa is very interesting. There was hardly any other Hindu dynasty in northern India that ruled uninterruptedly for a period of eight hundred years like the dynasty of Pushyavarman. Conquerors like Samudra Gupta, Yasodharman, Mahasena Gupta and Yasovarman could no doubt defeat the Kāmarupa kings in battle, but they could not include Kāmarupa within their territories. The repeated early Musalman invasions were succesfully repulsed by the kings of Kāmarupa which remained an independent kingdom till the last unconquered even by the Moghuls. The Ahom kings who succeeded the Koch kings became themselves *Hindus and erected numerous Hindu temples.* The extent of their kingdom was no doubt reduced and it came to be known as Assam, but even that small kingdom, with its limited resources, successfully resisted all Muhammadan invasions and continued to be independent till the advent of the British in 1826.

The kingdom continued to be known as Kāmarupa till the end of the Koch rule. I have, therefore, included in this book an account of the kings of Kamata and the Koch kings till the death of Naranārāyan. The history of the kingdom of

Kamata, which lasted nearly 250 years, is, however, dark. The kings of Kamata were probably the suzerains over a number of Bhuyan chiefs who actually ruled the country. These kings have left no epigraphic record for us. In my attempt to prepare a chronological list of these kings, therefore, I have been left, more or less, to conjecture. Some of my conjectures may be unfounded and if any one can present a more reliable history of this period, I shall be the first to congratulate him. Babu Nagendranath Basu, has, in his "Social History of Kāmarupa" tried to piece together a history of this period from the records of several well-known Kayastha families of Kamarupa, but his otherwise praiseworthy attempt has been vitiated by his eagerness to prove the Bengali origin of the Kayastha Bhuyans of Assam. He seems to have overlooked the fact that the inscription of Bhāskaravarman proves the existence of Kayasthas in Kāmarupa in the beginning of the seventh century, long before the period assigned to Adisur. Further, practically the whole of the country now known as northern Bengal was, in the old days, included in Kāmarupa and the Bengalis of northern Bengal, of the present day, were Kāmarupis some centuries back. Many Kayastha and Brahman families, originally settled in western Kāmarupa (northern Bengal) subsequently migrated into the modern Assam Districts of Kamrup and Goalpara as their family histories show and, as pointed out by Stapleton, such an exodus actually happened when, in the early part of the fifteenth century, Jalaluddin the son of Raja Ganesh, with the zeal of a new convert, began to compel the Hindus to accept Islam (1), but for that reason the descendants of the immigrants from northern Bengal cannot be claimed as Bengalis. The Aryans of the modern Assam valley were all originally immigrants from other parts of India, mostly from North Bihar. Even now Missers, Sukuls, Tewaris and Tirotias (belonging to Tirhut) are to be found among the Assamese Brahmans.

For the history of the Koch kingdom there are abundant materials. As Gait in his paper on the "Koch kings of Kāmarupa" and in his "History of Assam" and Mr. S. N. Bhattacharya in his "Moghul North-East Frontier Policy" have dealt with the history of Kāmarupa during this period rather fully, I have treated the subject very briefly omitting altogether the history of the kingdom after the death of Narnārāyan. During the reigns of Viswa Singha and Narnārāyan however Śankar Deva, the celebrated religious reformer of Assam, flourished and the Kāmarupi literature was greatly enriched. I have therefore added two small chapters on the Vaisnava reformation and the growth of literature towards the end.

The Chutia kingdom, in the extreme north-east of Kāmarupa, came into existence probably before the Ahoms entered Assam. It was after the conquest of this kingdom that the Ahoms secured a firm footing in eastern Assam. I have therefore added a short chapter wherein I have stated briefly the history of this kingdom from records so far availaable.

---

(1) J. P. A. S. B. vol XXI, 1930, No 2, Numismatic Number.

In the last chapter I have discussed the growth of the Kāmarupi literature. I deliberately use the word "Kāmarupi" because it was towards the end of the period dealt with by me in this book that the name Asam or Assam came to be applied to the eastern portion of the Assam valley which constituted the Ahom kingdom. Kāmarupa included the whole of the Assam valley till at least the accession of Dharmapāla. A proper discussion of this subject has been rendered possible by the collection of old *puthis* and the compilation of a descriptive catalogue - the work of my lamented friend, the late Pandit Hem Chandra Gossain. The credit of placing the late Pandit Gossain on deputation and subsequent preparation of the catalogue, however, belongs to Col. Gurdon and Sir Archdale Earle without whose active interest in the matter the *puthis* would never have been collected. The catalogue was actually published in 1929 by the Department of Historical and Antiquarian Studies, Assam, with a preface by Prof. S. K. Bhuyan. Pandit Gossain did not live to see it published. At the end of the book I have added three appendices containing the English translations of the three copper-plate inscriptions which were brought to light recently. I would also draw the attention of my readers to the "Addenda and Corrigenda" which adds certain matters which might have gone into the text of the book and wherein I have corrected certain mistakes and misprints that inadvertently crept into the book. For these and other unnoticed defects in the book, which I had to compile during such leisure as I could spare from my duties as Minister to the Government of Assam, I have to crave for indulgence from my readers.

In conclusion it is my pleasant duty to acknowledge the assistance which I received during preparation of this book - assistance in the shape of suggestions and discussions - from Pandit Padmanath Bhattacharya Vidyavinod, Rai Bahadur Ananda Chandra Agarwala, Rai Bahadur Padmanath Gohain Barua, Mr. H. E. Stapleton, Director of Public Instruction, Bengal, Mr. S. C. Goswami, Inspector of Schools, Assam Valley, Professors S. K. Bhuyan and Banikanta Kakati of the Cotton College, Dr. K. M. Gupta of the Murarichand College, Srijut Sonaram Chandhuri and Srijut Sarveswar Kataki of Gauhati. Mr. Bhuyan and Srijut Kataki have kindly helped me in obtaining photographs for some of the plates in this book and my nephew Mr. A Barah, M. A. Lecturer, Calcutta University, has supervised the execution of the blocks for the plates. My thanks are also due to the General Secretary of the Asiatic Society of Bengal and the Editor of the Journal of the Bihar and Orissa Research Society for their lending me certain blocks and permitting me to reprint some plates that originally appeared in their Journals. For similar permission I am also obliged to the Archaelogical Survey of India. I am indebted to Mr. N. K. Bhattasali, M. A., Curator, Dacca Museum and Mr. K. N. Dikshit, M. A. of the Archaelogical Department, for their interpretation of some of the old sculptural and architectural remains of ancient Kāmarupa.

K. L. B.

TABLE OF CONTENTS.

LIST OF ILLUSTRATIONS.

CHAPTER I.

PRAGJYOTISHA.

ITS EXTENT. The country known as Prāgjyotisha, in the most ancient times and as Kāmarupa in medieval times, has been mentioned both in the Rāmāyana and Mahābhārata. There is no doubt that the same country was called Prāgjyotisha in earlier times and Kāmarupa in later times. Of course the extent of the kingdom varied from time to time. The references in the Rāmāyana, as well as the Mahābhārata, indicate that the country stretched as far as the sea and that it was also, at least partly, a hilly country. In the Rāmāyana it is stated that the city of Prāgjyotisha was built on a gold-crested mountain called Varāha, which was 64 yojanas in extent and which stood or abutted on the fathomless varunālaya (sea). In the Mahābharata, Bhagadatta, the king of Prāgjyotisha, is called Śailālaya (dwelling among the mountains) and it is also stated that his troops consisted of Kirātas, Chinas and dwellers of the sea-coast. It seems that the Varāha (Boro ?) mountain, referred to in the Rāmāyana, was the Assam range, while the sea referred to was the very low-lying and water-logged country immediately to the south of these hills which, in the old days, was perhaps connected with the Bay of Bengal by the estuary of the Brahmaputra. This was no doubt the "eastern sea" known to the ancients. The low-lying parts of Sylhet and Mymensing are still called hāor (sāgara). In the Bhatera copper-plate inscription of Govinda Keśavadeva, king of Srihatta (*circa* 1049 A.D.) ,the sea or *sāgara* is mentioned as the boundary of certain lands granted. (1). It is therefore evident that, even till comparatively recent times, a part of Sylhet remained always submerged in water presenting the appearance of the sea. The Kirāta was perhaps the generic name of the Mongoloid people, but the name China was probably applied particularly to the Tibetans and the Bhutanese. The dwellers of the sea-coast were evidently the people living in the marshy regions of Sylhet, Mymensing and Tippera. All these allusions have led Pargiter to conclude that the kingdom known as Prāgjyotisha included, at the time of the Mahābhārata war, the greater part of modern Assam together with the Bengal districts of Jalpaiguri, Cooch-Behar, Rangpur, Bogra, Mymensing, Dacca, Tippera, part of Pabna and also probably part of east Nepal. (2). On the other hand, we again find from the Rāmāyana that Amurtarajas founded the kingdom of Prāgjyotisha close to

---

(1) Epigraphia Indica vol. XIX pp 277 to 286.

(2) "Ancient countries in Eastern India" J A S B, 1897, p 106.

Dharmāranya. This Amurtarajas was the son of Kuśa and grand-father of the famous *rishi* Viswāmitra. It is stated that Viswāmitra performed his austerities on the banks of the Kausika (modern Kosi). It seems therefore that Prāgjyotisha included, in the ancient times, the modern district of Purnea in Bihar and extended, on the north-west, as far as the Kosi. It is found from epigraphic evidence that, about the beginning of the sixth century A.D, the western boundary of Prāgjyotisha was the Kosi river. Prāgjyotisha therefore touched Videha(Mithila) on the west. *

It should, however, be stated here that though there is not much difference of opinion among orientalists as to the historicity of the conflict, as related in the Mahābhārata, between the Kauravas and the Pāndavas, which is assigned towards the end of the first millenium B. C., there is much controversy as to the date of the epics. European scholars generally place both of them towards the end of the *sutra* period when they were regularly

* The late Mr. A. Borooah in his Ancient Geography of India, prefaced to the third volume of his English-Sanskrit Dictionary wrote that to the east of the Kausika lay the country of the Pundras called also Gauda and that to the north-east of Pundra lay the important kingdom of Kamarupa. The latest opinion however is that the Pundras mentioned in the epics were to the south of Magadha, (see Map No. 5, Cambridge History of India Vol. I). It is perhaps a mistake to associate the Pundras with the stretch of country which came to be known as Pundra Vardhana during the Gupta period. Gauda is a still more recent name and it was evidently to the south of Kamarupa. To the east of Videha was ancient Pragjyotisha at a time when the names Pundravardhana, Gauda and Kāmarupa were unknown.

compiled from bardic tales. The geographical references as well as references to peoples, and tribes, contained in these two epics, are not therefore supposed, by these scholars, to possess the great antiquity with which Indian scholars generally clothe them. Whatever that may be, there is hardly any doubt that kings like Jarāsandha of Magadha and Bhagadatta of Prāgjyotisha were historical figures who ruled over powerful kingdoms during the period to which the Mahābhārata relates.

It is stated in the Kalika Purana that when Naraka was ruling in Prāgjyotisha his friend Bāna was ruling in Śonitpur which is identified with modern Tezpur. It is believed by some that the kingdom of Bāna included the whole of the modern district of Darrang and the North Lakhimpur subdivision. The Śiva temple of Mahābhoirab is attributed to Bāna who being a pre-Aryan was a devotee of Śiva. The Aryan writers give the following genealogy with regard to Bāna and his ancestors :—

Marichi
I
Kaśyap
I
Hiranyakaśipu
I
Prahlād
I
Virochana
I
Bali
I
Bāna.

The story of the secret marriage between Bāṇa's daughter Usha and Sri Krishna's grandson Aniruddha, the capture and confinement of Aniruddha and his subsequent release by Sri Krishna is told in Kumār Harana, the well-known Assamese poetical work. If, therefore, the story of Bāṇa is to be regarded as historical, it would seem that during the time of Naraka and Bhagadatta, eastern Assam Valley was outside Prāgjyotisha but subsequently the kingdom extended towards the east even beyond the Dikhoo river.

Even if we do not assign to the epic accounts a hoary antiquity, we can safely regard them at least as old as the Buddhist records and the Greek accounts of the fourth century B.C. All these confirm the supposition that about that time practically the whole of western Sylhet and south of eastern Bengal and part of south-west Bengal were under a sea though the delta was then beginning to form. The estuaries of the Ganges and the Brahmaputra formed this sea which was dotted with islands called *Dvipas*. The epic accounts give this sea the name Lohita Sāgara (estuary of the Louhitya). The Greek accounts make mention of islands in the estuary of the Ganges, the least width of which river even within Magadha was eight miles. The group of islands was very likely known as Vanga. The Buddhist Jatakas say that large sea-going vessels laden with merchandise could sail even from Champā (Bhagalpur). This shows that the sea then stretched far inland. The southern boundary of Prāgjyotisha about 1000 B.C. was therefore this sea. The western boundary was the Kauśika river and the northern boundary was the Bhutan hills and part ot Nepal. *

Babu Kedarnath Majumdar, in his History of Mymensing, has attempted to prove, from refer-

---

* In the Sabhā Parva of the Mahābhārata it is stated that Bhim, the second Pāndava, undertook the conquest of the eastern kingdoms and subdued the kings ot Pundra, Suhma, Vanga and Tamralipta as well as the mlechha kings near the sea-coast. It is also said that he went as far as the Lauhitya river but there is no mention of the conquest or Prāgjyotisha which is left to Arjuna to whom was entrusted the task of subjugating the kingdoms on the north. It is stated that Arjuna first vanquished the chiefs of Sakal dvipa and together with them attacked Bhagadatta, king of Prāgjyotisha, who with troops consisting of Kirātas, Chinas and the dwellers of the sea-cost, gave a stiff resistance. After conquering Prāgjyotisha Arjuna went to the north and having subdued all the mountainous kingdoms proceeded to Kashmere. Mr. Ramaprasad Chanda, writing in a Bengali magazine, wants to deduce from the above account that Pragjyotisha cannot be identified with the kingdom known as Kāmarupa in later times. It seems to us that it is now too late in the day to dispute this identity. Bhagadatta was a great hero and so the writer in the Mahābhārata made Arjuna, the hero of this epic, the conqueror of Prāgjyotisha. The mention of Kirātas, Mlechhas and the dwellers of the sea-coast precludes any possibility of Prāgjyotisha being anywhere in Central Asia near the country of the Sakas. Mr. Chanda considers that both Naraka and his son Bhagadatta are not historical figures and that the writer of Bhāskaravarman's Nidhanpur grant, in the seventh century A.D, made Naraka and Bhāgadatta the ancestors of Pushyavarman in order to enhance the reputation of the dynasty and thereby made Kāmarupa and Prāgjyotisha indentical. Mr. Chanda's statement seems to be self-contradictory for he himself admits that during the time of Kālidāsa, or two hundred years before the record of the Nidhanpur grant, Kāmarupa was known also as Prāgjyotisha. The Vāyu Purana, which is older than Kālidāsa's Raghuvansa, mentions the Prāgjyotishas as a nation living in the eastern part of India.

ences in the Manu-Sanhitā and the Mahabharata, that in the epic age at least three-fourths of modern Bengal, including the whole of the Mymensing district, was under the sea known as the *Lauhitya Sāgara* which extended, towards the north, almost up to the submontane tracts of the Himalayas and that the Brahmaputra fell into this sea without having to run a southerly course round the Garo Hills.(1). It seems that this was not the geographical condition at least about 1000 B.C. which was probably the period of the Māhabhārata war. Western Kāmarupa or northern Bengal to the east of Videha and as far south as the Rangpur district was then no doubt above water. According to local tradition, Bhagadatta had a pleasure seat, perhaps a sea-side resort, in the Rangpur district.

A subsequent Greek writer, Ptolemy, who wrote his Geography some 500 years after Megasthenes and Arrian, gives an account of the Gangetic coast from which we find that during his time, about the middle of the second century A.D., the Ganges fell into the sea through five mouths. This clearly indicates that the delta had then formed and the islands, comprising Vanga, that dotted the Lohita-Sāgara about 1000 B.C., had then been joined together to form a part of the southern Bengal mainland intersected by the several branches of the Ganges flowing into the sea. This stretch of country, elevated above the sea-level, subsequently got the name Samatata which was visited by Yuan Chwang some 500 years after Ptolemy. It is interesting to find that even

(1) Maimansingher Itihash, Chapter I.

then the country to the east of Samatata comprising southern Mymensing, western Sylhet and parts of Comilla and Noakhali were under the sea which was referred to by Yuan Chwang in the seventh century and by Alberuni in the eleventh century A.D. Ptolemy had however very hazy ideas about the geography of the countries to the north of the Ganges delta particularly of the north-eastern corner of India which then comprised Pragjyotisha. He gives numerous names of mountains, rivers, towns and tribes of this part of India and though scholars have tried to penetrate the disguise concealing the original forms of names distorted by him, satisfactory identifications have been rare. The Kirrhadia mentioned by Ptolemy is to be identified with the country inhabited by the Kirātas from the foot of the Garo and Khasi hills to the hill-tracts of Tippera along the eastern coast of the Brahmaputra estuary. These Kiratas and Mlechhas dwelling on the sea-coast are mentioned in the Mahābhārata. It is stated that in Kirrhadia the best *Malabathrum* (Tezpat) was produced. Up to this day *Tezpat* is grown on the southern slopes of the Khasi Hills and a considerable trade is carried on by the people of the district of Sylhet. Ptolemy mentions three mountain ranges, viz. Bepyrrhos, Maindros and Damassa or Dimassa. There is much difference of opinion as to the identification of these. It seems these were names of the different portions of the eastern Himalayas. The two rivers issuing from the Bepyrrhos and falling into the Ganges were probably the Kausika (Kosi) and the Trisrota (Teesta.) Other rivers mentioned are the Doanas which issued from the Damassa range and the Sobanos. The Doanas has been identified as the Brahmaputra and the Sobanos (probably the Subansiri) issued from the range known as Maindros (Mandāra or Mahendra). In the country to the south of the mountain ranges mentioned above Ptolemy asigns various tribes named Aminakhai, Indaprathai, Iberingai, Damassai, Nangalogai, Kakobai, Basanarai, Khalkitis, Koudoutai, Barrhai Indoi and the Doanai. The attempts made to identify these names, some of whom are clearly of Bodo origin, have been so far unsuccessful. The Damassai are supposed to be the Dimasas, a branch of the Kacharis. The Nangalogai (Nangalokas or naked men) were probably the Nagas. Koudoutai have been identified with the Kalitas. The Barrhai were perhaps the Barāhis and the Indoi were the Hindus. All these surmises are more or less unsatisfactory and one authority has gone to the length of identifying Alosanga with Shillong, as if a town of that name existed in the second century, which is of course absurd. (1) We need not therefore dwell further on Ptolemy's geography.

Yuan Chwang, the Chinese Pilgrim who visited the kingdom about 643 A.D., recorded that after travelling east above 900 li from Pun-na-fa-tan-na (Pundravardhana) and crossing a large river he came to Ka-mo-lu-po. The large river, which is called Ko-lo-tu in the Tang - Shu, is undoubtedly the Karatoyā. The country was more than a myriad li in circuit and its eastern boundary was a

(1) Researches on Ptolemy's Geography by Col. G. E. Gerini.

series of hills that reached the confines of China, thus indicating that about this time the extreme eastern portion of the Assam Valley was included within Kāmarupa. According to the Puranic accounts the temple of Kāmākshyā was in the centre of the kingdom which extended in all directions for one hundred Yojanas. According to the Yogini Tantra, which is clearly a much later work, Kāmarupa was bounded on the east by the Dikhoo river, on the west by the Karatoyā river, on the north by the mountain Kunjagiri and on the south by the confluence of the Lākshyā and the Brahmaputra.* It would appear from these accounts also that, even at a later period, the kingdom included not only the whole of the Assam Valley but also parts of northern and eastern Bengal, part of Bhutan, the Khasi and Garo Hills and the northern portion of the district of Sylhet. In any case it is clear that Prāgjyotisha or ancient Kāmarupa was a much larger kingdom than most of the other kingdoms mentioned in the Mahābhārata and most of the sixteen Mahājanapadas existing during the time of Gautama Buddha.

The kingdom came to be known as Kāmarupa during the Puranic times based on the legend that Kāmadeva, the God of love - the Indian Cupid - who was destroyed by the fiery glance of Śiva returned to life in this country. As already stated, the Chinese pilgrim, in the seventh century, mentions the name of the country as Ka-mo-lu-po. Three hundred years before Yuan Chwang, the

* **Till the last century the Brahmaputra flowed through the present district of Mymensing.**

famous *prasāsti* of Samudra Gupta mentions Kāmarupa as a frontier kingdom of India. (1).

The poet Kalidasa who, according to Vincent Smith, flourished in the first part of the fifth century also mentions Kāmarupa and Prāgjyotisha as names of the same kingdom. Rājaśekhara, the court poet of Mahipāla, the Pratihar King of Kanauj (910 - 940 AD), writing in the early part of the tenth century, however mentions Prāgjyotisha and not Kāmarupa as one of the countries of Aryavarta along with Magadha, Paundra, Tāmralipta and Suhma. On the other hand, the Arab writer Alberuni, in the eleventh century, mentions Tirhut, Mudgagiri (Monghyr), Nepal, Kāmarupa and Bhutan among the eastern countries of India.* It appears therefore that, since the beginning of the Gupta period down to the tenth century, the kingdom was known throughout Āryavarta both as Prāgjyotisha and Kāmarupa though its kings preferred to designate themselves as Lords of Prāgjyotisha down to the twelfth century. When the

(1) Corpus Inscriptionum Indicarum Vol. III, page 14.

* Alberuni writes:—

"Farther on, the country to the right is called Tilwat (Tirhut), the inhabitants Taru (Tharu), people of very black colour and flat-nosed like the Turks. Thence you come to the mountains of Kāmru which stretch away as far as the sea". (Alberuni's India p. 201). Quoting from Vāyu-Purana however the Arab writer gives a list of the people living in the east of India and this list includes the Magadhas, Mundas, Mallas, Vageyas, Tāmraliptakas and Prāgjyotishas. Again, quoting from Varāhamihira, he mentions Khasa (Khasis), Magadha, Mithilā, Samatata, Odra (Orissa) and Prāgyotisha as countries in the east.

Mussalmans came to Bengal, in the beginning of the thirteenth century, they found the country to the east of Karatoyā called Kāmrud or Kāmru. Latterly the Muhammadan historians referred to Kāmrud and Kamatā as if they were names of the same kingdom. As a matter of fact, the capital of the kingdom had then been removed to Kamatāpur, on the bank of the Dharla, the kings calling themselves Kamateswara and the kingdom extending from the Karatoyā on the west to the Barnadi on the east, including also a portion of Mymensing to the east of the Brahmaputra.

The country to the east of the Baranadi came to be specifically known as Saumāra and the Ahom kings of the time were called Rajas of Saumāra. In the beginning of the sixteenth century the Koch kings rose into power and the Kāmarupa of the Kamatā kings was their kingdom. Being pressed by the Muslim power of Bengal on the west and the Ahom power on the east the Koch kingdom did not long survive. Gradually when the Ahoms extended their sway westward and had to fight with the Muhammadans, during the sixteenth and the seventeenth centuries, the portion of Kāmarupa between the Karatoyā and the Mānas was permanently wrested by the Moghuls and included in Bengal. The Ahom kingdom to the east of the Mānas came to be known as Asam or Assam, after the Ahoms, and the name Kāmarupa has, since then, been restricted to the present district between the Mānas and the Barnadi.

Its Capital. The capital of the kingdom was named Prāgjyotishpur. There is a village two miles south of modern Gauhati which is still called "Dispur", indicating that the site of the city of Prāgjyotshpur was in or in the immediate vicinity of Gauhati. Prāgjyotishpur has been taken to mean the "City of Eastern Astrology" (1) or Astronomy. It is significant that to the immediate east of the town of Gauhati there is a temple, on the crest of a hill known as Chitrāchala, and this temple is dedicated to the Navagrahas or the nine planets. It is probable that this temple is the origin of the name Prāgjyotishpur. It is stated in the Kalika Purana that "here Brahma first created the stars and hence the city is called Prāgjyotishpur - a city equal to the city of Indra. (2)

It may be that Prāgjyotishpur was the seat of learning in astronomy or astrology in ancient India. It is not definitely known whether this learning was of Aryan or pre-Aryan origin. The temple of Navagraha is now in the hands of professional astrologers known as Daibagnas or Graha-bipras.* Gait says that the name Prāgjyotishpur "is interesting in connection with the reputation which the country has always held as a land of magic and incantation and with the view that it was in Assam that the Tantric form of Hinduism originated"(3). There is realy no connection between the name Prāgjyotishpur or the temple of Navagraha with the reputation of Kāmarupa as a land of magic or

(1.) Gait's History of Assam p. 15.

(2.) Kalika Purana.

*. Planetary worship in India is supposed to be a foreign importation, possibly of Magian origin (J.A.S.B. vol. XVI 1920 No. 3 p. 74)

(3.) Gait's History of Assam p. 15

sorcery or as the supposed original centre of Tantrik Hinduism. It is perhaps the temple of Kāmakshyā, on the west of Gauhati, which was associated with Tantrik Hinduism or magic and sorcery. It is now generally recognized that the cult of the *Yoni* and the *Linga* is of pre-Aryan origin. The shrine of Kāmākshyā, which represents the *Yoni*, is therefore properly associated with the pre-Aryan king Naraka who is reputed to have been the guardian of the shrine. Kāmarupa was not a stronghold of Buddhism when Yuan Chwang visited the country in the seventh century but some centuries after we find Kāmākshyā a reputed centre of the Vajrayāna system of Buddhism, known as the Sahajiā cult, along with Udyāna, Srihatta and Purnagiri. The very debased practices enjoined by this system of Tantrik Buddhism no doubt earned for "Kāmrup Kāmākshyā" the reputation mentioned above. It was to extirpate this system of debased religion that Mahāpurush Śri Śankar Deva began his preachings towards the end of the fifteenth century. During the next century he and his associates Śri Mādhava Deva, a Kayastha, and Śri Damodara Deva, a Brahman, with the help of their followers, succeeded in supressing the "Bauddha" rites and spreading the new Vaisnava tenet far and wide.

It is not known how long Pragjyotishpur or modern Gauhati continued to be the capital of the kingdom but it seems that some time after the death of Bhāskaravarman the Kāmarupa capital was removed to modern Tezpur which was then called either Hāruppeswara or Hātapeswara. In the rock inscription of Hārjaravarman, which has not yet been satisfactorily deciphered, the word has been read as Hāruppeswara but in the stray copper-plate of Harjaravarman, found and deciphered by Pandit Vidyavinod, the reading is Hātapeswara. The large tank known to this day as Hajarapukhri, in Tezpur, is still associated with the name of Harjaravarman. Hāruppeswara or Hātapeswara evidently continued as the capital at least from the reign of Harjaravarman in the early part of the ninth century till the extinction of the Sālastambha dynasty about the end of the tenth century when the capital was transferred to Sri Durjayā by Brahmapāla. His son Ratnapāla strengthened this city and named it Durjayā or "impregnable". Judging from the fact that the two copper-plate inscriptions of Ratnapāla have been found at Bargaon and Sualkuchi, not far from Gauhati, and a similar grant of Indrapāla, the grandson of Ratnapāla, has been found in Gauhati itself, it can be assumed with some degree of confidence that Durayjā was built near old Prāgjyotishpur on the bank of the Louhitya. About the end of the eleventh century the capital of Dharmapāla, the great-grandson of Indrapāla was at "Kāmarupanagar". Some would identify Kāmarupanagar with Kamatāpur or Kangur but such identification is not based on good grounds. As we shall show later, the expedition of Muhammad-i-Bukhtiyar, in the beginning of the thirteenth century, approached North Gauhati and his army was destroyed not far from that place while numismatic finds prove that the expedition led by Sultan Mughis-ud-din proceeded as far as Gauhati or North Gauhati towards the middle of the thirteenth century. The Kāmarupa capital had not till then been removed to Kamatāpur. In the middle of the twelfth century Vaidyadeva issued his land-grant, known as the Kamauli grant, from Hangshakonchi. As the suffix Konchi or Kuchi occurs in the names of numerous villages in the Kāmrup district it is almost certain that Hangshakonchi or Hāhkuchi was a town within that district. It will appear therefore that the capital continued to be somewhere within the present district of Kāmrup until after the middle of the thirteenth century when it was removed to Kamatāpur. At that time the eastern boundary of Kāmarupa extended only as far as Barnadi on the north bank and perhaps the Digaru river on the south bank.

The ruins of Hāruppeswara or Hātapeswara existing to this day are numerous and extensive but few of the antiquities of Prāgjyotishpur can now be seen in Gauhati. The Digholi tank and the various shrines within the town can be pointed out as the chief existing monuments of the old city of Prāgjyotishpur. Other scattered remains such as sculptured images, chiselled stone columns and bases, old bricks and pottery, have all been found from excavations within the town. A large number of old carved stones and bricks must have been used by the Ahom kings in re-building the temples at a much later age. North-Gauhati, which is probably to be identified wih Kāmarupanagar, still contains some temples with fine sculptured images and also a small stone bridge.

Its People. The earliest inhabitants of north-eastern India, were very probably of the Austric

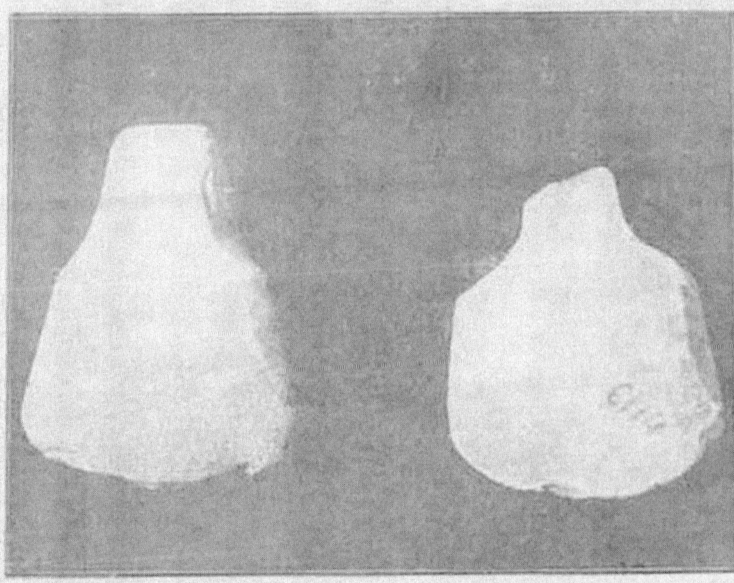

Shouldered stone implements found in Assam.

(By kind permission of the Asiatic Society of Bengal.)

stock. They were the pre-Dravidian aborigines who are now represented by the Monkhmer Khasis and Syntengs of Assam. The people akin to them in language are the Mundas of Chota Nagpur. Rapson writes that the "Austric languages which still flourish in Assam and Cambodia remain in India and Burma as islands of speech to preserve the record of a far distant period when Northern India (possibly Southern India also) and Farther India belonged to the same linguistic area" (1).

The people of the Austric stock may therefore be regarded as the representatives of the most ancient inhabitants of north-eastern India. They were a Neolithic people and the celts used by them have been discovered in various places in Assam. Particularly interesting is the find of two shouldered stone implements, one in Darrang and the other in the Cachar district which are very similar to the stone adzes found in Burma and also in Chota Nagpur and also the find, near Bishnath, of as many as six specimens of grooved stone hammers which are known to have been common in North America and which are the rarest of the numerous Neolithic stone implements recorded from Eastern Asia. The dolmen stones, sitting stones, flat monoliths and upright menhirs used by these people are still to be found in the plains as well as the hills of Assam. According to Hutton and Mills the upright menhirs and the sitting stones are to be interpreted "as providing phallic memorials through which the soul matter of

---

(1) Cambridge History of India, vol. 1. page 49.

the living or of the dead assists the fertilization of nature, the upright stone representing the male and the flat ones the female principles." The monoliths erected were both solid and hollow. These people used to burn their dead and the hollow monoliths were used as the receptacles of the ashes. It is therefore believed that these hollowed monoliths represent a specialized form of phallic ancestor cult which was widely prevalent among the earlier Mongolians of South-east Asia (1).

The Dravidians came subsequently as invaders from the west. Rapson writes:—"There is therefore nothing in the existing racial conditions and equally nothing in the existing physical conditions, to prevent us from believing that the survival of a Dravidian language in Baluchistan must indicate that the Dravidians came into India through Baluchistan in pre-historic times. Whether they are ultimately to be traced to a Central Asian or to a Western Asian origin cannot at present be decided with absolute certainty; but the latter hypothesis receives very strong support from the undoubted similarity of the Sumerian and Dravidian ethnic types" (2).

The Dravidians were not therefore the primitive inhabitants of India as supposed at one time. They were a cultured people, belonging to the Chalcolithic age who, in the remote past, inhabited the whole of northern India supplanting the Austric races. When the Aryans came they found

(1) J.P.A.S.B. New series, Vol. XXV, 1929

(2) Cambridge History of India, Vol. I, p. 43.

the Dravidians a more civilized people than themselves. They found Dravidian kingdoms not only in Southern India, but also in Northern India. Gradually the Aryans imbibed Dravidian culture and also religion. The cult of the *linga* and the *yoni* is now admitted to be of pre-Aryan Dravidian origin. Sir John Marshall writes:-

"Among the many revelations that Mohenjo-daro and Hārāppā have had in store for us, none perhaps is more remarkable than this discovery that Śaivism has a history going back to the Chalcolithic age, or perhaps even further still and that it thus takes its place as the most ancient living faith in the world" (1).

It seems that after the appearance of the Aryans, in India hordes of later Mongolians poured through the north-east. That they were later immigrants is proved by the fact that the Aryans designated them as Mlechhas thus indicating that they were foreigners. They came in probably at a time when the Austric people had already been driven to the hills by the Dravidian conquerors. The impact of the Mongolian thrust had therefore to be borne by the Dravidians who occupied the plains. The struggle must have been bitter and of long standing. At first the Mongolians seem to have carried everything before them but in course of time the new comers, who were themselves probably a Neolithic people, were vanquished by the Dravidians who used copper and bronze weapons and who ultimately recovered their supremacy as the ruling race.

(1) Mohenjo-Daro and the Indus Civilization, Vol.I. pp vi-vii.

These later Mongolians belonged to the Tibeto-Burman family of the Indo-Chinese group and their representatives of the present day are the Kacharis, Koches, Rabhas, Meches, Mikirs Lalungs, Garos, Nagas, Kukis and Chutias. Of these, the tribes speaking the Bodo (Boro) languages seem to have occupied the plains of Assam for a very long time. These Bodo people were no doubt the Kirātas and Mlechhas spoken of in the Mahābhārata. The Meches of Assam still preserve traces of the opprobrious name "Mlechha" applied to their forefathers by the early Aryans coming into Prāgjyotisha. The distinguishing feature of the Kirātas and Mlechhas, as recorded by Aryan writers, was their yellow complexion. It is stated in the Mahābhārata that the China and the Kirata troops of Bhagadatta shone like gold while Ghataka, the Mlechha King of Prāgjyotisha overthrown by Naraka, is described as a column of gold.

During the time of the Mahābhārata war, or even earlier, the Bodo tribes constituted the bulk of the population in the Assam Valley, northern and eastern Bengal and the surrounding and intervening hills. In the Surma Valley plains the Dravidians then formed the predominant element in the population as now.

The settlement of Aryans in the kingdom appears to have begun earlier than the period of the Mahābhārata war. It is stated in the Kalika Purrana that Naraka, who was probably a prince of Dravidian stock brought up in the family of the King of Videha, conquered Prāgjyotisha killing the Kirata king Ghataka and settled Aryans in his kingdom. In the Rāmāyana it is stated that Prāgjyotisha was founded by Amurtarajas a son of the great king Kusā "who was apparently an Aryan king in Madhyadesa" (1). From the Mahābhārata we find that Bhagadatta is described as the "aged friend" of Yudhisthira's father Pāndu. Bhagadatta came completely under Aryan influence and it can be reasonably supposed that Brahmans and other Aryans were settled in his kingdom. Apart from allusions in the epics or the Puranas, it is found from the inscription of Bhāskaravarman that about the fifth century A. D. there were Brahmans and Kayasthas in Kamarupa. According to Pandit Padmanath Bhattacharya Vidyavinod "it is remarkable that while in the neighbouring province of Gauda (Bengal) the alleged import by Adiśura of five Brahmans from Kanauj or the mythical creation of saptaśati (700) Brahmans is not attributed to a period earlier than the eighth century A.D. there should be so many Brahmans found in a single village in Kāmarupa two centuries earlier" (2). Yuan Chwang, who visited Kāmarupa in the seventh century, found hundreds of Deva temples in the country. Although the introduction of Aryans into Kāmarupa, at a very early period, is established, the fact remains that in early times, as now, the population was mainly of non-Aryan origin. According to the latest available census returns, the inhabitants of reputed Aryan descent in Assam, at the present

---

(1) Pargiter's, Ancient Countries in Eastern India.
(2) Epigraphia Indica vol. xix pp 115-125.

day, do not number more then ten lacs. Even now the people of Dravidian and Mongoloid origin largely predominate.

It is believed by some that a branch of the Aryans originally entered Assam from the north-east and that the descendants of these early Aryans are the Assamese Kalitās of the present day *. There is a tradition that there was a Kalitā country beyond the mountain range to the north-east of Assam. Some would advance the theory that certain tribes of the Mishmis living in these tracts were originally Brahmans or Aryans (1). They base this theory on the statement of Dalton that some of these Mishmis have Aryan features. The Aryan origin of the Kalitās of the Assam Valley does not seem to admit of any doubt but the same thing cannot be said with regard to the Mishmis.

---

* Mr. M. M. Chaterji writing in the J. P. A. S. B. vol. xxvi (1930) advances the theory that the Vaidyas of Bengal are the remnants of the Buddhist clergy overthrown by the Brahmans after the Brahmanic revival, in concert with the ruling Hindu king of Gauda in the eighth century. As we shall show later, these kings were really kings of Kāmarupa exercising suzerain power over Gauda. The Kalitas of Assam may also have been the original Aryan settlers in Kāmarupa who had adopted Buddhism and who were stigmatized by later Brahman immigrants, during the rule of the Pushyavarman dynasty, as Kula-lupta i. e. people who lost or dropped their caste or varna. It should be mentioned that there are Kultas or Kolitas in parts of Orissa also. In the Mudrarakshasam the Kulutas are mentioned as inhabitants of the Kuluta country under their king Chitravarman coming to the assistance of Malaya Ketu against Chandra Gupta Mourya. There are reasons to suppose that these Kulutas belonged to Eastern India.

(1) Social History of Kamarupa.

No reliance can be placed on the legend that Paraśurāma settled Brahman families in the region where the Paraśurāma Kunda now exists, nor is there any good authority for the supposition that a body of Aryans came into Assam through Tibet. We must therefore, in the absence of good and strong reasons, hold that the Aryans migrated into India only from the north-west and gradually spread over the whole of northern India. They therefore must have come into Assam through Videha or Magadha which were, in the most ancient times, almost coterminous with Kāmarupa. In fact when Bhagadatta was ruling in Kāmarupa the whole of northern Bengal and possibly central Bengal were within his kingdom the western boundary of which in the north, touched Viedha*. It is not therefore at all strange that Kāmarupa was Aryanized long before central or lower Bengal.

A word is necessary with regard to the theory of Babu Nagendranath Basu that the Koches of Kāmarupa are the descendants of the Vedic Panis

* It is interesting to note that the early Muhammadan writers such as the authors of the Ain-i-Akbari and the Riyaz, while giving an account of the earliest Hindu kings of Bengal (really northern and central Bengal), begin with Bhagadatta. It is said that the kings of his dynasty ruled Bengal for nearly 2200 years and then the sovereignty passed to Noz Gouria (Riyazus Salatin, Abdus Salam's translation) who was a Kayastha. His decendants ruled for 250 years and then Adisur became king. The fact is that the whole of northern and central Bengal, as far as Mithila to the west and the Ganges to the south, was within the kingdom of Bhagadatta and his successors held these territories for a long time until perhaps the rise of the Mouryas and thereafter the Guptas.

who were identical with the Phoenicians of old (1). Mr. Basu comes to the conclusion that the Koch is descended from the Vedic Pani and was driven into Eastern India by the Aryans. It is true that, as stated by Mr. Basu, the Vedic Panis were a sea-faring people and traders by occupation, but whereas the word Pani is derived from *pana* the word Pāni in "Pāni Koch" has nothing to do with *pana*. "Pāni Koch", literally meaning "Water Koch", evidently refers to the class of Koches who are considered clean enough to carry water for the high caste Hindus. Even to this day the process of gradual Hinduization is going on. A Kachari animist, as soon as he becomes a disciple of a Vaisnava Gossain, is called a Sarania Kachari or a Kachari initiated to the "eka śaran dharma" of the Vaisnava Gossains. His descendants, in the second or third generation having eschewed pork and wine for two or three generations, are raised to the status of Koches and are considered clean enough to carry water for Brahmans. This is how Koches swell in number. Ethnically they are of undoubted Mongoloid descent and cannot be the descendants of the Dravidians or the Sumerians or the Phoenicians as asserted by Mr. Basu who seems to have confused Pani with Pāni. The cult of the *linga* and the *yoni* may be associated with the Dravidians but not with the Mongoloid immigrants from whom the Koches can claim descent. Sir Edward Gait has shown conclusively that the Mongoloid type predominates in the

(1) Social History of Kamarupa.

Koches of Assam and that Dalton's theory that the Koches are of Dravidian origin is no longer held as correct. Head measurements by Colonel Waddell fully support the view that the Koches are of Mongoid origin (1).

There are good reasons to suppose that about the time of the Mahābhāratā war Kamarupa formed a Dravidian kingdom and that the kings of the dynasty of Naraka were of Dravidian origin like the Aikshākus of Ayodhya and the Janakas Videha, belonging to the solar race, who, according to Pargiter, were also Dravidians. Pargiter's theory has not however been widely accepted as correct. Besides, it may also be supposed that as the earliest Aryan colonists in Assam were the Kalitās the kings of the Naraka line were probably Aryan Kalitās. Whatever may have been the actual origin of Naraka and his descendants, there is no doubt that the Brahmans extolled them as Aryan Kshattriyas and made them perform the various caste ceremonies usually observed by Kshattriyas. After centuries they came to be looked upon as high class Kshattriyas and, as evidenced by the mention in the Rājatarangini, Kshattriya princes of northern India freely intermarried with them.

(1) Gait's History of Assam p. 47.
Assam Census Report for 1801.

CHAPTER II.

THE PREHISTORIC PERIOD.

The earliest mentioned king of Kāmarupa or Prāgjyotisha, as it was known in more ancient times, was a non-Aryan named Mahiranga Dānava. His name was evidently Mairang for a hill on the seventh mile of the Gauhati-Shillong road is still known as "Mairang Parbat". It is shown on the modern map as "Moiranka". The name Mairang was Sanskritized into Mahiranga. It is clearly a Bodo name and the people of this race who then inhabited the country were called Kirātas and Mlechhas as they were Mongolian immigrants. Mairāng is said to have been succeeded in direct descent by Hatakāsur, Sambarāsur and Ratnāsur. Mairang is called a Dānava but his descendants are called Asuras. This shows that epithets like Dānava and Asura were applied indiscriminately to all non-Aryans. After these kings came Ghatakāsur who is described as the ruler of the Kirātas. Perhaps he belonged to the same dynasty to which Hatak, Sambar and Ratna belonged. He was overthrown by Naraka who founded a new dynasty. Some historical records of this dynasty have been found and it appears that kings of this dynasty ruled over Prāgjyotisha for a considerable length of time.

The actual origin of Naraka, who though probably belonging to a different race was designated as Asura, has been obscured by the legend that the supreme God Vishnu in his incarnation of the Great Boar while lifting Prithivi (Earth) from the deluge with his tusks took her as his consort and had by her a son who was Naraka. It is for this reason that Naraka is called Bhauma (born of Earth) and on account of his supposed Divine origin all dynasties ruling in Kāmarupa claimed descent from him. Whatever his origin might have been, it is stated that Naraka was brought up by the king of Videha and that when he grew up he became a great warrior and conquered Prāgjyotisha by overthrowing the Mlechha king Ghatak. The people of the kingdom were then mostly Kirātas and Mlechhas who were evidently of Mongoloid origin. It is said that they were of rough appearance, gold or yellow complexion, with shaven heads and addicted to meat and drink (1). Their king Ghatak is described as tall and powerfully built and "being like a column of gold was bright and shining like the tongue of flame"(2). Naraka is said to have driven the Kiratas to the country near the sea-coast and

---

(1) Kalika purana.

(2) Ibid.

settled twice-born people (Aryans) in the country between the Karatoyā and the Lalitakāntā (1.) This was perhaps the earliest settlement of Aryans in Prāgjyotisha. He then built his citadel in a secluded place protected on all sides by hills and it is said that this stronghold was inaccessible even to Gods (2). About three miles to the south of modern Gauhati there is a village surrounded by low hills which is still known as "Narakāsur gaon". About two miles to the east of this village is the modern village of Dispur which is believed to be the abbreviation of "Prāgjyotish-pur". This village of Dispur is separated from "Narakāsur gaon" by a range of low hills on the highest peak of which stands the temple of Kāmākshyā. It appears that both Dispur and "Narakāsur gaon" were connected with the Kāmākshyā temple on the west and the Navagraha hill on the east by a semi-circular road. The citadel of Naraka was therefore actually protected by hills as stated in the Kalika Purana and was not far from Prāgjyotishpur.

After settling himself in Pragjyotisha Naraka married Māyā, the daughter of the king of Vidarbha. Pargiter holds that the Aikshākus of Ayodhya and the Janakas of Videha were not Aryans but Dravidians. It is reasonable to suppose that Naraka was also a Prince of the same race. It is probable that Prāgjyotisha was originally a Dravidian kingdom, that subsequently Mongolian hordes entering through the north-east overthrew

(1) **Kalika Purana.**
(2) **Ibid.**

the Dravidian dynasty and set up their own rule and that afterwards prince Naraka regained the kingdom with the help of the king of Videha. As a matter of fact the Dravidians who were designated as Asuras, Dānavas or Daityas were not the demons or goblins as painted by later Brahman writers but were perhaps more civilized than the Aryans themselves. Yayāti, an Aryan king, married Śarmishthā the daughter of a Daitya king. Aniruddha the grand-son of Śri Krishna is said to have married Usha the daughter of Bāna, another Daitya king. Prahlād, the great grand-father of Bāna, through a Daitya, was renowned as a pious and devout person. Māndhātri and Sagara who were probably pre-Aryan kings were suzereins over Aryan princes. Ethnologists hold that both the Aryans and the Dravidians were descended from the same dolichocephalic Caucasian stock, the former who lived in temperate regions were fair coloured while the latter living in tropical countries acquired the dark complexion. It is possible that the other differences in facial characteristics were also due to climatic conditions and environments. The last word has not yet been said as to the origin of those Indian pre-Aryans who built the wonderful cities now unearthed at Hārāppā, Mohen-jo-daro and Jhukar but there seems to be hardly any doubt that they were the Dravidians. It has been long recognized that the cult of the *linga* as well as the *yoni* originated from the pre-Aryans or Dravidians and that the Aryans, coming into India subsequently, had to adopt the same. The shrine at Kamakshya unmistakeably stands for the *yoni* worship and it is not therefore strange that Kāmakshyā was the deity worshipped by Naraka. The great antiquity of the shrine at Kāmākshyā is therefore established beyond doubt and the worship of this particular deity almost establishes the fact that Naraka was a king of Dravidian origin. That phallus worship obtained among the Chalcolithic people of the Indus Valley is proved by the discovery of terra-cotta phallic emblems in Hārāppā and Mohen-jo-daro.

Though probably of Dravidian origin, like the Janakas of Videha, Naraka being brought up in Videha was regarded as a Kshattriya for it is stated in the Kalika Purana that Gautama, the priest of the Videha king Janaka, performed the Keśavapana ceremony of Naraka strictly according to the Vedic rites and in accordance with the custom observed by Kshattriyas. It is further stated, in the same Purana, that Naraka was well-versed in the Vedas and devoted to the duties of the twice-born. Evidently his regard for Aryan culture did not last long. He subsequently reverted to the pre-Aryan worship of the *linga*. It is said that he came under the evil influence of a neighbouring Daitya king named Bāna who ruled over Sonitpur with his capital at Agni-nagara and who is believed to have established the Mahabhoirab temple containing a huge *linga*. Acting on the advice of Bāna, he ceased to worship the Aryan Gods and ill-treated the Ayran colony. He is said to have abducted a large number of Aryan damsels to gratify his lust. At length, when his iniquities grew numerous and it became impossible to tolerate him any longer, the Gods invited Śri Krishna to come and destroy him. Śri Krishṇa then came, all the way from Dwarakā, near the western sea-coast, and attacked Prāgjyotisha. All the powerful generals of Naraka were, one by one, vanquished and Naraka himself was at last defeated and slain by Śri Krishna who placed Naraka's son Bhagadatta on the throne of Prāgjyotisha.

The story of Krishna's march on Prāgjyotisha and overthrow of Naraka is a good illustration of history being obscured by subsequent interpolation of legends which extolled Krishna to the position of a deified personality. We know from the Mahābhārata that Krishna, an Aryan prince of the Yadava tribe, was the contemporary and friend of the Pāndavas. He is said to have referred to Bhagadatta in the following terms while addressing Yudhisthira, the eldest Pāndava :- "Bhagadatta is thy father's aged friend; he was noted for his deference to thy father in word and deed and he is mentally bound by affection and devoted to thee like a father." How could then Krishna attack and kill Naraka and place the "aged" Bhagadatta, a contemporary of Pāndu, on the throne?

In the Mahābhārata Bhagadatta is called the mighty king of the Mlechhas as his subjects were mostly people of Mongoloid orgin. He is also described as a warrior king "not inferior to Śakra (Indra) in battle." It appears that about the time he became king the kingdom of Magadhā was growing into power under

Jarāsandha a king of reputed Aryan descent but who was also stigmatized as Asura because his subjects were mostly pre-Aryans. In the Adi-parva of the Mahābhārata it is explained that Jarāsandha and Bhagadatta were, in their previous births, Asuras and that such was the case with Kangśa. At length Jarāsandha became Samrāt over a number of Aryan and pre-Aryan kings of northern India. Among his vassal kings we find the mention of Bhagadatta of Prāgjyotisha, and Vāsudeva of Pundra. In order to make Yudhisthira the Samrāt the Pāndavas had to deal with Jarāsandha first. This they did with the help of Krishna. Krishna with Bhima and Arjuna entered the city in disguise and killed Jarāsandha.

After this the Pāndavas began their conquering tour in order to proclaim Yudhisthira as the Samrāt. Some of the kings of northern India then voluntarily submitted to the Pāndavas while the rest were compelled by force to acknowledge Yudhisthira as their over-lord. Among the larger kingdoms joining the Sāmrājya of Yudhisthira we find the mention of Prāgjyotisha, Chedi, Magadha, Pundra, Tāmralipti and Suhma (west Bengal). Bhagadatta did not tamely submit to the Pāndavas who had to fight strenuously for eight days to vanquish him. The Pāndavas then arranged a grand assemblage of the ruling princes at Indraprastha. It is noteworthy that the architect selected to construct and decorate the assembly-hall was a pre-Aryan named Maya Dānava. This is a striking proof of the fact that, even at so late an age as the period of the Mahābhārata war, the despised Asuras and Dānavas – the descendants of those pre-Aryans who built the mangnificent cities now unearthed at Hārāppā and Mohen-jo-daro – were superior to the Aryans in artistic and architectural skill.

The Rājasuya ceremony was however a failure. A trouble arose over a question of precedence in formally receiving the assembled princes. By order of Yudhisthira precedence was given to Śri Krishna, his friend and adviser. A large number of the princes felt humiliated at this as Śri Krishna was not a ruling prince. Śiśupāla, the king of Chedi, could not control his feelings and, getting up, delivered a speech abusing both Śri Krishna and Yudhisthira. Śri Krishna then flew into a great rage and instantly killed Śiśupāla with his *chakra* (discus) in the presence of the assembled princes and their retinue. This asassination led to a great uproar and the ceremony ended in confusion. Soon after, a confederacy was secretly formed against the Pāndavas and Duryodhana was the leader of this confederacy. The adherants of the Pāndavas joined the opposite confederacy and the princes of India were thus ranged in two hostile camps. Bhagadatta, king of Prāgjyotisha, joined the confederacy headed by Duryodhana. In Bengal and Assam there is a tradition that Duryodhana married Bhānumati the daughter of Bhagadatta. In the Bengali

Mahābhārata by Kaśiram Das this is expressly stated but there is no mention of such a matrimonial relationship in the original Sanskrit epic. At length the great battle of Kurukshetra, which lasted for several days, was fought. In this battle Bhagadatta, then an old warrior, fell fighting. It is stated in the Mahābharata that Bhagadatta was so old that the wrinkles on his forehead covered his eye and he had therefore to tie a rag round his forehead at the time of fighting so that he could draw the bow-string and aim the arrow. On the advice of Śri Krishna Arjuna cut the rag with an arrow whereupon the vision of Bhagadatta was obstructed and, during this opportunity, Arjuna killed him. Arjuna then did ***pradakshin*** round the fallen hero who was a friend and contemporary of his father. It is also stated that, during the war, the army of Kalinga followed the lead of Bhagadatta who was therefore an important general of the allied army. The Pāndava confederacy was at length victorious and all the Kuru princes were killed. Yudhisthira once more aspired for the position of a Samrāt. This time the *Aswamedha* or the horse-sacrifice was arranged. At this ceremony the old custom of receiving the assembled princes, according to precedence, by offer of the *Argha*, was discarded on the advice of Śri Krishna himself. The ceremony was a success and Yudhisthira was proclaimed a Samrāt. Vajradaatta, who succeeded Bhagadatta in Prāgjyotisha, acknowledged

Yudhisthira as his over-lord but not without a stiff fight. In the *Harshacharita* of Bānabhatta Puspadatta and Vajradatta are mentioned as the successors of Bhagadatta but in none of the inscriptions of the kings of Bhagadatta's dynasty do we find the name of Puspadatta. In the Karna-parva of the Mahābhārata we find that a son of Bhagadatta was killed in the battle of Kurukshetra and this prince might have been Puspadatta. It may be that Vajradatta was the younger brother of Puspadatta, but the writers of the inscriptions of Vanamāla, Balavarman III and Ratnapāla erroneously mentioned him as brother of Bhagadatta instead of as brother of Puspadatta. Pandit Vidyavinod supposes that Banabhatta meant Pushya (Puspa) varman by Puspadatta (1).

This *Sāmrājya* established after much bloodshed did not last long. After Parikshit and Janmejaya the empire shrank into a small kingdom which again was split up into two smaller kingdoms, one branch continuing to rule at Indraprastha and the other ruling at Kauśambi. Udayana, the king of Kauśambi, was a contemporary of Gautama Buddha and king Bimbisāra of Magadha.

Gradually, since the time of Gautama Buddha, the kingdom of Magadha grew more and more powerful, as ancient Indian history tells us, and frontier Indian kingdoms like Kamarupa which figured prominently in the previous age dwindled into insignificance.

---

(1) Kāmarupa Sasanavali pp 10-11.

We do not know who were the successors of Vajradatta but a copper-plate inscription of Bhāskaravarman who ruled over Kāmarupa in the early part of the seventh century A. D. states that a period of three thousand years elapsed between the death of Vajradatta and the accession of Pushyavarman, the ancestor of Bhāskaravarman eleventh in ascent from him. Yuan Chwang, the Chinese pilgrim who visited Kāmarupa during the reign of Bhāskaravarman, records that there were one thousand generations after Vishnu the progenitor of Naraka and before the birth of Bhāskaravarman. It can be well conjectured that both the writer of the copper-plate inscription and Yuan Chwang calculated that about 600 A.D, when Bhāskaravarman had ascended the throne, 3301 years of the Kali Yuga had already expired and Hindu tradition places the battle of Kurukshetra some hundred years after the beginning of the Kali Yuga. In fact according to Kahlan, the author of the Rājatarangini, the Pāndavas flourished about 650 years after the commencement of the Kali age. These two accounts therefore do not help us to fix any historical chronology.

Whatever that might be, although it can be safely assumed that the kings of Kāmarupa came under Aryan influence since the time of the Mahābhārata war or probably earlier, the long period of history intervening between Bhagadatta's successor and Pushyavarman is dark. There are no doubt somewhat conflicting local traditions about the successors of Bhagadatta. According to one account the successors of Bhagadatta in direct line of descent were Dharmapāla, Karmapāla, Prithvipāla and Subāhu. According to another account there reigned in Kāmarupa, in the Satya yuga, a king called Sambarāsur whose son was Mahiranga who had his capital in Moiroka (Mairang) hill within the Beltola muza. His son was Ghataka who was overthrown by Naraka of a different dynasty. Naraka's son was Bhagadatta who was succeeded by Dharmapāla and Kamapāla in direct descent. After 19 kings of this dynasty, beginning from Naraka, had ruled Subāhu became king. He stopped the sacrificial horse of Vikramāditiya and was overthrown. After this a Dravidian name Jitāri becamed king of Kāmarupa. It is stated in another account that Jitāri or Jitārikshya was known also as Dharmapāla.

In the absence of any epigraphic record we can not place any reliance on these traditional accounts. It may be that these accounts do not give names of kings in chronological order. This is the great defect of Indian traditional accounts. Even the historical accounts of Kahlan, the Kashmiri chronicler, is not free from this defect. Further, such accounts usually mention the popular names of kings whereas epigraphic records like copper-plate inscriptions, rock inscriptions and inscriptions on stone slabs or pillars generally contain the honorific names of kings. We know from the Nidhanpur copper-plate inscription that Susthitavarman, the father of Bhāskaravarman, was popularly known as Mrigānka In the traditional accounts of Kāmarupa Mrigānka is actually the name of a Kāmarupa king.

The early Buddhist records mention the existence of sixteen *Mahājanapadas* during the time of Buddha in the sixth century B.C. These do not include Prāgjyotisha though they include both Anga and Magadha on the borders of Prāgjyotisha. The Greek writers of the fourth century B.C. mention the Prasioi and Gangaridae as the easternmost nations in India ruled over by a king called Agrammes. Some of the Greek writers give names of tribes, places and rivers which cannot be easily identified. They mention the Kalingas of Orissa as well as the Mundas and Savaras of Chota Nagpur. They mention also the Kausika or Kosi river (Cosoagus) which was perhaps the western boundary of Prāgjyotisha at the time. They do not, however, mention Prāgjyotisha, either as a country or as a nation, unless we take Prasioi or Prasii as the Greek abreviation of Prāgjyotisha. They however distinctly state that the Prasioi nation had Palimbothra (Pātaliputra) as their capital. Whether the Prasioi nation included also the Prāgjyotishas, to the east of Videha, is a doubtful point. Both geographically and ethnologically the people of Mithila and Western Prāgjyotisha (Northern Bengal) could combine with the Magadhas into one nation. The Gangaridae, who are supposed to have been the people living near the mouth of the Ganges, were, however, separated from the Magadhas by the people of Chota Nagpur who are separately mentioned. It is not, therefore likely that the two widely separated peoples, the *Prāchyas* of Magadha and the dwellers of the Ganges delta, combined to form one kingdom.

The Puranas which chronologically come next to the Greek accounts refer to Prāgjyotisha. The Brahmānda, Vāyu, Matsya, Agni, Garuda and the Mārkandeya Puranas, which can be assigned to this period, make mention of Prāgjyotisha, but the dynastic lists of "future kings" given in some of these, in the form of prophesies, do not include the kings of Prāgjyotisha through they include the Andhras and even the Andhravrityas. The fact probably is that before the rise of the dynasty to which Pushyavarman belonged, Prāgjyotisha was either included within the Mourya empire or it disintegrated into petty principalities ruled over by local chiefs like the Bhuyans of the fifteenth century. It is also possible that during the long interval between Vajradatta and Pushyavarman further influx of *mlechhas* took place leading to chaos and disorganization. It is true that the Kashmere chronicler mentions that a Kashmere prince named Meghavāhana married a Prāgjyotisha princess in the first century A.D. As we shall, however, show later, Meghavāhana cannot be placed earlier then the fifth century A.D.

Since the time of Bimbisāra, who in the sixth century B.C. conquered Anga, the Magadha kingdom gradually extended towards the east and ultimately, during the time of the Nandas or the Mouryas, absorbed western Prāgjyotisha or Northern Bengal. Subsequently during the rule of the Imperial Guptas the tract of the country between the Kausika and Trisrota, to the south of Jalpaiguri district, became the Pundravardhana bhukti.

CHAPTER III.

KAMARUPA IN THE GUPTA PERIOD.

In the Nidhanpur plate of king Bhāskaravarma Deva (1) the genealogy of the kings mentioned therein is traced from Naraka, his son Bhagadatta and his grandson Vajradatta. There is really no inherent impossibility in the same dynasty ruling from the time of the Mahābhārata war down to the seventh century A.D. We know that a Paurava king, who must have descended from Puru, the remote ancestor of Yudhisdthira of the Mahābhārata fame, ruled over a part of the Punjab in the fourth century B.C. when Alexander the Great invaded India. Prāgjyotisha was a frontier kingdom of India, girt on all sides except the west, by natural defences. It is possible that its kings, after Vajradatta, either acknowledged the overlordship of other more powerful kings of northern India or, being out of the way, were not

---

(1) **Epigraphia Indica vol. XII.**

molested by any of them but, as already stated, the fact that the kingdom came to play no part in the history of northern India within historical times from the rise of Bimbisāra in Magadha, in the sixth century B.C. down to the time of Samudra Gupta in the fourth century A.D, is rather striking and leads one to suppose that probably there might have been some upheaval within the kingdom which reduced it to an insignificant position. Any way, in the absence of clear proof to the contrary, we can assume as correct Bhāskaravarman's claim of descent, in unbroken line, from Naraka, as stated in the Nidhanpur copper-plate inscription.

It is rather significant that the names of some of the Kāmarupa kings follow closely those of the illustrious emperors of Aryavarta. Pushyamitra Sunga usurped the Mourya throne about 185 B.C. He revived the ancient horse sacrifice or *Aswamedha* and became renowned. He died about 149 B.C. The name of the Kāmarupa king Pushyavarman was probably given after the renowned Sunga king of Magadha. Similarly we find Pushyavarman's son named Samudravarman after Samudra Gupta, the famous Gupta emperor who ruled from 330 to about 385 A.D. Even Samudravarman's queen bore the same name as the queen of Samudra Gupta. This goes to show that Samudravarman probably ruled a short time after Samudra Gupta whose illustrious name was then green in the memory of the people of northern India.

The first epigraphic record which mentions

Kāmarupa is the famous Allahabad inscription of Samudra Gupta which was once regarded as posthumous but which historians now believe to have been engraved during the life-time of the famous emperor. In this inscription Kāmarupa is mentioned as a frontier kingdom along with Samatata, Davāka, Nepal and Kartripura the kings of which fully gratified the imperious commands of Samudra Gupta "by giving all kinds of taxes and obeying his orders and coming to perform obeisance" (1).

The "pratyanta nripati" of Kāmarupa who submitted to Samudra Gupta was very probably no other than Pushyavarman. Gait has placed him tentatively in the first half of the fifth century but this is probably not correct. As we shall show later, his accession to the throne took place not later than 380 A.D.

We know that Samudra Gupta celebrated the horse-sacrifice but it does not appear that his son Chandra Gupta II, who assumed the title Vikram-

(1) Fleet Corpus Inscriptionum Indicarum vol. III p 14.

The country named in the inscription as Davāka has not yet been satisfactorily identified. It can not obviously be identified with modern Dacca (Dhaka) which was perhaps included in Samatata. Very probably, the present Cachar district, including the north Cachar hills and the Kopili valley, which in later times constituted the Kachari Kingdom, was known as Davāka. Even now the Kopili valley, comprising an area of about 400 square miles, is known as Davakā. From Yuan Chwang's account we find that in the seventh century this area was included within Kāmarupa and that large herds of wild elephants roamed in this tract. Part of the present Sylhet district was within Kāmarupa and the other part was perhaps under the sea.

āditya, performed the same ceremony. In the traditional accounts of Kāmarupa it is however stated that a king of the Naraka dynasty named Subāhu detained the sacrificial horse of Vikramāditya who then invaded Kāmarupa and put Subāhu to flight. Subāhu might have been the popular name of Pushyavarman as Mrigānka was the popular name of Susthitavarman and Samudra Gupta was the Vikramāditya referred to in the traditional account. It is quite possible that, following the ancient custom, Samudra Gupta, in his *digvijaya*, prior to the *Aswamedha*, led his sacrificial horse and challenged all the kings to detain the horse. Those who accepted the challenge had to fight while those who wanted to avoid fight acknowledged the overlordship of the conqueror and allowed the horse to pass unrestricted. Pushyavarman, otherwise known as Subāhu, having stopped the horse had to fight and being worsted acknowledged the suzerainty of the Gupta emperor and performed obeisance.

Pushyavarman was succeeded by his son Samudravarman who was perhaps the contemporary of Chandra Gupta II Vikramāditya and the celebrated poet Kālidasa. In the Nidhanpur inscription it is stated that there was no "mātsya-nyāya" in his kingdom and that Samudravarman was like the fifth ocean (1). The word "mātsya-nyāya" has been explained as anarchy due to the absence of a strong ruler when the powerful people oppress the weak just as the larger fish devour the smaller fry. The mention of this word

(1) Epigraphia Indica vol. XII.

seems to indicate that there was such anarchy during the reigns of his predecessors. It may be that after such anarchy was ended Pushyavarman rose to power or that after the accession of Pushyavarman the anarchy ended.

Some scholars believe that the poet Kālidāsa who was in the court of Chandra Gupta II Vikramāditya, really narrated in canto iv of his Raghuvansha, the conquering tour (*digvijaya*) of Samudra Gupta under the poetic disguise of Raghu. At any rate, Kālidāsa in the beginning of the fifth century A.D. must have recorded the facts concerning the countries of India mentioned in his book according to his own knowledge of those countries. For instance, the hydrographical condition of Bengal at that time is clearly referred to in canto iv, verses 34 to 38. The poet mentions that Raghu's son Aja selected the king of Kāmarupa as his best man in his marriage with Indumati. This shows that the king of Kāmarupa of his time, who was probably Samudravarman, was a very important monarch belonging to an old and reputed dynasty, otherwise the poet would not have made him the best man of the son of his hero.

With regard to the next king Balavarman I, the son of Samudravarman by his queen Dattadevi, the Nidhanpur inscription states that"his irresistible troops constituted his armour". It appears therefore that he was a powerful king and a conqueror. There is mention in the Kashmere chronicle Rājatarangini that king Meghavāhana of Kashmere married a Prāgjyotisha princess named Amritaprabhā. It is stated that the king of Prāgjyotisha held a *svayamvara* for the marriage of the princess. Of all the princes assembled Amritaprabhā's choice fell upon the Kashmere prince Meghavāhana. It is recorded that "there in the presence of the kings he (Meghavāhana) received from the princess Amritaprabhā the bridegrom's garland while the parasol of Varuna cast its shade upon him. By this the people knew his future greatness as by the west wind the gathering of clouds. Because this parasol, which king Naraka had carried away from Varuna cast its shade on no one but a sovereign of the whole globe (Chakravartin)"(1). This parasol or umbrella is mentioned also in the *Harsha-Charita* of Bāna wherein it is stated that it was an heirloom of the kings of the dynasty of Naraka. It is also stated there that king Bhāskaravarman, through his envoy Hangshavega, presented this umbrella to Sri Harshavardhana. It is stated that queen Amritaprabhā erected in Kashmere a lofty *Vihāra* for the benefit of the foreign *bhikshus* and that this *Vihāra* was known as Amritabhavan. It is further stated that Amritaprabhā took to Kashmere a Tibetan Buddhist scholar named Stunpā who was a preceptor of her father, the Kāmarupa king. This Stunpā erected a *stupa* in Kashmere known as "Lo-stunpa" (2). If the above statements are to be believed as true it would appear that Buddhism had spread into Kāmarupa long before the visit of Yuan Chwang, that a remote ancestor of Bhāskaravarman was a Buddhist and that the cultural connection between

(1) **Rajatarangini Book II p. 148-150.**
(2) **Rajatarangini Book III p. 9.**

Kāmarupa and Tibet, to which reference will be made in a subsequent chapter, began as early as fifth century A.D.

According to Kahlan, the author of the Rājatarangini, Meghavāhana was succeeded by Sresthisena and the latter by Toramāna. If this Toramāna is identical with the Ephthalic king Toramāna, the father of the famous Mihiragula, the king of the white Huns who ruled over the Punjab and possibly also over Kashmere, then he cannot be placed earlier than the third quarter of the fifth century A.D. The identification would probably be correct for, according to Kahlan, Toramāna struck coins in his name extensively and such coins have, as a matter of fact, been discoverd in large quantities. These bear the name of Toramāna in characters of the Gupta period. This being so, Meghavāhana may be placed about the second quarter of the fifth century though Kahlan's chronology places him in the first century and he was probably the son-in-law of the Kāmarupa king Balavarman I. This matrimonial alliance and the celebration of the *Svayamvara* indicates that Prāgjyotisha or Kāmarupa was then an important kingdom in northern India and that it was no longer a mere frontier kingdom as in the days of Pushyavarman.

Vincent Smith mentions that in the year 428 A.D., during the reign of emperor Kumāra Gupta, an embassy was sent to China by an Indian king named Yue-ai (Moon-loved) who was lord of the Ka-pi-li country. Lt. Col.

Wilson has identified Ka-pi-li with the Kapili river of Assam named in the Kalika purana as *Kapila-Gangâ*, and Vincent Smith has tentatively accepted this identification (1). As we have already suggested, the Kapili valley, which is still called Davakā, may be identified with the kingdom of Davāka mentioned in the Allahabad inscription of Sumudra Gupta. The embassy may therefore have been sent by the king of Davāka whose name was either Chandra-Priya or Chandra-Vallabha. It should however be mentioned that there was a king of Kāmarupa named Chandra-mukha (moon-faced) who was the great-grandfather of Bhāskaravarman. He cannot, however, be assigned to the second quarter of the fifth century. It seems that in the sixth or the seventh century this kingdom of Davāka was absorbed by Kāmarupa, for according to Yuan Chwang's account the Kapili valley was included in Kāmarupa.

The kings after Balavarman were Kalyānavarman, Ganapativarman, Mahendravarman and Nārāyanavarman who do not appear to hāve been much renowned. According to the Nidhanpur inscription, Ganapativarman was generous in his gifts while Nārāyanavarman was, like king Janaka, deeply versed in the knowledge of the self. Nārāyanavarman was succeeded by his son Mahābhutavarman who is named in the *Harsha Charita* as Bhutivarman. It was he who granted, to a large number of Brahmans, lands in the Chadrapuri vishaya. The copper-plate relating to this grant

(1) Vincent Smith's Early History of India, p. 316.

having been destroyed by fire his great-great-grandson Bhāskaravarman recorded, what is known as the Nidhānpur grant, to confirm the gift made by his ancestor. Originally only three plates of this inscription were discovered by Pandit Padmanath Bhattacharya Vidyavinod who contributed a paper on them in Epigraphia Indica vol XII. Subsequently two more plates found were described by Pandit Vidyavinod in vol.XIX of the Epigraphia Indica. The third lost plate was again discussed by him in the same journal. One more plate is still missing. These newly discovered plates mention the names of Chandrapuri vishaya, Kāusika river and Mayura-Sālmala agrahāra. The occurrence of the word "agrahāra" seems to indicate the existence of a temple for the maintenance of which and its *shebaits* the lands were granted. As the inscription begins with the adoration of ash-besmeared Mahādeva it is clear that these Kāmarupa kings were all devotees of Śiva. As a matter of fact Śiva is invoked in the inscription as the *ista-devatā* of the donor. Further in the *Harsha Charita* it is stated that Bhāskāravarman worshipped only the lotus-feet of Śiva. So it may be assumed that the agrahāra mentioned in the inscription was no other than a Śiva temple. The newly discovered plates contain the names of the donees who number more than 200. From this list we find such names as Vishnu-Ghosha, Arka-Datta, Rishi-Dama, Dama-Deva, Dhruva-Soma, Vishnu-Palita, Gayatri-Pala, Yājna-Kunda, Padma-Dassa, Tosha-Naga and Gopala-Nandi. It is curious that the surnames Ghosha, Datta, Dama, Deva, Soma, Palita, Pala,

Kundu, Dasa, Naga and Nandi are now confined to Kayasthas of Bengal but not to Brahmans. One authority (Dr. Bhandarkar) has pointed out that identical surnames were used by the Nāgar-Brahmans. It is not known when and how such a colony of Brahmans came to be settled in Kāmarupa near the Kosi river as early as the beginning of the sixth century. Pandit Vidyavinod's surmise that most of the Brahman families in the neighbouring province of modern Bengal are the descendants of these Brahmans from Kāmarupa seems to rest on good foundation (1). The Nidhanpur inscription is an epigraphic record of very great historic value.

In the first part of the sixth century during the reign of Nārāyanavarman or his son Mahābhutavarman Yāsodharman king of Malwa, who defeated Mihiragula, the leader of the white Huns, is said to have conquered the whole of northern India from the Louhitya (Brahmaputra) to the western ocean. This is recorded in his Mandasor pillar inscription (2) wherein it is emphasized that Yasodharman conquered territories which even the Guptas (on the east) and the Huns (on the west) failed to penetrate. It is possible to detect here a reference to Kāmarupa which was always outside the Gupta empire. The invasion of Kāmarupa by Yasodharman is here indicated. It is not known how far this invasion was successful. Any way, the conquest of Eastern India by Yasodharman, in the early part of the sixth century, shows that about that period the Gupta power in Magadha was nearly extinct.

(1) Epigraphia Indica vol. XIX page 246.
(2) Fleet Corp. Ins. Ind. page 146.

As a matter of fact the Imperial Guptas ceased to rule after the close of the fifth century and, as remarked by Vincent Smith, that line passed by an obscure transition into what is known as the dynasty of the "Later Guptas of Magadha." This dynasty did not exercise sovereignty even over the whole of Magadha, part of which came under the sway of the Varmans of Maukhari. Taking advantage of the decline of the Gupta power the Kāmarupa kings appear to have extended their kingdom towards the west. Down to the end of the fifth century the tract of country between the Teesta and the Kosi formed the Pundravardhana Bhukti of the Gupta empire.* In the first quarter of the sixth century we find this tract within the Kāmarupa kingdom. Mahābhutavarman's grant referred to

* It has been recently announced in the newspapers that Prof R. G. Basak has discovered a copper-plate in the Bogra district which bears the date 128 Gupta era equivalent to 447 A.D. The grant is not however from the Gupta emperor Kumara Gupta I who was reigning at the time. It is stated that the plate simply records the purchase of some revenue-free state lands. That the occurence of the Gupta era in any particular locality does not necessarily mean the ascendancy of the Gupta power in that locality is proved by the use of that era in Harjaravarman's rock inscription at Tezpur some 350 years after the extinction of the Gupta power. Kāmarupa never formed a part of the Gupta empire but it appears that the Pundravardhana Bhukti, which included the districts of Bogra, Dinajpur and Rajshahi, was for some centuries within the Gupta empire though both before and after the existence of this empire these districts, or at least parts of them, were included in Kāmarupa . There was no local era in Bengal prior to the twelfth century A.D.

above may be dated about 525 A.D. This grant consisted of lands in the Chandrapuri Vishaya within the present district of Purnea for, according to the Nidhanpur inscription, the lands granted were on the banks of the old channel of the Kausika or Kosi (1). Rennell's map of Bengal (1783) shows the position of the old channel of the Kosi. It appears that this river originally took an easterly course and flowing to the west of Purnea fell into the Ganges at Rajmahal or nearly forty miles below its present confluence with the Ganges. It appears from the Nidhanpur inscription that the river had already abandoned its old channel by the time Bhāskaravarman confirmed his ancestor's grant. That the Kausika, mentioned in the inscription, is the Kosi river in modern Bihar admits of no doubt, but certain writers have attempted to identify Kausika with the Kusiara river in Sylhet (2). These writers conveniently forget that in the ninth century another Kāmarupa king, named Vanamāla, granted lands adjoining the Chandrapuri Vishaya and, in order to localize the lands more definitely, he stated in his inscription that the lands lay to the west of the Teestā (*Trisrotāyāh paschimatah*). After this, any attempt to locate the Chandrapuri Vishaya anywhere in the Sylhet district cannot but be regarded as childish.

Towards the close of the sixth century the

(1) Kāmarupa Sasanavali page 41.
(2) I.H.Q. vol. VII. No. 4.

dynasty of the Later Guptas produced a powerful king named Mahāsena Gupta. By checking the Maukharis in mid-India he re-established the Gupta power to some extent. After this he turned his attention towards the east where the Kāmarupa kings had appropriated to themselves the whole of the Pundravardhana bhukti. He was therefore compelled to declare war against the then Kāmarupa king Susthitavarman, the father of Bhāskaravarman. It appears that Susthitavarman sustained a crushing defeat and Mahāsena Gupta earned a great victory which was glorified by his grandson in the Aphshad inscription. It is stated in this inscription that Susthitavarman was defeated by Mahāsena Gupta "whose mighty fame, marked in honour of victory over the illustrious Susthitavarman (and white) as a full-blown Jasmine flower or water-lily, or as a pair of necklace of pearls pounded into little bits, is still constantly sung on the banks of the Lauhitya, the surfaces of which are (so) cool, by the Siddhas in pairs, when they wake up after sleeping in the shade of the betel plants that are in full bloom" (1). This panegyric was justified for the victory had really important political consequences. Mahāsena Gupta recovered the whole of the Pundravardhana bhukti and the Kāmarupa boundary was pushed back to the Teesta- Karatoya.* The result was that the territories which included the lands donated by Mahābhutavarman in the

(1) Fleet Corp, Ins, Ind. vol III page 206.

* Before 1784 the Karatoya was only a branch of

previous century were lost to Kāmarupa. When in the early part of the seventh century Śaśānka was overthrown, Bhāskaravarman re-acquired the lost tracts and confirmed the grant of his ancestor. This explains why the confirmation was issued immediately after the overthrow of Śaśānka and from the victorious camp itself where Bhāskaravarman was "accompanied by a fleet of war-boats, war-elephants, cavalry and infantry."

Susthitavarman, though defeated, was a great king and therefore in the Aphshad inscription he is described as "illustrious". The victory over him and the recovery of the territories were therefore regarded as a great triumph as the text of the inscription indicates. Susthitavarman could not retalliate the defeat during his life-time. He left this duty to his worthy son Bhāskaravarman.

We can now tentatively suggest the chronology of the kings of the dynasty of Pushyavarman as follows:-

Name of king.	Approximate reign.
Pushyavarman	380-400 A.D.
I	
Samudravarman	400-420 "
I	

the Teesta and bifurcating from it flowed towards the east through Ghoraghat (Rennell's Bengal Atlas, Map no. V). The Karatoya is now a river to the west of the Teesta (The "ten-mile" Atlas of India, vol. 1, Map no. 41-10).

Balavarman I 420-440 „
I
Kalyānavarman 440-460 „
I
Ganapativarman 460-480 „
I
Mahendravarman 480-500 „
I
Nārāyanavarman 500-520 „
I
Mahābhutavarman 520-540 „
I
Chandramukhavarman 540-560 „
I
Sthitavarman 560-580 „
I
Susthitavarman (Mrigānka) 580-600 „
I
Bhāskaravarman (Kumāra) 600-650 „

The starting fixed point in the above chronology is the reign of Bhāskaravarman, the contemporary of Harshavardhana - Siladitya or Śri Harsha and the Chinese pilgrim Yuan Chwang. Śri Harsha ruled from 606 to 648 A.D. It appears that Bhāskaravarman was older than Śri Harsha, for in the procession at Kanauj in 644 A.D. Śri Harsha himself dressed as Indra while Bhāskaravarman personated as Brahmā. The role of Brahmā would not have been assigned to Bhāskaravarman if he was not older than Śri Harsha. We can therefore place Bhāskaravarman's accession to the throne about 600 A.D. From this point, by allowing on an average 20 years for the reign of each king we can place Pushyavarman's accession about 380 A.D., but probably he ruled earlier. The allowance of 20 years for each reign can not be considered extravagant in view of the long reign of Bhāskaravarman himself which covered nearly fifty years. The names of the above mentioned kings, as given in the inscription, can be partly verified from two sources. The first is the clay-seal of Bhāskaravarman which was discovered during excavation of the Nalanda ruins. This seal contains the names of all the kings and queens from Ganapativarman to Bhāskaravarman. The second is the *Harsha Charita* of Bāna who flourished in the court of Śri Harsha and was therefore a contemporary of Bhāskaravarman. In this work the names of the Kāmarupa kings and queens from Mahābhutavarman are given. The only difference is that Mahābhutavarman is mentioned in the *Harsha Charita* as Bhutivarman. As a matter of fact, in line 51 of the Nidhanpur inscription itself Mahābhutavarman is referred to as Bhutivarman. Evidently he was popularly known as Bhutivarman.

CHAPTER IV.

KAMARUPA OF BHASKARAVARMAN.

Susthitavarman, known also as Śri Mrigānka, had two sons viz. Supratisthitavarman and Bhāskaravarman. It is stated in the *Harsha Charita* that the second son Bhāskaravarman was the direct successor of his father on the throne of Prāgjyotisha. On the other hand it is stated in Bhāskaravarman's inscription that "surrounded by learned men and accompanied by an well equipped army consisting of war-elephants his (Supratisthitavarman's) birth (rise) was for the good of others." Pandit Vidyāvinod detects here an indication that Supratisthitavarman actually succeeded his father and having ruled for a few years died (probably without leaving any issue). He supposes that during his short reign Supratisthitavarman introduced various reforms the good results of which were enjoyed by his brother who succeeded him (1). Previously

---

(1) Kāmarupa Sāsanavali p. 31 Footnote (3)

however, the learned Pandit supposed that, during the life-time of his father, Supratisthitavarman, as heir-apparent, introduced various measures of progress and reform in the administration of the kingdom the beneficial effects of which he could not himself enjoy as king but which were actually enjoyed by his younger brother Bhāskaravarman when he became King (1). We think the Pandit's previous supposition was correct. The reference to the "*Supratisthita Kataka*" indicates that the army was re-organized. Supratisthitavarman must have witnessed the defeat sustained by his father at the hands of the Magadha king Mahāsena Gupta. His first duty, as heir-apparent, was therefore to strengthen the army, particularly that arm of it which consisted of war-elephants. Unfortunately it seems he died during the life-time of his father and could not therefore succeed as king but his brother, on ascending the throne, found himself at the head of a strong and well-equipped army with the aid of which he subsequently defeated Śaśanka and conquered Bengal. Bhāskaravarman therefore actually enjoyed the fruits of the labours of his deceased brother and this is exactly what the writer of his inscription seems to have meant.

It is however significant that Bhāskaravarman, even after he succeeded to the throne, used to be known as Kumāra (Prince). In this respect a parallel can be found in his celebrated contemporary

(1) Pandit Vidyāvinod's paper on Bhāskaravarman's copper-plate inscription, published in the Annual Report of the Kāmarupa Anusandhān Samiti for the year 1916 - 17, edited by Chandra Nath Sarma, B. L.

Harshavardhana of Thaneswar who in 606 A.D., on being invited to ascend the throne, after the murder of his elder brother Rājyavardhana, at first refused to consent but after consulting a Buddhist oracle agreed to carry on the government designating himself as Prince Silāditya till 612 A.D. when his formal coronation took place (1). As we have already shown, Bhāskaravarman became king earlier, probably about 600 A.D. and so it can not be said that he emulated the example of Harshavardhana and styled himself as Kumāra or Prince. Rather the reverse might have been the case. The actual reasons why Bhāskaravarman was called Kumāra are not quite clear. It can be suspected that he was a bachelor throughout his life. In any case it seems that he occupied the throne on his father's death and soon gave abundant proofs of his political sagacity which, in the words of his panegyrist, the writer of the Nidhanpur inscription, "earned for him the reputation of a second *Brihaspati* well known to others."

On ascending the throne Bhāskarvarman found two strong rival powers growing in northern India, viz. one in central and northern Bengal under Śaśanka Deva and the other in mid-India under Prabhākaravardhana, the father of the famous Śri Harshavardhana. The origin of Śaśānka is shrouded in mystery. Some scholars suppose that he belonged to the line of the later Guptas of Magadha and Pandit Vidyāvinod seems to have found no difficulty in assuming that he was a son of Mahāsena

---

(1) Vincent Smith's Early History of India pp.350-351

Gupta (1). It is however curious that the Aphshad inscription of Adityasena, the grandson of Mahāsena Gupta, makes no mention of Śaśānka. It is known that Śaśānka was a devotee of Siva while the Guptas were Vaisnavas. His descent from the Gupta line is therefore extremely doubtful. In the Rhotasgarh rock-inscription of a seal one Saśānka Deva is mentioned as Mahasāmanta (2). It seems therefore that Saśānka Deva was at first only a local chief or sāmanta owning allegiance to a superior over-lord who was probably Mahāsena Gupta. As already stated, the Kāmarupa kings had extended their sway over northern and perhaps central Bengal after the decline of the Gupta power. About the last quarter of the sixth century, Mahāsena Gupta tried to check the growing aggressions of the Kāmarupa kings. It seems that Śaśānka gave powerful aid to Mahāsena Gupta who inflicted a defeat on Susthitavarman, the king of Kāmarupa. The Magadha king thus recovered northern and central Bengal over which Śaśānka Deva was appointed as Mahā-sāmanta or governor. Subsequently, taking advantage of the death of Mahāsena Gupta and the weakness of his minor son Mādhava Gupta, Śaśānka proclaimed himself as independent king of central and northern Bengal and also struck coins.* Babu Nagendra Nath Basu surmises that

(1) Kāmarupa Sāsanavali p.15 (Introduction).

(2) Fleet Corpus Inscriptionum Indicarum vol. III p. 284.

* From numismatic evidence Mr. Bhattasāli has proved that Sasānka did not belong to the Gupta line but was almost certainly the successor of Samachāra Deva two

he was a Kayastha of the Deva family (1). In the Ganjam inscription of Mādhava Varman also he is named "Mahārājadhirāja Śaśānka Deva" (2). As he was king of central and northern Bengal he is mentioned by Yuan Chwang as king of Karnasuvarna (central Bengal) and by Bānabhatta as king of Gauda (northern Bengal). He soon attained to such power that he not only challenged the feeble Magadha ruler Mādhava Gupta on the west and the Kāmarupa power on the east but also subjugated the whole of lower Bengal, Chota Nagpur and Orissa on the south. About 600 A.D., evidently after the death of Mahāsena Gupta, he appears to have successfully invaded Magadha where his zeal for the orthodox system of Hindu religion led him to perpetrate acts which gained for him notoriety for ever. He is said to have uprooted the sacred Bodhi-tree in Gayā and thrown into the river the sacred stone bearing the footprints of Gautama Buddha. The Guptas of Magadha were noted for their benign toleration of Buddhism during centuries. It is hardly conceivable that a scion of that noble family did not scruple to perform such acts of sacrilege. The theory that he belonged to the Gupta family is therefore quite untenable. Towards the west of Kāmarupa, Śasānka

---

of whose coins, like the one of Saśānka, also bear on the reverse the legend *Narendra vinata* thus showing that Narendra or Narendra Gupta was not the name of Śaśānka as originally supposed from this legend. (J.P.A.S.B. vol XIX 1923 No. 6. Numismatic number).

(1) Banger Jātiya Itihās, Rājanya Kānda.

(2) Epigraphia Indica vol. VI. p. 143.

appears to have held possession of that portion of territory which included the lands granted by Mahābhutavarman to a large number of Brahmans. It is therefore unnecessary to stress why he was regarded as the natural enemy of Bhāskaravarman who must have been waiting for a favourable opportunity to regain the lost dominions and to retalliate the defeat inflicted on his father. Śasānka was however too powerful a ruler to be dealt with and Bhāskaravarman therefore wisely refrained from precipitating matters by himself launching an attack on Karnasuvarna, the capital founded by Śaśānka. The long looked for opportunity came at last. On the death of Prabhākaravardhana his eldest son Rājyavardhana ascended the throne at Thaneswar. It appears that a branch of the Gupta family then ruled at Malwa. Deva Gupta of this family had overthrown the Maukhari king Grahavarman who was the brother-in-law of Rājavardhana. Deva Gupta had insulted Rājyaśri, the sister of Rājyavardhana, who at once marched to the assistance of Grahavarman. In the meantime, Śaśānka appears to have marched to the assistance of Deva Gupta. The fact that he allied with Deva Gupta led R.D. Banerji to suppose that he belonged to the Gupta family. Whatever that may be, Rājyavardhana easily defeated Deva Gupta but Śaśānka managed to invite him to his camp on a false promise and there treacherously murdered him. This incident is mentioned not only by Bāna but also by the Chinese pilgrim Yuan Chwang. On getting this information Śri Harsha resolved to take revenge on the murderer. " He made preparations to subdue the arrogant and powerful king of Gauda and had just started on his march when he was met by Hangsavega, an ambassador from Bhāskaravarman of Kāmarupa, with valuable presents. The *Harsha Charita* of Bāna gives a detailed account of Hangsavega's meeting with Śri Harsha. When the chamberlain announced that Hangshavega "a confidential messenger" sent by the Kumāra Raja of Prāgjyotisha was waiting at the gate, Śri Harsha commanded "admit him at once" (1). The chamberlain then entered with Hangsavega "whose very exterior, delighting the eye with graceful flexions, belied the weight of his qualities" (2). The messenger was followed by a long train of men carrying munificent presents" (3). When Hangsavega had gone through the usual ceremonies of paying homage Śri Harsha asked, " Hangsavega, is the noble prince well? Hangsavega replied, " At this moment he is well, since your majesty so respectfully inquires with a voice bathed in affection and moist with a flow of friendship." After this Hangsavega began to unfold the presents one by one saying " excepting only a heart replete with respect, a present worthy of your majesty, who is the vessel for the grandeur of governing the four oceans, is with difficulty attainable in the world" (4). Nevertheless, Hangsavega made particular mention of the royal umbrella named Ābhoga which the Kumāra raja sent and which was a

(1) Harsha Charita (Cowell's translation).
(2), (3), (4), Ibid.

"family heirloom" derived from Varuna (1). He declared that "fire does not burn it, nor wind tear it away, nor water wet it, nor dust defile it, nor age corrode it" (2). The king inspected all the presents and this done he dismissed all the servants and addressing Hangsavega said "explain your errand." Hangsavega then said:— "In former times, your majesty, the holy earth having through union with the Boar become pregnant, gave birth in hell to a son called Naraka. * * It was he who won this umbrella, the external heart of Varuna. In the posterity of this hero, when many great Meru—like kings such as Bhagadatta, Puspadatta and Vajradatta had passed away, there was born a Mahārājadhirāja named Susthiravarman, a splendid hero famous in the world as Mrigānka, great grandson of Mahārāja Bhutivarman, grandson of Chandramukhavarman and son of Sthitivarman. * * * * * * To this auspiciously named king was born, by his queen Syamādevi, a son and heir Bhāskaradyuti otherwise named Bhāskaravarman. * * Now from childhood upwards it was this prince's firm determination never to do homage to any being except the lotus-feet of Śiva. Such an ambition, so difficult of attainment in the three worlds, may be reached by one of three means viz. by a conquest of the whole earth, by death or by a friend like your majesty. * * * The friendship of monarchs again has regard to utility. And what possible contribution of utility could incline your

(1) Harsha Charita (Cowell's translation).
(2) Ibid

majesty to friendship? Wealth is but a remote consideration to your majesty whose aim is to amass fame. One who relies upon his arm alone has no occasion for desiring the assistance of his other members, much less of a stranger. To one greedy to seize the four combined oceans what qualification is there even in the proffered gift of a part of the earth? * * * * Seeing therefore that ours is an object attainable only by impossible expedients, let your majesty, graciously regarding a mere petition, hear. The sovereign of Prāgjyotisha desires with your majesty an imperishable alliance. * * * If your majesty's heart too is inclined to friendship and can comprehend that friends enter upon a slavery disguised under a synonym then enough! Commission me to say that the sovereign of Prāgjyotisha may enjoy your majesty's, as Mandāra Vishnu's, hearty embrace. * * * * * In this moon-like face * * * let the glory of the sovereign of Prāgjyotisha at length indulge to satiety the longing of her eyes. If your majesty accepts not his love, command me what to report to my master" (1).

This remarkable speech of the consummate diplomat seems to have moved the youthful Śri Harsha. "When the messenger ceased speaking the king, who from previous reports of the prince's great qualities had conceived a very high respect for him and whose affection had been raised to a climax by the affair of the umbrella Ābhoga, replied almost bashfully with profound respect :—"How

(1) **Harsha Charita (Cowell's translation).**

could the mind of one like me possibly even in a dream show aversion, Hangsavega, when such a great and noble spirit, such a treasure of virtue and captain of the worthy bestows his love as an absent friend upon me? * * * * * The ten regions are the unhired servants of the sweet qualities of this noble. * * * * The Prince's design too is excellent. Stout-armed himself, with me, a devotee of the bow, for his friend, to whom save Śiva, need he pay homage? This resolve of his increases my affection. The heart respects the lion, though a brute, for his pride" (1).

After this Hangsavega suitably replied to the king and took his leave. It appears that Śri Harsha sent "a load of answering gifts in charge of eminent envoys."(2). An offensive and defensive alliance was thus formed between Śri Harsha and Bhāskaravarman. This alliance was disastrous for Śāsānka for while Śri Harsha's cousin and general Bhandi probably attacked from the west, Bhāskaravarman at once attacked from the east and occupied Karna Suvarna* which was near to Kāmarupa. From his Nidhanpur copper-plate inscription it appears that Bhāskaravarman attacked with a strong navy of huge boats, which must have passed down the Brahmaputra and then proceeded up the Ganges, and that his army consisted of war-elephants, cavalry and infantry (*Mahā nau hastyaswa patti*). Being attacked from two

(1) & (2). Harsha Charita (Cowell's translation).

* Karnasuvarna has been identified with modern Rangamati on the western bank of the Bhagirathi in the Kandi subdivision of the Murshidabad district.

sides and thus outflanked Śāsanka fled towards Orissa. The Nidhanpur copper-plate grant was issued from Bhāskaravarman's victorious camp at Karnasuvarna (*Jaya sabdārtha skandhābhārāt Karnasuvarna vāsakāt*) (1). Thus the defeat of his father was avenged and the lost dominions were regained. Bhāskaravarman now became the master or overlord of practically the whole of Gauda excluding only Magadha which was included in the dominions of Śri Harsha.

Sir Edward Gait, relying on Vincent Smith and Pandit Padmanath Vidyāvinod, holds that Bhāskaravarman came into possession of Karnasuvarna after the death of Śri Harsha. This supposition is evidently incorrect. Śaśanka held sway over central and lower Bengal and also perhaps over part of Magadha and Orissa. It appears that being overthrown by Bhāskaravarman in Karnasuvarna he retired to the south and continued to rule there as evidenced by the Ganjam inscription of Mādhavavarman, a *Samanta* under him (2). This inscription is dated 619 A.D. and from this fact Pandit Vidyāvinod and some other scholars have wrongly assumed that Śaśānka continued to rule at Karnasuvarna till 619 A.D.* Babu Nagendranath

(1). Epigraphia Indica, vol. XII. p. 78.
(2). Epigraphia Indica Vol. VI. p. 144.

* In his recent work "Kāmarupa Śāsanāvali', Pandit Vidyavinod admits that Saśānka was driven out of Karnasuvarna earlier through the combined efforts Sri Harsha and Bhāskaravarman, but he holds that Bhāskaravarman only temporarily occupied Karnasuvarna which was included in the dominions of Sri Harsha. There is, however, no basis for this statement.

Basu believes that after the alliance between Śri Harsha and Bhāskaravarman, Śaśānka lost Karnasuvarna and was obliged to retire to the hilly country in the south (1). He holds also that probably Śri Harsha allowed Bhāskaravarman to rule over Gauda and Karnasuvarna and established Mādhava Gupta, son of Mahāsena Gupta, in Magadha as a vassal ruler. This was probably the actual fact. R. D. Banerji also thinks that Śaśanka was overthrown by the combined efforts of Bhāskaravarman and Śri Harsha (2). In his latest work, the History of Orissa, R. D. Banerji writes :—

"Whatever be the real origin of Śasānka, there is no doubt about the fact that eventually he was driven out of Karnasuvarna. It is quite possible that this event had taken place before the date of the Ganjam plate and at that time he had lost his possessions in Bengal and was the master of Orissa only."

The theory of Sir Edward Gait and Vincent Smith that Bhāskaravarman acquired Karnasuvarna after the death of Śri Harsha is therefore quite incorrect. It is reasonable to suppose that Śaśānka was driven out of Karnasuvarna about 610 A.D. The coronation of Śri Harsha took place about 612 A.D. after Saśānka had been overthrown and Bhāskaravarman had come into possession of Karnasuvarna. A writer in the Indian Historical

(1) Bangalar Jātiya Itihash vol. 1. pp. 65-66.
(2) Bangalar Itihash vol. 1. pp. 87-88.

Quarterly (1) points out that Śri Harsha's sway never reached Bengal and that Śaśānka's kingdom passed to Bhāskaravarman as otherwise he could not have controlled the sea-route to China and promised a safe passage to Yuan Chwang (2). It appears clear from Bana's *Harsha Charita* that after the alliance with Bhāskaravarman Sri Harsha felt at ease concerning the conquest of Gauda and despatching his cousin Bhandi to invade Gauda (perhaps in collaboration with Bhāskaravarman), he himself set out to search for his sister Rājyaśri who had escaped to the jungles of Vindhyā. Karnasuvarna was actually conquered by Bhāskaravarman as stated in the Nidhanpur plate. Another well known scholar, Mr. Ramaprasad Chanda, writing in a Bengali magazine, rejects Vidyāvinod's theory that Bhāskaravarman occupied Karnasuvarna only temporarily and holds that during the seventh century Gauda was included within the kingdom of Kāmarupa (3). Beal, in his introduction to the biography, states, " Bhāskaravarman the king of Kāmarupa and probably former kings of that kingdom had the sea-route to China under their special protection ". (4). Perhaps Beal would have been more correct if he had stated that Bhāskaravarman and his successors had the control over the Tamralipti region and the sea-route for at least 100 years after the death of Bhaskaravarman.

(1) " Finger-posts of Bengal History " by Bejoynath Sarka. (Indian Historical Quarterly. vol. VI. pp. 442-443)

(2) Life of Hiuen Tsiang, translation by Beal. p. 188.

(3) Prabasi, Baisakh 1339 B.S. pp. 62-66.

(4) Beal's introduction to the Life of Hiuen Tsiang p. XVI

The biographers of Yuan Chwang mention Kumāra Raja as the Lord of Eastern India and this was the appellation applied by subsequent Chinese writers to the kings of Kāmarupa. The "five Indies" of the Chinese writers were Northern India, Western India, Central or Mid-India, Southern India and Eastern India. "Eastern India" comprised modern Assam and Bengal proper including the whole of the delta of the Ganges together with Sambalpur, Orissa and Ganjam (1). The fact that both in the biography and the Si-yu ki, Pundravardhana, Samatata, Karnasuvarna and Tāmralipti are separately mentioned, does not mean that these countries were then independent principalities. As a matter of fact it is significant that the names of the kings of these countries are not mentioned but the name of the reigning king of Kāmarupa is mentioned. They were probably then administered by local chiefs who were vassals of the king of Kāmarupa. In his Nidhanpur inscription the kings who were vassals of Bhāskaravarman are referred to and it is stated that he "equalled the prowess of the whole ring of his feudatories by the strength of his own arm" (2). The pilgrim while describing his travels in mid-India similarly mentions countries like Brahmapura, Ahi Khetra, Virasana, Kapitha, Kanauj, Ayodhyā, Prayāga, Kausambi, Kapilavasthu, Kusinagara, Benares and Magadha over all of which Śri Harsha was admittedly the suzerain power.

---

(1) Cunningham's Ancient Geography of India.
(2) Epigraphia Indica vol. XII. p. 78.

Yuan Chwang mentions Saśānka as a "recent king" of Karnasuvarna, but in his account of his visit to Karnasuvarna he makes no mention of the reigning king of that principality as he does in the case of Kāmarupa. The fact is that nearly 20 years before he arrived in India Śaśānka had been overthrown and driven out of Central Bengal over which Bhāskaravarman became the overlord. Yuan Chwang makes no mention of any king reigning in Samatata which was near the sea, but when the next Chinese traveller I-Tsing visited Eastern India about 670 A.D. one Rājabhata was the Raja of Samatata. This Rājabhata was either a vassal under the Kāmarupa king or Samatata was outside the dominions acquired by Bhāskaravarman.

Beal mentions that according to the records left by I-Tsing, respecting other pilgrims visiting India shortly after Yuan Chwang, a Korean priest named Hwui Lun, otherwise known as Prajnāvarma, visited India, some years after the departure of Yuan Chwang. He was evidently a contemporary of Adityasena, the author of the Aphshad inscription, for it appears he recorded that at Nalanda "recently a king called Sun-army (Adityasena) built, by the side of the old temple, another which is now newly finished"(1). It is further mentioned in the records that "formerly a Maharaja called Śri-Gupta built this temple (the Deer temple) for the use of Chinese priests. He was prompted to do so by the arrival of

(1) Beal's introduction to the Life of Hiuen Tsiang p. XXVII

about twenty priests of that country who had travelled from Sz'chuen to the Mahābudhi temple to pay their worship. Being impressed by their pious demeanour he gave them the land and the revenues of about twenty villages as an endowment. This occurred some 500 years ago. The land has now reverted to the king of Eastern India, whose name is Deva Varma, but he is said to be willing to give back the temple land and the endowment in case any priest came from China" (1). Śri Gupta mentioned in the above extract, was undoubtedly the grand-father of Chandra Gupta I, the founder of the Gupta empire. Śri Gupta was only a local chief in Magadha with his capital at Patna or its vicinity. So the twenty villages endowed by him, must have been within his small principality, probably not very far from Nalanda. It appears that after Śri Harsha's death these twenty villages of Magadha came into the possesion or Bhāskaravarman, the king of "Eastern India", from whom they were inherited by Deva Varma who was perhaps his immediate successor. It is not possible to trace a king called Deva Varma of another dynasty ruling in Eastern India at that time. The Varmans of Maukhari belonged to Madhya-desha or mid-India. The kings of Kāmarupa used the suffix "Varma Deva" after their names. The full name of Bhāskaravarman, given in the Nidhanpur plate, is "Bhāskara-varma-Deva".

(1) Beal's introduction to the Life of Hiuen Tsiang p. XXVII.

It is therefore very probable that the Korean priest transposed "Varma-Deva" into "Deva Varma". In any case, it seems certain that the king named as Deva-varma was a Kāmarupa king. It is therefore clear that even after Bhāskaravarman at least the Eastern part of Magadha with perhaps the whole of modern Bengal, excepting probably Samatata, was under the overlordship of the Kāmarupa kings. This supremacy lasted for at least 100 years till the overthrow of the Kāmarupa king Śri Harsha Varma Deva about 750 A.D.

Yuan Chwang came to India with the object of studying Buddhistic lore and seeing for himslf the various Buddhist shrines in India. He had no idea of visiting Kāmarupa which according to him had no trace of Buddhism till that time. In fact after his first stay at Nalanda he set out to see the sacred Buddhist places and though visiting Karna-Suvarna and Samatata which contained Buddhist *stupas* he did not care to enter Kāmarupa proper. After traversing through southern India and western India he returned to Nalanda and had decided to return to China when by chance he came to visit Kāmarupa and thereafter meet emperor Harsha-Vardhana. Had it not been for his visit to Kāmarupa under unforeseen circumstances and the subsequent meeting of the two kings on the banks of the Ganges perhaps he would not have been present at the great assembly at Kanauj. The circumstances leading to his visit to Kāmarupa are therefore interesting and these can be gathered from the biography of Yuan Chwang written by his disciple Hwui-li and subsequently enlarged by Yen Thsang. It appears that a certain Brahman from "Eastern India" who was a heretic (probably a non-Buddhist or at least a non-believer of the Mahāyāna system) came to Nalanda when Yuan Chwang was residing there with Śilabhadra, the great Buddhist professor. The Brahman came to dispute with the monks at Nalanda. He was defeated and returning to Kāmarupa he told Kumāra Raja about the high qualities of the Chinese monk. Bhāskaravarman then sent an invitation to the Chinese traveller addressed to Śilabhadra. Before the message was received Yuan Chwang chanced to meet a naked *Nirgrantha* and asked him to foretell whether he would be able to return to China safe together with all the sacred books and images collected by him. The *Nirgrantha* then took a piece of white stone and drew a figure on the ground, and after casting the lot he replied "Do not be anxious. Siladitya raja and Kumāra raja will themselves despatch men as escort. The Master will successfully return without accident." Yuan Chwang then asked, "As to these two kings I have never yet seen them. How then can such a kindness befall me?" The *Nirgrantha* replied, "Kumāra raja has already sent messengers to invite you to go to him. In two or three days they should arrive. After you have seen Kumāra you will also see Siladitya." The *Nirgrantha* then went away. After two days the messengers sent by Kumāra raja of "Eastern India" arrived and presented a letter to Śilabhadra. The letter ran as follows: —

"Your disciple wishes to see the great priest come from China. I pray you, respected sir, to send him and so gratify this imperial thought of mine". On getting this message Śilabhadra called the congregation and said that as Yuan Chwang had already agreed to come to Śri Harsha's capital for a disputation with the exponents of Hināyana he should not go to Kāmarupa. He then replied to the messenger in the following terms:—"The priest of China is anxious to return to his own country and so is unable to comply with the king's request." On hearing this reply Bhāskaravarman again despatched another messenger with the following letter:—"Although the Master wishes to return home, yet for a little while let him come to your disciple. There shall be no difficulty about his departure. I pray you comply with my humble request and do not again decline to send". Śilabhadra having again refused to consent Bhāskaravarman was greatly enraged and sent yet another messenger with a personal despatch for Śilabhadra to the following effect:— "Your disciple like a common man has followed the way of worldly pleasure and has not yet learnt the converting power residing in the law of Buddha. And now when I heard the name of the priest belonging to the outside country my body and soul were overjoyed; expecting the opening of the germ of religion (within me). But you sir, have again refused to let him come here, as if you desired to cause the world to be for ever plunged in the dark night (of ignorance). Is this the way in which your Eminence hands down and transmits the bequeathed law for the deliverance and salvation of all the world? Having an invincible longing to think kindly of and show respect to the Master I have again sent a messenger with a written request. If he does not come, your disciple will then let the evil portion of himself prevail. In recent times Śaśānka raja was equal still to the destruction of the law and uprooted the Bodhi tree. Do you, my Master, suppose that your disciple has no such power as this? If necessary then I will equip my army and elephants and, like the clouds, sweep down on and trample to the very dust that monastery of Nalanda. These words are true as the Sun, Master, it is better for you to examine and see what you will do". The threat uttered towards the end of the message had the desired effect for Śilabhadra having read the letter addressed Yuan Chwang thus: — "With regard to that King, his better mind is fast bound and weak; within his territories the law of Buddha has not widely extended. Since the time that he heard your honourable name he has formed a deep attachment for you. Perhaps you are destined to be, in this period of your existence, his good friend. Use your best diligence then and go. You have become a disciple in order to benefit the world; this then is perhaps your just opportunity; and as when you destroy a tree you have only to cut through the root and the branches will of themselves wither away, so when you arrive in that country only cause the heart of the king to open to the truth and then the people will also be converted. But if you refuse and do not go, then perhaps there will be evil deeds done. Do not shrink from this slight trouble ".

Yuan Chwang agreed and soon after left for Kāmarupa accompanied by the envoy. When he reached the capital of Kāmarupa he was received by Bhāskaravarman and his high officers in state and conducted to the palace. Every day the king arranged music and banquets with religious offerings of flowers and incense. In this way more than a month passed. At this time, while on his way back from the Ganjam campaign, Śri Harsha heard that Yuan Chwang was then a guest of Bhāskaravarman. Being much annoyed he despatched a messenger peremtorily asking the Kumāra raja to send the Chinese priest at once to him. Bhāskaravarman did not like the tone of the message and haughtily replied " He (Śri Harsha) can take my head but he can not take the Master of the Law yet." Śri Harsha was greatly enraged on receiving this message and calling together his attendants he said " Kumāra raja despises me. How comes he to use such coarse language in the matter of a single priest ?" Then he sent another messenger to Kāmarupa with the following imperial order: – " Send the head. that I may have it immediately by my messenger who is to bring it here." On receipt of this message Bhāskaravarman realized the folly of his language and the danger of courting a conflict with the more powerful monarch who had been his ally in disposing of Śaśānka. He therefere at once ordered an army of "20,000 elephants and 30,000 ships" to be equipped. Then embarking with Yuan Chwang they together " passed up the

Ganges" and reached a place called Kio-shu-ho-kio-lo (Kajurgira) where Śri Harsha was encamping. Keeping Yuan Chwang in a pavilion-on-travel * erected on the north bank of the Ganges, Bhāskaravarman with his ministers himself proceeded to meet Śri Harsha who received the Kumāra raja courteously and enquired where the Chinese priest was stopping. Kumāra replied, "He is staying in a certain pavilion-on-travel." Śri Harsha again asked, "And why did he not come with you?" To this Kumāra replied, "Mahārāja has respect for the virtuous and loves religion. Why not send for the Master to come to confer with the King?" Śri Harsha then realized that he should himself come and see the priest at the pavilion. During the night Śri Harsha came and visited Yuan Chwang with whom he had a long discourse. Śri Harsha at length declared that he proposed to call a grand assembly at Kanauj and "command the Sramans and Brahmans and heretics of the five Indies to attend in order to exhibit the refinements of the Great Vehicle (Mahayāna) and demolish their abusive mind, to make manifest the exceeding merit of the Master and over-throw their proud thought of self." Then at the beginning of the winter Śri Harsha having issued invitations to the leading princes and religious professors of all sects marched all the way to Kanauj in procession accompanied by Bhāskaravarman and Yuan Chang. It is related

* Pavilions-on-travel called Bāhor were used by the Assam kings and are still used by the more influential Vaisnava Gossains of Assam.

that Śri Harsha marched in state along the south bank of the Ganges while Bhāskaravarman marched along the north bank at the head of 500 elephants, clad in armour, both keeping pace with each other. They reached Kanauj after a march of 90 days. At Kanauj itself daily processions took place. At these processions the image of Buddha was carried. Śri Harsha, attired as Indra, held the *chattra* over the image while Bhāskaravarman, dressed as Brahmā, waved a white *chameri*. There were assembled no less than 18 vassal kings of different countries of India besides three thousand Buddhist priests, about the same number of Brahmans and Nirgranthas and about a thousand monks from Nalanda. It is said that of all the kings assembled only "Śri Harsha and Bhāskaravarman wore tiaras like the Devas with flower wreaths and jewelled ribons."

We have given above rather full quotations from Yuan Chwang's biography, written by his favourite disciple, to show the importance of Bhāskaravarman and the kingdom of Kāmarupa at this time. It is clear that emperor Śri Harsha treated Bhāskaravarman, in every way, as a respected ally and friend and not as a vassal king.* Even Śri Harsha's own son-in-law, Dhruvabhatta, the king of South India, was treated as a monarch

* In own his drama named Priyadarsikā Śri Harsha himself distinguished between his vassals (Pādapadmopajibiua) and his allies (rāja samubena). Mr Kale says that the latter included the kings of Kāmarupa and Valabhi.

(Priyadarsika of Śri Harsha, edited by M.R. Kale).

inferior to Bhāskaravarman in rank.

After the assembly in Kanauj was dissolved Śri Harsha arranged a grand distribution of charity at Allahabad at the confluence of the two holy rivers, the Ganges and the Jumna. Śri Harsha accompanied by all the 18 kings went there. The camp of Śri Harsha was on the north bank of the Ganges while that of Kumāra raja was on the south of the Jumna, by the side of a flowering grove. In the morning the military followers of Śri Harsha and Kumāra raja embarked in ships and the attendants of Dhruvabhatta mounted their elephants and, so arranged in an imposing order, proceeded to the place of the assembly. The kings of the eighteen kingdoms joined the cortege according to arrangement. Śri Harsha distributed untold wealth to Buddhists, Brahmans, heretics, the poor and the destitute. Even his own gems and wearing garments were given away. At length the king had to beg from his sister a second-hand garment to put on. Such was charity as was understood and practised by the ancient Hindu kings of India. It is fortunate that an eminent foreigner - a savant - was present to witness this distribution of charity and that he left a record of what he saw with his own eyes.

After this ceremony was over, Yuan Chwang took leave of Śri Harsha and the Kumara raja. Both of them were affected during the leave-taking. The Kumāra raja addressed Yuan Chwang thus :— "If the Master is able to dwell in my dominions and receive my religious offerings I will undertake to found one hundred monasteries on the Masters' behalf." Yuan Chwang replied, "The country of China is very far from this and has but recently heard of the law of Buddha. Although it has received a general knowledge of the truth yet it has not accepted it in its entirety. On this account therefore I have come to inform myself how to put and end to differences. And now having completed my aim (I remember) how the learned men of my country are longing to fathom to their depth the points I have ascertained. Therefore I dare not delay a moment remembering the words of the Sutra: "whoever hinders men from a knowledge of religion shall for generation be born blind." If then you hinder my return you will cause countless disciples to lose the benefit resulting from a knowledge of the law; how then will you escape the dread of being deprived of sight?" To this Kumāra raja replied, "Your humble disciple admires and values the virtue of the Master; and I would ever look up to and serve him; but to stand in the way of the benefit of so many men would truly cause my heart to be filled with fear. I leave the Master to his choice, to go or to stay; but I know not, if you prefer to go, by what route you propose to return. *If you select the southern sea route then I will send official attendants to accompany you.*" The italics are ours. This shows that the southern sea-route from Tāmralipti was then under the control of Bhāskaravarman. Yuan Chwang replied that he would return through North-west India. Kumāra raja then asked, "I pray you let me know what provision you stand in need of." Yuan Chwang replied that he required nothing. Kumāra raja said, "It is impossible to permit you to go thus" and he offered money and valuable articles. Similarly Śri Harsha also offered presents. Yuan Chwang refused to accept anything except a cape called *ho-la-li* made of coarse skin lined with soft down, a present from Bhāskaravarman, which was designed to protect one from rain and cold. Thus the eminent Chinese traveller took his departure with the escort provided by Śri Harsha. Three days after, Śri Harsha, accompanied by Kumāra raja and Dhruvabhata, took several hundred light horsemen with them and, overtaking the pilgrim, accompanied him for some time and then finally returned.

Certain conflicting statements in the Si-yu-ki or the "Record of Western lands" concerning the pilgrim's visit to Ka-mo-lu-po require to be explained. In his first volume "On Yuan Chwang's Travels in India" Watters quotes from the text to show that after the pilgrim had returned to Nalanda finishing his itinerary and had arranged to return to China he received the invitation from Bhāskaravarman and after much hesitation decided, on the advice of Śilabhadra, to accept the king's invitation (1). He then proceeded to Bhāskaravarman's capital straight from Nalanda. In the second volume of Watters' work however it is quoted from the text of the Si-yu-ki to show that the pilgrim, when he started from Nalanda on his travels to the east and south of India, first

(1) Watters on Yuan Chwang vol. 1 p. 348.

came to Irānaparvat in the east and thence to Champā (Bhagalpur). From Champā the pilgrim travelled above 400 li to Ka-chu-wo-ki-lo (Kajughira or Kajangala). According to Cunningham this place is Kunkjol, now called Rājmahal. From this place travelling east he crossed the Ganges and came after a journey of more than 600 li to a country called Pun-na-fa-tan-na (Pundravardhana) which was more than 400 li in circuit. Proceeding east another distance of above 900 li he crossed a large river and came to Ka-mo-lu-po "which was more than a myriad li in circuit." According to the text the pilgrim proceeded from Kāmarupa to Samatata, thence to Tamralipti, thence to Karnasuvarna and thence to Orissa and the south. This narrative conflicts with the account given in the pilgrim's biography and also in the Si-yu-ki itself as stated above. Watters in his second volume says that "we need not suppose that the pilgrim made the journey as indicated in the text" and again in the same volume he states that "notwithstanding the statements of our text, however, we must consider him to have travelled in the manner indicated in the Life" (1). We think Watters is right and Gait has also rightly followed the account given in the biography and made the pilgrim visit Kāmarupa towards the end of his stay in India. As already stated, the pilgrim, though he passed near Kāmarupa at the earlier stage of his itinerary, did not actually enter Kāmarupa as it contained,

(1) Watters on Yuan Chwang vol. II pp. 187 & 192.

till then, no trace, of Buddhism. Watters thinks that at least three fourths of the text, as we have now, were the compilation of Yuan Chwang himself, the remainder being additions or interpolations by Pein - Chi and others(1). The biography is however an authoritative work. Cunningham in his Ancient Geography of India holds that Yuan Chwang visited Kāmarupa twice (2). This is quite improbable because till his visit to Kāmarupa about 643 A.D. he had not met Bhāskaravarman before. Whatever that may be, we find from the text of the Si-yu-ki that the pilgrim found the western boundary of Kāmarupa proper to have been a large river about 900 li to the east of Pundravardhana and that the country was more than a myriad li in circuit. In a subsequent Chinese work, the Tang-shu, the large river is called Ko-lo-tu which is evidently equivalent to Karatoya and not the Louhitya or Brahmaputra as supposed by Watters (3). According to the text of the Si-yu-ki the circumference of the capital of Kāmarupa was thirty li and the king who was named "Sun-armour" (Bhāskaravarman) was a Brahman by caste. His other name was "Youth" or Kumāra. He was a lover of learning and his subjects followed his example. Men of ability came from far lands to study in Kāmarupa. Though the king was not a Buddhist he treated accomplished *sramans* with respect. The reigning king was descended

---

(1) Watters on Yuan Chwang vol. I page 3.
(2) Ancient Geography of India p. LXIX.
(3) Watters on Yuan Chwang vol. II p. 187.

from a stock which originated from Nārāyana Deva (Vishnu) and the sovereignty had been transmitted in the family for 1000 generations. In his Nidhanpur copper-plate inscription Bhāskaravarman is said to " have revealed the light of the Arya religion (*prakāsit āryadharmālō-ka*) by dispelling the accummulated darkness of Kali age, by making a judicious application of his revenues; who has equalled the prowess of the whole ring of his feudatories by the strength of his own arm, who has derived many a way of enjoyment for his hereditary subjects whose loyal devotion to him was augmented by his steadiness, modesty and affability, who is adorned with a wonderful ornament of splendid fame made of the flowery words of praise variously composed by hundreds of kings vanquished by him in battle; whose virtuous activities, like those of Sivi, were applied in making gifts for the benefit of others; whose powers, as of a second precep-tor of the Gods (Brihaspati), was recognized by others on account of his skill in devising and applying the means of politics that appear in suitable moments; whose own conduct was ador-ned by learning, valour, patience, prowess and good actions" (1). It appears that Vasuvarna, the writer of the inscription, did not overdraw the picture of the illustrious king. The reference to the "ring of feudatories" seems to suggest that his vassal rulers combined to throw off the suzereignty of the Kumāra Raja but were unsuccessful.

(1) Epigraphia Indica vol. XII p. 78.

With regard to the country it is stated by the pilgrim that it was low and moist and that the crops were regular. Cocoa-nuts and jack-fruits grew abundantly and were appreciated by the people. The climate was genial. The people were honest, small of stature and black-looking. Their speech differed a little from that of mid-India. They were of violent disposition but were persevering students. They worshipped the Devas and did not believe in Buddhism. The Deva-temples were some hundreds in number and the various systems had some myriads of professed adherents. The few Buddhists in the country performed their acts of devotion in secret.

The pilgrim ascertained from the people that to the east of the country was a series of hills which reached as far as the confines of China. The inhabitants of these hills were akin to the "Man and the Lao". In the south-east of the country elephants were plentiful. This shows that the kingdom then included the whole of the valleys of the Kopili and the Dhansiri which even now contain herds of wild elephants.

The above description, it should be noted, is of Kāmarupa proper and not of the extensive dominions of Bhāskaravarman towards the west. Evidently the pilgrim came into the present district of Kāmarupa and the capital of that time was probably the old Prāgjyotishpur or Gauhati. The pilgrim, with the king and his retinue, must have therefore proceeded down the Brahmaputra and reached the Ganges by a stream which connected the two rivers and then going up the

Ganges reached Rājmahal*. The countries passed through were both Kāmarupa and Karnasuvarna (Central Bengal). Bhāskaravarman would not have selected this route if Karnasuvarna was not then under his sway†. According to the account given in the Si-yu-ki the circumference of Kāmarupa was about 1700 miles. As Gait has pointed out, this circumference must have included the whole of the Assam Valley, the whole of the Surma Valley, a part of North Bengal and a part of Mymensing. The question whether Sylhet was included within the kingdom at that

---

* Prior to 1783 the Brahmaputra did not meet the Ganges at all. The combined waters of the Brahmaputra and the Megna fell into the sea separately. There were, however, navigable rivers connecting the Brahmaputra with the Ganges. From Rennel's map of 1783 we find that the Jenni river, issuing from the Brahmaputra near Sherpur (Sherpur Dashkāhaniā) joined the Ganges near Juffergunj, below Pubna and Ruttongunj, and that the Karatoya, coming from the north, also fell into the Ganges at this place. Perhaps the river Jenni subsequently got the name Jabuna.

† Mr. Ramaprasad Chanda, writing in the Prabasi, holds that as Sri Harsha transferred his capital from Thaneswar to Kanauj, so Bhāskaravarman, after his conquest of northern and central Bengal, also transferred his capital to Karnasuvarna, and this is supported by the statement in Yuan Chwang's biography that embarking on boats together wih Yuan Chwang he "passed up the Ganges" to meet Sri Hrasha at Rājmahal. This is not probable because Yuan Chwang came to the Kāmarupa capital travelling east 900 li from Pundravardhana and Karnasuvarna cannot be to the east of Pundravardhana. It is, however, possible that after some weeks' stay at Prāgjyotishpur Yuan Chwang was taken by Bhāskaravarman to his newly conquered capital Karnasuvarna where he received the summons from Sri Harsha. From that place, therefore, both of them

time is a matter of some doubt. The Nidhanpur copper-plate was found in Panchakhanda within the district of Sylhet. Gait argues from this that Sylhet was within the dominions of Bhāskaravarman. One authority has recently pointed out that the lands mentioned in the Nidhanpur copper-plate were given to a number af Nagar

---

proceeded up the Ganges and reached Rājmahal where Sri Harsha was encamping. This was no doubt towards the close of the year 643 A.D. The Nidhanpur grant was issued from Karnasuvarna long before this, probably about 610 A.D. and then Karnasuvarna was merely the "victorious camp" and Bhāskaravarman was there with his victorious army consisting of war-boats, war-elephants, cavalry and infantry *(Mahânou hastyaswa patti)*.

We are not, however, prepared to reject Mr. Chanda's conjecture *in toto*. Very probably Bhāskaravarman used Karnasuvarna as his capital for some time in order to consolidate his rule over the newly acquired territories. It was probably from Karnasuvarna that he sent assistance to the Chinese envoy Wang-hiuen-Tse about 649 A.D. Even before Sri Harsha's death his kingdom had extended as far as the Kausika (Kosi). It seems that during the confusion, after Sri Harsha's death, he managed to extend his dominions further to the west and acquired the eastern part of Magadha. During the eventful years towards the close of his reign, political considerations compelled him stay away from Kāmarupa proper and that probably explains how, on his death, Sālastambha could usurp the throne setting aside the rightful successor.

Another significant fact is that Sri Harsha encamped at Rājmahal and waited there for Bhāskaravarman. Rājmahal then stood at the junction of the Kosi and the Ganges and Sri Harsha therefore actually had his camp just outside the boundaries of Bhāskaravarman's dominions. This also indicates that Sri Harsha's sway never extended to any part of northern or central Bengal over which Bhāskaravarman was the acknowledged ruler.

Brahmans as indicated by their surnames which are now curiously confined to Kayasthas in Bengal, but which were usually borne by Nagar Brahmans of that time(1). It is also pointed out that the deity which the Nagar Brahmans worshipped was Śiva named Śri Hatakeswar. It is assumed that the name of the country known as Śri Hatta (Sylhet) was derived from Śri Hatakeswar*. On the other hand, Pandit Padmanath Bhattacharya Vidyāvinod, who is himself a native of Sylhet, does not support this view (2). He points out that while in Samatata the pilgrim came to know of six other countries which he could not visit, and one of them was Shih-li-cha-ta-lo which was to the north-

(1) I.H.Q. vol. VI No. 1 (March 1930).

* Dr K. M. Gupta of the Sylhet College in his paper "On some castes and caste-origins in Sylhet" writes :—"The kings of Kāmarupa, which included Sylhet, seem to have adopted a systematic policy of inviting Brahmans to their kingdom. It is apparently for this reason that Kāmarupa became a centre of Brahmanical faith. * * * We further note that the tutelary deity of the Nagar Brahmans was, and still is, Hātakeswara. * * * * Hātakeswara Śiva, is also known as Hatta-nātha or Hattanātha Śiva, and I have no doubt that the very name Srihatta (Sylhet) is derived from this sept-deity of the Nāgar Brahmans. The conclusion is irresistible that the emperors of Kāmarupa pursued a systematic policy of colonising Sylhet with Nāgar Brahmans and thereby introducing orthodox Hinduism in the outlying parts of the empire." Dr Gupta's theory about the origin of the name Srihatta and the inclusion of Sylhet within Kāmarupa during the 5th–7th centuries is probably correct but, as already pointed out, his theory that the lands granted by Bhutivarman were situated within Sylhet is certainly incorrect.

(2) Epigraphia Indica vol. XII p. 67.

east of Samatata among the hills near the sea. Pandit Vidyāvinod identifies shih-li-cha-ta-lo with Srihatta and points out that it is to the north-east of Samatata or East Bengal and is confined on the north and the south by the Assam range and the Lushai hills respectively. Further the western portion of Sylhet and part of Mymensing are even now very low-lying resembling a sea in the rainy season and which are still popularly called *haor* (sāgara) or sea. If Sylhet was within the kingdom of Kāmarupa the pilgrim would not have mentioned it as a separate country. On account of the mention of the sea some scholars identify shih-li-cha-ta-lo with Srikshetra but this is evidently incorrect as Srikshetra is not to the north-east of Samatata and is not girt by hills on both sides like the Sylhet plain. Vidyāvinod's identification of shih-li-cha-ta-lo with Srihatta may probably be correct but, as has been already pointed out, the mere mention of Srihatta as a separate country, and not as a separate kingdom, does not necessarily prove that it was outside the dominions of Bhāskaravarman.

Śri Harsha died in the year 648 A.D four years after Yuan Chwang left India, but Bhāskaravarman was reigning till about 650 A.D. Just after Śri Harsha's death his minister Arjun or Arjunāswa usurped the throne. At that time an embassy arrived from the emperor of China. Alas, Śri Harsha who had shown so much respect to the pious Chinese pilgrim who, on his return, must have prompted the Chinese emperor to despatch this friendly mission, was no longer living to receive the envoy in a befitting manner. On the contrary the usurper Arjun actually ill-treated the members of the mission and killed some of them. The rest, led by Wang-hiuen-tse, escaped to Nepal and sought the aid of the kings of Nepal and Tibet and of Bhāskaravarman. It appears from the Chinese accounts that the kings of Nepal and Tibet assisted with forces and Shi-kien-ma (Sri Kumara), the "King of Eastern India" sent him "thirty thousand oxen and horses and provisions for all his army, to which he added bows, scimitars and collars of great value" (1). With such assistance Wang-hiuen-tse defeated the usurper Arjun and capturing him took him as a prisoner to China. Bhāskaravarman probably did not continue to reign long after this event.

Bhaskāravarman was perhaps the most illustrious of the monarchs of ancient Kāmarupa. His name has been immortalized by the accounts which Yuan Chwang and his biographers have left. It appears that during his time Kāmarupa was one of the most advanced kingdoms in India. It would be profitless now to discuss whether he was a Brahman, Kshatriya or a Hinduized Koch by caste. Suffice it to say that he was a Hindu by religion spreading "the light of Ārya Dharma" though he had great reverence for learned Buddhist priests and professors of his time and was distinctly inclined towards Buddhism. The text of his messages to Śilabhadra

---

(1) Indian Antiquary vol. IX p. 14.

leave no doubt on this point. The very high functions allotted to him during the famous religious assembly at Kanauj by the Hindu emperor Śri Harsha proves that he was not a Hindu of the despised low caste. He was undoubtedly looked upon as a good Kshatriya, as his surname Varma indicates, whatever might have been his origin. In any case he was certainly not a "Hinduized Koch." All the kings of his dynasty beginning from Pushyavarman were Kshatriya monarchs. When Yuan Chwang visited the kingdom he found hundreds of Hindu temples there and evidently there were large numbers of Brahmans and other high caste Hindus living within the kingdom which was a seat of learning for we are told that people of other countries came there for study. Even during the reign of Mahābhutavarman, the ancestor of Bhāskaravarman, in the early part of the sixth century, we find a colony of Nagar Brahmans in the kingdom. The *Vyavahhâri* named in the Nidhanpur grant was a Kayastha named Hardatta. He is mentioned as Kayastha and not as Karana or Karanika*. It appears that the caste name Kayastha had then come into use and that Kayasthas were among the earlier Aryan settlers in Kāmarupa. The word *Vyavahâra* occurs also in the rock-inscripition of Harjaravarman and Mahamaho-

* This proves the hollowness of the statement of R.D. Banerji that "in genuine North Indian inscriptions the word "Kayastha" does not occur before the 8th century A. D." (J. P. A. S. B. vol. X. Nos, 10 & 11, November and December 1914 p. 43.)

padyaya Pandit H. P. Sastri has translated it as a law suit. The *Vyavahāri* was therefore a lawyer. Hardatta Kayastha was either engaged by the Brahman donees to plead their case as against the revenue officers who had assessed the lands to revenue or he was the king's lawyer to see to the correct legal drafting of the grant. In any case it was evidently at the instance of this lawyer that the following line at the end of the inscription was recorded:-

"Because after the burning of the plates, these newly written letters are of different form (from those of the previous inscription), therefore they are not forged."

Evidently in those days the Kayasthas not only acted as District and Revenue officers but were also professional lawyers.

The eastern part of the present district of Purnea, bounded on the west by the Kosi river, formed a part of Mithilā. A part of Mithilā was therefore within Kāmarupa at least from Mahābhutavarman's reign till the reign of Susthitavarman and again from the time of Bhāskaravarman till the rise of the Pāla power after the overthrow of Sri Harshavarman in the eighth century. The Brahmans and Kayasthas of Mithilā therefore spread to other parts of Kāmarupa including perhaps Sylhet. Even now many Brahman families in Assam trace their origin from Mithila. On the north-eastern boundary of the Purnea district is the modern district of Jalpaiguri which continued to be included in Kāmarupa even till the time of the Koch king Naranārayan.

There was therefore very close connection between Mithila and Kāmarupa. The old Kāmarupi language was a variety of eastern Maithili and that is why Yuan Chwang remarked that the spoken language of Kāmarupa differed only a little from the language spoken in mid-India i. e. Magadha and Mithilā. In prehistoric times Mithilā (Videha) supplied a prince who founded the famous "Bhauma" dyansty in Prāgjyotisha. During historic times it was through Mithilā that Aryan culture and civilization spread into the rest of Kāmarupa. It was again from Kāmarupa in the north that the Aryans gradually spread towards the south to Gauda, north of the Ganges, and to Samatata, south of the Ganges. This is proved by the wide diffusion of the surnames of the Nagar Brahmans of Kāmarupa, such as Ghosha, Datta, Dama, Deva, Soma, Palita, Pala, Kundu, Dasa, Naga and Nandi throughout modern Bengal and Sylhet. Curiously enough, neither the Brahmans nor the Kayasthas of the modern Assam valley, except those who migrated to Assam from Bengal during the Ahom rule, appear to have used these surnames though among the oldest Assamese Brahman families there are still Misras, Sukuls, Tewaris and Tirotias (coming from Tirhut). According to Bhandarkar these Nagar Brahmans subsequently became Kayasthas (1).

The Nidhanpur grant was issued from Karnāsuvarna and the text of the inscription must therefore have been composed by a pandit of that part

(1) Indian Antiquary, March 1932, p 52.

of the country who was named Vasuvarna. This probably explains the occurrence in this inscription of expressions and passages which we do not find in subsequent Kāmarupa inscriptions, but which used to be inscribed in plates issued by the Gupta kings of Magadha and Pundravardhana and the subsequent Pāla rulers of Gauda and Magadha. For instance, the expression *Bhumi-Chhidra* does not occur in other inscriptions of the Kāmarupa kings but it occurs in several of the Pāla rulers of Gauda. The expression *gangina*, meaning perhaps a dried up channel, is also peculiar to Gauda. The penultimate stanza in which two *slokas* from the *Vrikaspati Sanhita* have been quoted was also due to observance of a Gaudian custom. The only other Kāmarupa king in whose inscription we find this quotation is Vaidya Deva who was himself a Gaudian. There are also names of offices mentioned in this inscription which do not occur in subsequent Kāmarpupa inscriptions. The "officer issuing hundred commands who has obtained the *pancha mahâ sabda*" is not mentioned in subsequent inscriptions. It seems that Bhāskaravarman after his conquest of Karnasuvarna and Gauda, finding himself in the exalted position of an emperor, introduced this high office, probably in imitation of the Gupta emperors. The expression "*prâpta pancha mahâ sabda*" probably means the holder of five offices each of which is styled *Mahâ* or great such as Mahāsāmanta, Mahā-sainya-pati (*vide* stray-plate of Harjara), Mahā-sāndhivigrahik and so forth. It is interesting to note that the person named in this inscription, who was to mark out the boundaries of the lands comprised in the grant, was one Srikshi kunda, the headman of Chandrapuri. The donees named in the plate, who were all Nagar Brahmans, included seven persons with the surname Kunda. Srikshi Kunda, the headman of Chandrapuri, was therefore himself also a Nagar Brahman. The *nyâya karanika*, was evidently a judge and it appears that this office existed till the Ahom regime when it was styled "*nyâya sodhā Phukan*". The *Bhândâragâradhikâra* meant the officer in charge of the royal treasury. This office also, though not mentioned in subsequent inscriptions, existed till the time of the Ahom kings when the name of the office was *Bar bhândâra Barua*. The revenue collector is called *Utkhetayità* and the engraver of the inscription on the copper-plate is called *Sekyakâra*. One Kāliyā was the engraver of this inscription and it is a common Kāmarupi name even till now.

Arts and industries had then advanced to a remarkable extent. From the *Harsha Charita* of Bāna we find a list of the presents which Bhāskaravarman sent to Śri Harsha through his trusted envoy Hangshavega. These presents included, as already mentioned, an ingenuously constructed royal umbrella of exquisite workmanship studded with valuable gems, *puthis* written on *Sāchi* bark, dyed cane mats, Āgar-essence, musk in silk bags, liquid molasses in earthen pots, utensils, paintings, a pair of Brahmani ducks in a cage made of cane and overlaid with gold and a considerable quantity of silk fabrics some of which were so even and polisbed that they resembled *Bhurjapatra* (probably *Mugā* and *pāt* fabrics). This list alone is sufficient to show that the arts and industries of Kāmarupa, at such a distant period, reached a very high state of perfection. The Chinese accounts say that Bhāskaravarman could muster a fleet of 30,000 ships and an army of 20,000 elephants clad in mail. This may have been an over-estimate but, even making due allowances for exaggeration we can conclude that Bhāskaravarman was a very powerful monarch and that during his time boat-building was a flourishing industry in Kāmarupa and that iron, which must have been then available in abundance from the Khasi Hills, was largely manufactured into accoutrements of war. The manufacture of molasses in liquid form, from sugar-cane juice, is still a peculiar practice in the modern Kāmrup district. Agar-essence is still prepared in Assam from the resin produced from the Agar tree (Aquilaria Aglochia). The Assamese *Mugā* and *pāt* silk fabrics are still produced in abundance. *Puthis* written on *Sachi* bark an still abundant in Assam and musk is still an important product of the Bhutan hills.

Bhāskaravarman's close connection with Śri Harsha and Yuan Chwang led to his association with the famous Buddhist university of Magadha, for his seal has been discovered recently at the site of Nalanda in the company of two fragmentary seals of Śri Harsha. The seals were found by Dr. Spooner during the excavation of the ruins of Nalanda in the year 1917-18. Mr. K. N. Dikshit in his "Epigraphical notes of the Nalanda finds" referred to this seal and stated that the kings mentioned therein were not known to belong to any north-India dynasty. This was corrected by the late Mr. R. D. Banerji in the Journal of the Bihar and Orissa Research Society (Vol. V). The corrected reading of the text of the seal as subsequently given by Mr. Dikshit is as follows :—

1. *Sri Ganapati Varma Sri Yajnavatyam Sri Mahendra Varma.*

2. *Sri Suvratayam Sri Narayanavarma Sri Devavatyam Sri Mahabhuta varma.*

3. *Sri Vijnana Vatyam Sri Chandramukha Varma Sri Bhogavatyam.*

4. *Sri Sthitavarma tena Sri Nayana Sobhayam (Sri Susthitavarma.)*

5. *(Sri Syama Lakshmyam) Sri Supratisthita Varma.*

6. *Sri Bhaskara Varmeti. (1.)*

This genealogy agrees with that given in the Nidhanpur plate and also in the *Harsha Charita* of Bana. The mother of Susthitavarma is however named "Nayana Shova" instead of Nayana Devi and the mother of Bhāskaravarman is named Syamālakshmi instead of Syamādevi as appearing in the Nidhanpur plate. The importance of this discovery requires no emphasis. Mr. Dikshit thinks that the seal probably accompanied Bhāskaravarman's letter to Śilabhadra inviting Yuan Chwang (2). As however it was found in the company of

(1) J.B.O.R.S. vol. VI. (1920) p 151.
(2) Ibid.

the two Śri Harsha seals the probability is that both Śri Harsha and Bhāskaravarman, on their march from Rājmahal to Kanauj, visited Nalanda together with the Chinese pilgrim and, to commemorate their visit, left their respective seals at the university. This custom was evidently in vogue, for a considerable number of similar broken seals were discovered at the site, during the excavation. These seals being impressed upon clay tablets or plaques are decipherable though they were entombed under debris for so many centuries.

Nidhanpur Inscription of Bhaskaravarman.

APPENDIX I

COPPER-PLATE INSCRIPTION OF BHASKARAVARMAN

Translation in English.

(Reprinted from Epigraphia Indica Vols XII and XIX)

Om. (Verse 1.) Having saluted the god who is lovely with the moon as head-gear, the wielder of the bow (pinākā), adorned with particles of ashes, I once again make clear (what was already) plain words (i.e. of the destroyed plates) for the benefit of the (spiritually) prosperous Brāhmans.

(Line 2.) Hail. From the camp located at Karnasuvarna, with the appropriate epithet of victory owing to possession of splendid ships, elephants horses and foot-soldiers.

(V. 2.) Victorious is the form of the great Lord (Mahādéva), never forsaken (in contemplation by the devotees), bedecked with its own splendour, that has a girdle made of the lord of snakes, (and) that destroyed the body of Kāma (Cupid) at a mere glance.

V. 3.) Victorious is (also) Dharma (Religion), the sole friend of the creation, the cause of prosperity in both the worlds (this and the next), whose form is the good of others, unseen (yet) whose existence is inferred from the results.

(V. 4.) Naraka, the chief of the rulers of the earth, was the son of the wielder of the Chakra (i.e. Vishnu), who with a view to lift up the Earth from (beneath) the Ocean, assumed the distinguished form of a boar.

V. 5.) From that Naraka, by whom *naraka* (hell) was never seen, was born king Bhagadatta, the friend of Indra, who challenged in fight Vijaya (i.e. Arjuna), renowned for conquests.

(V. 6.) Of that killer of (his) enemies (there) was a son named Vajradatta whose course was like (that of) the thunderbolt (Vajra), who with an army of uninterrupted progress always pleased in fight the performer of hundred sacrifices (i.e. Indra).

(V. 7.) When the kings of his family having enjoyed *the position (of rulers) for* three thousand years had (all) attained the condition or gods, Pushyavarman became the lord of the world.

(V. 8.) His son was Samudravarman, who was like a fifth samudra (Ocean), during whose reign there was no anarchy, shining with gems, and quick in duels.

(V. 9.) That king had a son born of (his queen) *Dattadevi, (named) Balavarman, whose* force and armour *never broke up and whose army* would easily march against enemies.

(V. 10.) His son born of (queen) Ratnavati was the king named Kalayānavarman, who was not the abode of even very small faults.

(V. 11.) From him (queen) Gandharvavati begot a son Ganapati (by name) who was incessantly raining gifts as (the god) Ganapati (rains) ichor, who was endowed with innumerable qualities, for the extermination of strife (as Ganapati) is born to destroy the Kali age.

(V. 12.) His queen Yajnavati, brought forth a son Mahendravarman, as the sacrificial fire (produces) fire, who was the repository of all sacrificial rites (like fire).

(V. 13.) From him who mastered his self, Suvrata generated a son Nārāyanavarman for the stability (of the rule) of the world, who like Janaka (or his father) was well versed in the principles of the philosophy of the (supreme) Self.

(V. 14.) From him, Devavati, like Prakriti from Purusha, bore Mahābhutavarman, the sixth Mahābhuta (element) as it were, for the steady succession of (all) the properties.

(V. 15.) His son was Chandramukha, who was charming by (possessing) all the arts as the moon (by the digits), whom Vijnānavati brought forth, as the Sky did (the moon), a dispeller of (all) gloom (as the moon dispels the darkness).

(V. 16.) Thereafter (queen) Bhōgavati of (good) enjoyment became the cause (of birth) of Sthitavarman, the supporter of the world, who had innumerable (sources of) enjoyment, (just as) Bhogavati (the city of the Snakes of the nether regions) is (the source) of prosperity of the chief of the Snakes, the supporter of the earth, who has a myriad of hoods.

(V. 17.) From that king of unfathomable nature, of innumerable gems, and the spouse of the (goddess) Lakshmi, was born Sri-Mrigānka, who had no blemish, *just as the moon, free from spots, is born from the milky* ocean, whose substance is unfathomable, whose pearls cannot be counted, and from which Lakshmi was produced.

(V. 18.) His (i.e. Sthitavarman's) son king Susthitavarman was born of Nayanadēvi, he who held the kingdom in his own hand, and was renowned as Sri Mrigānka.

(V. 19.) By whom was given away to supplicants as if it were (a clod of) earth, that shining Lakshmi (i.e. wealth) whom (god) Hari like a miser bears with joy in his bosom.

(V. 20.) From him Syāmādēvi, (divine) like that goddess (Syama) of the Krita (i.e. golden) age, generated a son Supratishthitavarman, the moon as it were to dispel (all) gloom.

(V. 21.) Whose prosperity was for the benefit of

others, who was possessed of elephants and attended by the chief among the learned, and possessed of a well established capital like a kulachala, whose height is for the benefit of others, which is haunted by the chief of Vidyadharas, is rich in elephants, and has a ridge.

(V. 22.) The same Syamadevi also brought forth his younger brother Sri-Bhaskaravarman, who like the sun was of incalculable rise and the abode of all light-

(V. 23.) Who though being only one, is, on account of his character, much and simultaneously reflected in the hearts of people, pure like mirrors turned toward, him.

(V. 24.) Whose mark (i.e. picture) was seen in the houses of kings, untarnished on account of great lustre, like the disc of the sun in several water pots.

(V. 25.) Who is without cruelty, easily accessible, of immense effects, and the soles of whose feet are surrounded by people who resort to his protection, like the wish-yielding tree which holds no snakes, which is well growing, abounds in rich fruits, and whose roots are surrounded by people who want shade.

(Lines 34-44.) Moreover he (Bhaskaravarman, who has been) created by the bold lotus-born (god), the cause of the rise, the arranging and the destruction of the Universe, for the proper organization of the duties of (various) castes and stages (of life) that had become mixed up; who by (his) rise has made the circle of (related) powers become attached like the Lord of the World (the Sun), whose disc becomes coloured when it rises; who has revealed the light of the Arya religion by dispelling the accumulated darkness of (this) *Kali* age by making a judicious application of his revenues (like the sun that dispels the accumulated darkness in the *Kali* age by spreading the mass of its pleasant rays), who has equalled the prowess of the whole ring of his feudatories by the strength of his own arm; who has devised many a way of enjoyment for his hereditary subjects, whose (loyal) devotion (to him) was augmented by his steadiness (of purpose), modesty and affability; who is adorned with a wonderful ornament of splendid fame made of the flowery words of praise variously composed by hundreds of kings vanquished by him in battle; whose virtuous activities, like (those ot) Sivi were applied in making gifts for the benefit of others; whose powers, as (of) a second preceptor of the gods (Brihasdati), were recognised by others on account of (his) skill in dividing and applying the means of politics that appear in suitable moments; whose own conduct was adorned by learning, valour, patience, prowess and good actions; who was avoided by faults as if they were overcome on account of (his) taking to the other (i.e. Virtue's) side; by whom the Lakshmis (deities of luck) of Kāmraupa were, as it were, attracted with a staunch incessant excessive passion of love; to whom was exhibited, with a fast embrace, the course of love for the a bhigāmikagunas (by the Lakshmi of Kāmarupa drawn by an excessive sentiment of constant affection) who is, as it were, the breath ot the holy Dharma whose person has been seized by the powerful Kali (Iron age), the abode of politics and good qualities, the receptacle of friends, the shelter of the terrified, the abode of good luck, whose dignified power was shown by the elevated rank obtained in order of succession from (Naraka) the son of Vasumati (Earth), the king of kings, the illustrious Bhāskaravarman, in sound health, commands the present and the future district officers, as well as the courts of justice in the district of Chandrapuri (thus): let this be known to you (all), that the land of the Mayurasālmalagrahāra (grant to Brāhmanas) lying within this district granted by issuing a copper-plate charter by king Bhutivarman has become liable to revenue on account of the loss of the copper-plates, so by the Maharaja having informed the senior respectable persons (and) having issued orders for making a fresh copper-plate grant, the land has been awarded to the Brāhmans who had been enjoying the grant already in the manner of *bhumi-chhidra*, so that no tax is levied on it as long as the sun, the moon and the earth will endure. These are the names of the Brāhmans (donees).** For *bali* (worship) *charu* (oblation) and *satra* (hospitality) seven shares are allotted. The produce of the land that is increased by the Kausikà (river) will go to the Brāhmans, the donees of the grant, but the land which is enlarged by the Gangini shall be equally divided by the Brāhmans as recorded. These are the boundaries :-- to the east, lies the dried Kausika, to the south-east, that very Kausika marked by a (piece of) hewn fig tree, to the south east, a (piece of) hewn fig tree;

(Lines 45-51.) To the (south-) west the dried river bed marked by a cut down fig tree; to the west now the boundary of the dried river bed; to the north-west a potter's pit and the (said) dried river bed, bent east wards; to the north a large *jatali* tree (i.e. Bignonia suaveolens); to the north-east the pond of the tradesman Khāsoka and that dried (river) Kausika. The officer issuing hundred commands is Srigopala who has obtained the five great *sabdas*. The officer who marks the boundaries is the headman of Chandrapuri (named) Srikshikunda. The *nyayakaranika* (is) Janārdana Svāmin. (Witnesses (?) are) the lawyer Haradatta, the Kayastha, Dundhunatha and others. *Sasayitri* and writer is Vasuvarman. Master of the treasure (is) the *Mahasamanta* Divakaraprabha. Tax collector (is) Dattakara Purna. Engraver (is) Kāliya.

(Here follow two of the customary imprecatory verses).

(V. 28.) Because after the burning of the plates, these newly written letters are of different form (from those of the previous inscription), therefore they are not forged.

CHAPTER V.

THE DYNASTY OF SALASTAMBHA.

Bhāskaravarman died about 650 A.D. We are inclined to suppose that he was a bachelor throughout his life and therefore died without leaving any issue. The fact that he was known as Kumāra-Raja till his death lends support to this supposition. It seems that shortly after his death the line to which he belonged came to an end and the line commencing with Sālastambha began, his immediate successor being deposed by Sālastambha who usurped the throne. The name Sālastambha is given in the inscriptions of Harjara, Vanamāla, Balavarman III and Ratnapāla but it seems to have been a *birud* name. In the inscription of Balavraman III his father Virabāhu is called "Rana-stambha" and in the second inscription of Indra Pāla "Saugrāma-stambha" is stated as one of the thirty-two *birud* names of that king. Both Rana-stambha and Sangrāma-stambha mean the same thing i.e. one who like a pillar takes resolute stand in battle. Sāla-stambha may be translated as a Sāl-column or one immovable like a pillar of Sāl or a Sāltree. The immediate successor of Sālastambha is named as Vijaya in the inscription of Harjara and, Vigraha -stambha in the inscription of Ratnapāla. Vigraha-stambha, which means one like a pillar in conflict, is clearly *birud,* the real name being Vijaya Varma-Deva. Similarly Sālastambha had probably another name with the suffix Varma-Deva. He might have been the king referred to as Varma-Deva, or its transposed form Deva-Varma, in I-Tsing's records mentioned in Beal's introduction to the biography of Yuan Chwang. The Chinese writers, including Yuan Chwang, always referred to Bhāskaravarman simply as "Kūmāra." In the same way the Korean priest mentioned only the suffix of the real name of Sālastambha who ascended the throne about 655 A.D. and ruled till about 675 A.D. He was therefore a contemporary of Ādityasena of Magadha.

The Bargaon copper-plate inscription of Ratnapālavarman deciphered by Dr. Hoernle mentions that "after this for several generations kings of Naraka's dynasty had ruled the whole country, a great chief of the Mlechhas, owing to a turn of adverse fate, took possession of the kingdom.This was Sālastambha" (1). The exact text is as follows:—

Evam vangsha kramena kshitimatha nikhilam bhunjatām Narakanam rājyam Mlechhādhinātho vidhi chalana vasadevā Jagrāha rāyam."

Hoernle suggests that the word "mlechha" means a foreigner. We think the word undoubtedly

(1) J.A.S.B. vol LXVII part I, 1898 p. 99.

means the non-Hindu Mongoloid people of the kingdom. A tribe of these people is still known by the name " Mech" which is clearly the abridged form of " Mlechha". The word "adhinatha " may mean a ruler, master, governor or even a commander. So the word "*mlechhādhinātha*" may mean the " governor of the Mech country. At this time Kāmarupa had grown into such a large kingdom that governors were probably appointed to administer particular localities. It is therefore reasonable to suppose that when Bhāskaravarman died, Sālastambha who was the governor of the Mech country organized a revolt and that he dethroned the immediate successor of Bhāskaravarman and proclaimed himself as king. He probably belonged to the dynasty of Bhagadatta for ordinarily nobles of the royal family were appointed as governors. What the writer of the Bargaon inscription evidently meant was that the person who could claim the throne rightfully, being the nearest relative of the deceased king, was pushed aside and Sālastambha of another line usurped the throne. As a matter of fact Rājyamati, the daughter of Śri Harsha Varma Deva, who belonged to the line of Sālastambha, was described, in the Nepal inscription of Jayadeva, as *Bhagadatta rāja Kulajā* or a descendant of Bhagadatta's royal line. Vanamāla and Balavarman III, who were kings of the line of Sālastambha also claimed descent from Bhagadatta. It is suggested by some that Prālambha and Harjara were *mlechha* names thus indicating that they belonged to a *mlechha* dynasty founded by Sālastambha, but the immediate successors of

Sālastambha were Vijaya, Pālaka, Kumāra, Vajradeva, Śri Harshadeva and Balavarman and none of these can be called *mlechha* names. It is true that in the inscription of Vanamāla the name Prālambha is considered strange (*Prālambha ityadbhuta nāmadheya*); but in the same breath it is stated that " this slayer of enemy-heroes was born in the family of Bhagadatta." In the beginning of the stray plate of Harjaravarman after certain lines which can not be read, the following occur:- " Oh son of the Earth (*Pārthiva*) for these reasons your descendants will be known as *Mlechhas*." The reasons given may have been contained in the undeciphered lines or in the first plate which is missing. It is probable that the kings of the line to which Vanamāla belonged were actually regarded as *Mlechhas* and that is why the writer of the inscription attempted to explain the reasons. More than a century after, the panegyrist of Ratnapāla also tried to lower the origin of this line and extol that of Brahmapāla the founder of the Pāla line.

A writer in the Journal of the Asiatic Society of Bengal has attempted to prove that Viśākhadatta the author of the *Mudrarakshasam*, the well-known Sanskrit drama, was a native of Kāmarupa. It is believed that Viśākhadatta flourished towards the end of the seventh century. In some manuscripts of the *Mudrarakshasam* the name Avantivarman occurs in the place of Chandra Gupta, found in other manuscripts, in the last *sloka* of the drama. The translation of the last *sloka* would thus be as follows:

"May king Avantivarman with his prosperous connections and servants long protect the earth, he who is a kingly manifestation of that self-existent God, to whose tusk, when He had assumed the form of the Boar, fitted to grant protection, the Earth of yore clung amidst universal destruction, and on whose arms she now leans being frightened by the *Mlechhas*."

The writer in the J.A.S.B., Mr. Jogendra Chandra Ghosh, thinks that this Avantivarman was no other than the son of Bhāskaravarman. Avantivarman, the father of Grahavarman of Moukhari, was a king of the sixth century A.D. while Viśākhadatta lived in the latter part of the seventh century. Mr. Ghosh writers:- "Who this Avantivarman might then be? Although history is silent about any descendant of Bhāskaravarman of Kāmarupa, the reference to the *Varaha avatara* leads us to think that this Avantivarman might be the immediate descendant of Bhāskaravarman who claimed his descent from the *Varāha-avatāra*. That Bhāskaravarman had his sway over northern Bengal is evidenced by the fact that he had issued his Nidhanpur copper-plate grant from his victorious camp at Karnasuvarna in Bengal" (1). Although not noticed by him, Mr. Ghosh's supposition is strengthened by the fact that the danger of the *Mlechha* revolt, as referred to in the *sloka*, was actually imminent in Kāmarupa when the strong rule of Bhāskaravarman ended with his death. As already hinted by us, Bhāskaravarman's continued stay in Karnasuvarna

---

(1) J.P.A.S.B. Vol. XXVI. No. 1 pp 241--245.

and absence from Kāmarupa proper, during the latter part of his reign, facilitated the fomenting of the revolt and when he died it appears that Sālastambha, the leader or governor of the *Mlechhas*, usurped the throne by deposing Bhāskaravarman's immediate successor. The danger which the author of the *Mudrarakshasam* feared actually materialized. It seems to us that Avantivarman or Avanti-varma-Deva, as the direct successor of Bhāskaravarman, did not reign for more than five years at the longest and that Sālastambha occupied the throne of Kāmarupa about 655 A.D. after dethroning and probably killing him.

The successors of Sālastambha have been partially named in the copper-plates of Harjaravarman, Vanamāla and Balavarman III who all evidently belonged to the same dynasty and also in the inscription of Ratnapāla who belonged to another line, probably of the same dynasty. The inscription of Harjaravarman, of which only the middle plate has been found, being anterior in point of time, we must rely on it for the order of succession. According to this record Sālastambha was succeeded by his son Vijaya. The immediate successors of Vijaya were Pālaka, Kumāra and Vajradeva. Then came the illustrious Harshavarman who possessed many good qualities and who loved his subjects. His son and succesor was Balavarman II who was a powerful king and after whom there were born in the dynasty Chakra and Arathi both of whom being unrighteous could not succeed to the throne which was occupied by the son of Arathi who is not named but who was clearly Prālambha for it is stated in the Vanamāla grant that Prālambha's brother was Ārath (son of Arathi), who was killed in battle while fighting against enemies. The stray plate of Harjaravarman's grant therefore introduces the names of three kings viz. Kumāra and Vajradeva who were predecessors of Śri Harshadeva and Balavarman II who was the son and succesor of Śri Harshadeva. It is not known whether Chakra and Arathi were the sons of Balavarman II or of his successor but it is clear that none of these two brothers could succeed to the throne and Prālmmbha the son of Arathi became king. Ārath, the elder brother of Prālambha, was evidently killed in a battle before Prālambha became king.

From Sālastambha to Vajaradeva there were, both inclusive, five or six kings and allowing, on an average, sixteen years for the reign of each king we can place the accession of Śri Harshavarma Deva about 730 A.D. and, as we shall presently see, he reigned for about 20 years till 750 A.D. Rājyamati the daughter of Śri Harsha Deva was married to Jayadeva King of Nepal. It is stated in the Nepal inscription that Jayadeva "wedded, as if she were fortune, Rājyamati possessed of virtues befitting her race, the noble descendant of Bhagadatta's royal line and daughter of Śri Harsha Deva, lord of Gauda, Odra, Kalinga, Koshala and other lands, who crushed the heads of hostile kings with the club-like tusks of his rutting elephants"(1). Jayadeva's Nepal

(1) Indian Antiquary vol. IX p 181.

inscription was recorded in the year 153 of a certain era. This era was formerly supposed to be the Śri Harsha era and the date of the inscription was taken to be 759 A. D. Sylvain Levi has however pointed out that it was a Tibetan era 11 years earlier than the Śri Harsha era. The year 153 of this era would therefore correspond to 748 A.D. We thus get another fixed point in the chronology of the Kāmarupa kings. It seems fairly certain that Śri Harsha Deva was ruling when this inscription was recorded and that his overthrow by Yasovarman took place some time after 748 A.D. There is hardly any doubt that he had a long reign during which he extended his conquests. We can therefore tentatively fix his reign from 730 to 750 A.D.

Sālastambha, Vijaya, Pālaka, Kumāra, and Vajradeva who followed Bhāskaravarman appear to have held undisputed possession of the territories which their illustrious predecessor, the Kumar Raja, admittedly acqiured. No historical record exists to show that they were dispossessed of these territories by any one. After them came Śri Harsha Deva who not only bore the name of the famous emperor of India who flourished in the previous century but also became an emperor himself by subjugating Odra (Orissa) and Kalinga (Ganjam) on the south and Koshala (North Bihar) on the west. The statement in the Nepal inscription that he was "*Gaudodradi-Kalinga-Koshala pati*" has been accepted as correct by the historians and scholars of Bengal and elsewhere but Sir Edward Gait has unfortunately dismissed it as an "instance of poetic exaggeration indulged by panegyrists of early Hindu Kings"(1). He evidently forgot that Bhāskaravarman himself was the master of the whole of Kāmarupa and Gauda perhaps as far south as the sea. He and his successors were the protectors of the sea-route from Tāmralipti. It is not at all improbable that about 80 or 90 years after his death, the territories acquired by him having been thoroughly consolidated by his successors, Śri Harsha Deva was powerful enough to conquer new territories towards the south and the west in which two directions only the kingdom was capable of extension. The empire of Śri Harshavarma Deva therefore comprised all the three present provinces of Assam, Bengal and Bihar and Orissa with the addition, perhaps, of the eastern portion of the United Provinces and the northern portion of the Madras Presidency. While ridiculing the "panegyrists of early Hindu kings" Sir Edward Gait inadvertently and unintentionally failed to refer to the most glorious chapter in the history of Kāmarupa—a period during which Kāmarupa was the suzerain power over nearly the half of northern India from Sadiya in the east to Ayodhya in the west and from Himalayas on the north as far as the Bay of Bengal and Ganjam to the south.

Mr. Ramaprasad Chanda supposes that after conquering Odra (Orissa) Śri Harsha Deva established probably a relative of his named

---

(1) Gait's History of Assam p 30.

Kshemankara Deva as ruler of Orissa (1). He makes this conjecture as Kshemankara Deva and his successors Sivakara I, Suvakara and Sivakara II claimed themselves to be "*Bhaumas*" i.e. descendants of Naraka (2). As a matter of fact copper-plate inscriptions prove that these kings ruled in Orissa in the eighth and ninth centuries (3). It may be that after Śri Harsha Deva's death, about 750 A.D. Kshemankara Deva, the first king of this line, proclaimed himself independent and hence we find Subhakara and his son Sivakara II describing themselves as Parameswara-Mahārājādhiraj Parama bhattāraka (4). It is also found that Subhakara Deva sent an embassy to China in the year 795 A.D (5). We can therefore easily place his grandfather Kshemankara Deva's accession about 745 A.D, the year in which, probablv, Śri Harsha Deva of Kāmarupa conquered Orissa.

Śri Harsha Deva was not however destined to hold this extensive empire long. He at length found a rival in Yasovarman of Kanauj, who aspired to be a conqueror of northern India and with whom he inevitably came into conflict. Yasovarman advanced against him and the decisive battle was fought within Bihar. In this battle Śri Harsha Deva was completely defeated and killed. The court poet of Yasovarman, named Vākapati, has left a poem styled *Gauda-vāho* (Gaudavadha) or "overthrow of Gauda" to

---

(1) Prabasi vol. XXXII No. 1.
(2) R.D. Banerji's History of Orissa vol. 1 p 159.
(3) Ibid p 146
(4) Ibid p 148
(5) Ibid p 146

commemorate this victory which was evidently regarded as a great military triumph.* Unfortunately Vākapati has not named the kings of Gauda and Vanga overthrown by Yasovarman. If he had done so much controversy would have been set at rest. The noted Bengali historian, R.D. Banerji, claims that Jivita Gupta, the grandson of Adityasena was then the reigning king in Gauda and Magadha but that the name of the Vanga king subdued by Yasovarman in not known (1). His theory is hardly probable for the sway of Adityasena or any of his successors over Gauda has not been proved. R.D. Banerji himself admits that Śri Harsha Deva must have ruled over Gauda before 748 A.D. (2). On the other hand, Yasovarman's attack on Magadha and Gauda can be placed between 740-750 A.D. A writer in the Indian Historical Quarterly has correctly stated that on the overthrow of some successor of Bhāskaravarman by Yasovarman of Kanauj anarchy ensued in Bengal (3). This is supported by Prof. Krishnaswami Ayengar who also surmises that Śri Harsha Deva of Kāmarupa and lord of Gauda, Odra, Kalinga and Koshala was the Gauda ruler who was overthrown by Yasovarman and whose defeat

---

* It is stated in the Gaudo vaho that the king of Gauda or the Magadhādhipa was pursued and slain but that the Vanga king subsequently submitted to Yasovarman and acknowledged him as suzerain. Possibly the Vanga king was only a vassal under Śri Harsha Deva.

(1) Bangalar itihash vol. 1 page 105.

(2) Ibid.

(3) I. H. Q. vol. VI p 443.

was the occasion for the glorification in the Gaudo-vaho (1). R.D. Banerji, who is an acute historian, again writes that it is not known whether Gauda was conquered by Śri Harsha Deva or by his predecessor but that probably during the first quarter of the eighth century Gauda, Odra, Kalinga and Koshala were under the kings of Kāmarupa and that about that time Yasovarman of Kanauj attempted to conquer the whole of northern India (2). The fact is that Gauda was not conquered by Śri Harsha Deva but by his predecessor Bhāskaravarman more than a century before and R.D. Banerji knew this very well. His difficulty seems to have been his leaning towards the theory that on the overthrow of Śaśānka Bengal was occupied by Bhāskaravarman only temporarily, that the dominions of Śaśānka passed on to Śri Harsha of Kanauj and not to Bhāskaravarman and that on the death of Śri Harsha, when Aryunāswa usurped the throne, either Mādhava Gupta or his son Adityasena became independent, thus suggesting that either of them recovered the possession of Bengal from Bhāskaravarman or his successor (3). There is absolutely no historical basis for this supposition. As already stated, there is no doubt at all that Bhāskaravarman conquered practically the whole of Bengal, with the exception perhaps of Samatata, after overthrowing Śaśānka. There is nothing to

(1) Journal of Indian History vol. III (1927) pp 313-30.
(2) Bangalar itihash vol. I pp 104-105.
(3) Ibid p 95.

show that Śri Harsha's sway extended to Bengal, nor is there anything to indicate that either Mādhava Gupta or Adityasena reconquered Bengal. The Aphshad inscription of Adityasena boasts of the victory of Mahāsena Gupta over Susthitavarman but makes no mention of any conflict between himself and the successor of Bhāskaravarman. In his Deoghar inscription, which is obviously much later in date, he boasted of having performed the *Aswamedha* sacrifice on his return from the Chola country, but even in this record no mention is made of any conflict with the successor of Bhāskaravarman in northern or central Bengal (1). It seems clear that Adityasena's activities were confined to south Bihar, Chota Nagpur and Orissa and that he left the Kāmarupa kings in undisturbed possession of practically the whole of Bengal. It should be noted here that neither the later Guptas nor the Pāla rulers were actually indigenous kings of Bengal but while the supremacy of the Pāla kings, who actually ruled in Magadha, over the greater part of Bengal, between the ninth and the twelfth centuries, is an undisputed fact there is practically no evidence to show that the later Guptas held sway over Bengal after the overthrow of Śaśānka and prior to the rise of the Pāla power. R.D. Banerji himself admits that the rule of the later Guptas came to a close about the end of the seventh or the beginning of the eighth century (2). On the other hand Yasovarman attained to power during the second quarter of the eighth century.

---

(1) Fleet Corpus Inscriptionum Indicarum p 213.
(2) Bangalar itihash vol I page 97.

According to Vincent Smith he sent his embassy to China about 731 A.D. Yasovarman was a conqueror. The ancient Hindu kings fought more for renown than for acquisition of territories. Yasovarman marched all the way from Kanauj, not to fight against an insignificant local ruler like Jivita Gupta II, but to have a trial of strength with the new conqueror, Śri Harsha Varma Deva, who had then extended his sway as far west as Koshala. After the trial was over and Śri Harsha Deva had been crushed, Yasovarman returned to Kanauj where he, in his turn, was subsequently defeated and overthrown by another conqueror Lalitāditya Mutapida, king of Kashmere.

Now the question is when was Śri Harsha Deva overthrown by Yasovarman. It could not have been prior to 748 A.D, the year in which the Nepal inscription of Jayadeva was recorded, because the very laudatory references to Śri Harsha Deva in that inscription would not have been made if by that time he was no longer the master of Gauda, Odra, Kalinga and Koshala. We may therefore tentatively place the date of the decisive battle about 750 A.D. When Śri Harsha Deva was overthrown and killed the *mātsyanyāya* began in Bengal because his powerful rule was then ended. This anarchy did not last for more than thirty or forty years. During this period, it appears, various kings of India overran Bengal taking advantage of the absence of a strong ruler. It is stated in the Ragholi plate of Jayavardhana that a son of Sauvardhana killed the Paundra king and subjugated the whole country (1). We also find that the Gurjara king Vatsarāja invaded Bengal and carried away two royal umbrellas which were subsequently acquired by the Rāstrakuta king named Dhruvadhārāvarsha (2). There was none to resist all these invasions. Ultimately Gopāla, the first king of the Pāla dynasty, rose to power about the end of the eighth century. Both he and his illustrious son Dharmapāla at length consolidated their power over Magadha and the greater part of Bengal. Dharmapāla ruled during the first quarter of the ninth century.

A writer in the Indian Historical Quarterly has attempted to place Gopāla about the second half of the seventh century and suggests that the *Mātsyanyāya* in Bengal began when Bhāskaravarman died and that Gopāla, who was a *Samanta* under Bhāskaravarman, ultimately became ruler of Gauda and Magadha. He identifies Gopāla with the "Śri Gopāla" mentioned in Bhāskaravarman's inscription as the "officer issuing hundred commands who has obtained the five great sounds." It is curious that such a theory has been seriously put forward in a historical magazine. If Gopāla became king during the second half of the seventh century, who was the ruler of Gauda who was overthrown by Śri Harsha Deva? Who was again the Gauda ruler killed by Yasovarman towards the middle of the eighth century? We have a fixed chronological point in the inscription of the Nepal king Jayadeva. We must therefore make Śri Harsha

---

(1) Epigraphia Indica vol. IX p 41
(2) Indian Antiquary vol. XI p 167.

Deva the suzerain over Gauda, Odra, Kalinga and Kośala shortly before 748 A.D. On the other hand, it does not appear that Gopāla or any of his immediate successors, viz. Dharmapāla and Devapāla was overthrown by any king of Kāmarupa or by Yasovarman of Kanauj. The writer has made no attempt to reconcile these inconsistencies of his theory.

As already stated, Śri Harsha Deva was overthrown and killed in battle. Gait assumes that the line of Sālastambha ended with Śri Harsha Deva (1). In the Tezpur grant of Vanamāla, the grandson of Prālambha, it is however stated that Sālastambha and Śri Harsha Deva were the ancestors of Prālambha who himself belonged to the dynasty of Naraka. All doubts on this point have been set at rest by the discovery and decipherment of the stray plate of Harjaravarman wherein it is stated distinctly that Harshavarman (Śri Harsha Deva) was succeeded by his son Balavarman II (2). With Śri Harsha Deva's death the empire which Bhāskaravarman acquired and which he largely extended also fell to pieces. Practically the whole of Gauda passed out of the hands of the Kāmarupa kings. Only a small stretch of country in northern Bengal appears to have been retained in Kāmarupa for we find that Vanamāla, who ruled in the ninth century, granted lands within this area.

Kāmarupa proper probably remained unaffected by the anarchy which overtook Gauda but its kings were no longer overlords. After Śri Harsha Deva

(1) Gait's History of Assam p 29.
(2) Kamarupa Sāsanavali pp 48--51.

the next king was his son Balavarman II who is said to have been powerful. After him probably there were two kings whose names have yet to be recovered. Then came Prālambha the son of Arathi who seems to have been the contemporary of the first Pala ruler Gopāla. In the Vanamāla inscription he is described as the descendant of Bhagadatta and as Lord of Prāgjyotisha (1). " He was against those who were enemies to his ancestors from Sālastambha down to Śri Harisha (Śri Harsha Deva) who are all deceased" (2). There is a reference in this inscription to Prālambha's brother who is not named but simply called Ārath or son of Arathi who seems to have been the chief general of the army (3). According to Gait, Prālambha "killed or banished all the members of the former ruling family." We do not find any authority for this statement. It is only in the inscription of Vanamāla that we find any direct mention of him. In this inscription he is described as *Kshyata-boeri-vira* (destroyer of the enemy heroes) but not as destroyer of the members of the former ruling family. There is no mention anywhere of the murder or banishment of the relatives of the former kings. Gait's statement is evidently based on an incorrect translation. Prālambha's queen was named Jivadā by whom he had a son named Harjara (4). It is stated that Harjara was "like Yudhisthira in truth, like Bhima to his enemies and like Jishnu in

(1) J.A.S.B. vol. IX part II pp 767--771.
(2) Ibid.
(3) Ibid.
(4) Ibid.

battle"(1).

Harjaravarman, whose rock-inscription at Tezpur is dated 510 Gupta era, equivalent to 829 A.D., probably ruled *Circa* 820-835 A.D. This date is another very valuable fixed point in the chronology of the Kāmarupa kings. It also shows the use of the Gupta era in Kāmarupa. It may be that the Gupta era was better known and more popular than the Harsha era or because the Gupta emperor Samudra Gupta had at least conquered Kāmarupa and made the then Kāmarupa king his vassal whereas Śri Harsha of Kanauj was not the overlord of the Kāmarupa king but his friend and ally. It does not appear that there was any local era in use in Kāmarupa at any time. In their inscriptions the kings mentioned only their regnal years. Harjaravarman was probably the contemporary of the second Pāla king Dharmapāla. He was evidently an illustrious king, for in the Nowgong inscription of Balavarman III it is stated that after Pālaka, Vijaya and other kings had followed in succession "there arose in the land a great king Harjara by name who was an affliction to his enemies" (2). The inscription on the stray plate discovered by Vidyāvinod shows that the smaller kings of the submontane tracts, who used to fight amongst themselves, all acknowledged the suzereignty of Harjaravarman. In this inscription, recorded at Hatapeswara, Harjaravarman is designated as "Parama

(1) J.A.S.B. vol. IX part II pp 767--771
(2) J. A. S. B. (1897) pp 293-297.

Ruins of Haruppeswara. Plinth Mouldings.

Parameswara, Parama Bhattāraka Parama Māheswara". Only the middle-plate of this inscription has been found. It appears that this inscription contained an order issued by prince Vanamāla, who is mentioned as *Yuvaraja*, from Hatapesvara which is described as "*Jayaskandhavara*". On the other hand in his rock-inscription Harjara himself described Haruppeswara as a *pura* (city). There is no doubt that Hatapeswara or Haruppeswara was the capital of Harjara and not merely a victorious camp. During the reign of his son and successor Vanamala this city had wide streets and was adorned by numerous lotus-covered lakes. It was also the abode of many learned and holy men. It is not known however whether this capital was founded by Harjara or any of his predecessors. Vidyāvinod supposes that it was established as capital by Sālastambha, after he usurped the throne, when the old capital Prāgjyotishpur was very likely sacked and destroyed.

There is some doubt as to the real name of the city. In the stray copper-plate of Harjaravarman it is called Hātapeswara but in his rock inscription, which however has not yet been very satisfactorily deciphered, the name is Hāruppeswara. The inscription of Vanamāla which describes the grandeur of the city mentions the name as Harayeshana, according to the decipherment made by Pandit Kamalakanta. As the copper-plates are no longer available it is not possible now to say whether Pandit Kamalakanta's reading was correct. Pandit Vidyavinod however seems to be definite that in the subsequent inscriptiou of Vanamāla's grandson Balavarman III the name Hāruppeswara is clearly legible. Both Pandit Vidyāvinod and Rai Bahadur A.C. Agarwala have suggested different meanings of the name Hāruppeswara which was very probably the name of a *linga*. Probably this *linga* represented *Hetuka* or *Hātaka Sulin* whose fallen temple Vanamāla is said to have rebuilt and the ruins of which are probably those now lying in Tezpur town. In that case the name of the *linga* should have been Hātakeswara instead of Hāruppeswara or Hātapeswara and the *linga* itself was probably of gold as the word *Hātaka* means gold. The Muslim historians state that when Mahammad Bukhtiyar was surrounded by the troops of the Kāmarupa king in 1206 A.D. he took refuge in a temple which contained a huge image of solid gold. This was probably another Siva temple containing a gold *linga*. Whatever that may be, during the reign of Vanamāla the city was of considerable dimensions extending probably from the Bamuni hill on the east to Dah-Parbatia on the west with the modern town of Tezpur in the centre where evidently the king's palace stood.

The rock-inscription of Harjaravarman purports to be an ordinance regulating the plying of boats in the Brahmaputra within certain boundaries specified therein. It seems the dispute was between fishing boats and boats belonging to the royal navy during the incumbency of the Commander-in-chief Mahā-Sāmanta Suchitta. It was ordained in the inscription that fishing boats must restrict themselves to midstream and that any violation of the order would be punishable with a fine of 100 cowries. The boats belonging to the navy being large they could be propelled upstream by means

Ruins of Hāruppeswara. Lotus-carved Capital.

of ropes only and therefore it was necessary to keep the shoreside of the river clear for them. The order was inscribed in bold characters on a huge rock-boulder on the bank of the river so that it may be visible to all boats passing up and down. This inscription was recorded about the ninth year of the king's reign.

Harjaravarman had by his queen Tārā a son named Vanamāla who has left a copper-plate inscription from which we find that he was a conqueror and his kingdom extended as far as the lines of forest near the sea-shore or sea-like waters. (*Jala nidhi tata vanamāla simāvadhi medini patistasya yogya iti nāma dhāta chakre vanamāla iti*). This probably means that Sylhet and Mymensing, bordering on the low-lying sea-like country, were under his sway. This inscription was recorded in the nineteenth year of the king's reign which shows that he had a long reign. By his inscription Vanamala granted lands to a Brahman in the village Abhissura-vataka near Chandrapuri on the west of the Trisrota (Teesta)*. The inscription gives a vivid and poetic description of the city of Hāruppeswara, the river Lauhitya (Brahmaputra) on which it stood and the line of boats that adorned the river-side. It is stated that in Hāruppeswara

---

* In 1875 Blochman in his "History and Geography of Bengal" (J. A. S. B) wrote:-

"We have to bear in mind that the Karatoyā. in former times, was connected by branches with the Teesta (Trisrota) and that the Teesta, before 1784, flowed west of the Karatoyā, joined the Attrai and fell into the main branch of Ganges (Pudma)."

Thus it would appear that the lands granted by Vanamāla lay between the Teesta and the Kausika;

people of all castes and occupations lived happily, that this city was the residence of numerous learned and pious men, that its streets were wide but crowded with elephants, horses and chariots, on which were mounted the kings and the notables, and the horizon was clouded by the massing of elephants, cavalry and infantry. A very poetic description is given of the river the water of which became pure by constantly washing the waist of the Kāmakuta hill which contained the temple of Śiva and His consort Mahā Gauri. The boats were adorned (perhaps with flags and buntings). Chauries waved from them and *Kinkinis* were attached to them to make sounds while being propelled; they were variously painted and moved very fast. Perhaps the scribe was describing a boat-race on the Brahmaputra organized for the pleasure of the king. One could see such crocodile-headed, painted and bedecked race-boats on the Brahmaputra on festive occasions down to the eighties of the last century. A picture of such a boat is given in the *Darrang rāj Vansāvali* by Suryakhari Doibogna who wrote the book towards the end of the eighteenth century. It is further stated in the inscription that the sounds of music arising from the numerous temples, the incantations of the priests engaged in performing Yajnas and the many lotus-flowered beautiful lakes proclaimed the glory of Vanamāla Varma in all countries. Even now the small town of Tezpur is a town of beautiful lotus-covered lakes.

According to the Nowgong inscription of Balavarman III Vanamāla "erected a row of palaces

Distant view of Hajarapukhri in Tezpur.

which had no equal in the world and being extensive possessed many rooms and though gay with general ornamentation was also furnished with true pictures" (1). This palace was in the ancestral camp of Hāruppeswara which was also the capital of Harjara. The Nowgong inscription also states that Hāruppeswara was on the bank of the Brahmaputra for it is stated that "near that pure river Louhitya, the current of which was agitated by the foreheads of his victorious elephants, there stands that ancestral camp of his (*paitāmaha Katākam*)." The name of Harjaravarman has been preserved in Tezpur by the magnificent tank constructed by him and which is still known as Hajarapukhuri. The extensive architectural remains in and around Tezpur, which will be fully described in a subsequent chapter, testify to the building activities of his son Vanamāla as recorded in the Tezpur copperplate inscription.

There is no doubt that Vanamāla was succeeded by his son Jayamāla but there is disagreement as to whether Virabāhu was the son of Jayamāla or whether Virabāhu was another name of Jayamāla. Dr. Hoernle takes the word Vanamāla in stanza 16 as adjective of Jayamāla and holds that it was Jayamāla who "having observed that his son had finished his education and attained adolesence made made over to him the (royal) umbrella of moonlike whiteness together with the two (royal) chameris and then bravely enduring the rite of starvation became absorbed into the light of the Divine

(1) J. A. S. B. vol. LXVI part 1 pp 285-297.

Being". Vidyāvinod thinks that it was Vanamāla who thus abdicated in favour of his son Jayamala. According to thim "Sri Virabāhu" mentioned in stanza 18 refers to Jayamāla. In other words after becoming king he assumed the *birud* name Virabāhu. Vidyāvinod is right for it is not stated in the inscription that Jayamāla had a son named Virabāhu. In the absence of such a statement we may assume that Jayamāla was known also as Śri Virabāhu.

On the abdication of his father Virabāhu ascended the throne and married a princess named Ambā of of rank equal to his own or in the language of the inscription "equal to himself in point of family, beauty and age." It was probably this king who was a contemporary of the Pāla king Deva Pāla whose cousin Jayapāla is stated, in the Bhagalpur inscription of Nārāyana Pāla, to have come to friendly terms with the Lord of Prāgjyotisha. Dr. Hultzch thinks that the stanza in the inscription may be taken to mean that Jayapāla supported the king of Prāgjyotisha successfully against the king of Utkala but other scholars do not accept this interpretation. The stanza seems to mean that Jayapāla, in obedience to the orders of Deva Pāla, having marched out at the head of a mighty army for the conquest of all quarters, the king of Utkala, being frightened by his very name, left his own capital whereas the king of Prāgjyotisha having resolved not to equip for war remained in friendly neutraliti surrounded by a host of suitors. In any case R. D. Banerji's interpretation that Jayapāla subdued the king of Prāgjyotisha is not correct(1). According to the Nowgong inscription " when the appointed time came through the power of his maturing *Karma* king Virabāhu, while distinguishing himself in war was attacked by a disease contracted through neglect of medical advice.* Considering that the world is vain and human life unstable like a water-drop he bethought himself of what remained for him to do. So, on an auspicious day, the king transferred, in the prescribed form, his throne and crown to that son of his who was tall of body, in appearance like a lion-cub" (2). Virabāhu thus, like his father Vanamala, abdicated in favour of his son Balavarman III who was not perhaps his eldest son but whom he selected as the most fit to succeed him in the throne.

Balavarman III is described in his inscription as a powerful monarch, who "conquered all potentates in dire contest by his arm which showed dark against the numerous flashes of his drawn sword-blades", who was "fearful of disgrace, harsh towards enemies, gentle towards religious preceptors, truth-speaking, not contentious nor vaunting, generous and purified from sin through the reverence shown to his father and mother." Balavarman III probably ruled during the last quarter of the ninth century. His inscription was recorded in the eighth year of his reign.

---

(1) Bangalar Itihash vol. I p 183.
(2) J. A. S. B. No. IV (1897) p 295.
* Vidyavinod thinks that the disease was one not curable by physicians and not one contracted through neglect of physicians' advice.

In the inscription of Balavarman III it is expressly stated that the lands mentioned in the grant would be free from all interference and annoyance caused by Rājni, Rāja-putra, Rānaka, Rājavallabha, the elderly woman employed in guarding the female apartments in the palace, those engaged in fastening boats or elephants, policemen in search of thieves and stolen properties or engaged in punishing criminals, persons pitching the royal umbrella or tent and the officers employed in collecting the tenants' taxes or other imposts. In the land-grant of Ratnapāla, about a century after, similar exemptions are set forth in a stanza which Hoernle has translated thus:-

"The king sends his greetings and commands to all and several who reside there : to the common people of the Brahman and other castes, headed by the district revenue officers and their clerks as well as to the other (higher class) people, such as the Rājanakas, Rājaputras, Rāja-vallabhas etc., and above them the Rānakas, Rājnis and Rājas and in fact to all who may reside there in future at any time:- Be it known to you that this land together with its houses, paddy-fields, dry land, water, cattle-pastures, refuse-lands etc. of whatever kind it may be, inclusive of any place within its borders, and freed from all worries on account of the fastening of elephants, the fastening of boats, the searching for thieves, the inflicting of punishhments, the tenants' taxes, the imposts for various causes and the pasturing of animals such as elephants, horses, camels, cattle, buffaloes, goats and sheep, as set forth in this charter".

The above mentioned ordinances, which are not to be found in the land-grants of the earlier kings such as Bhāskaravarman and Vanamālavarman, are interesting in that they give us a glimpse of the system of administration then obtaining and also indicate the extent of prestige and influence gained by Brahmans over the later kings. It appears that the Raja (King), the Rājni (Queen) and the Rānaka (war-lord) took precedence over the Rājaputra (prince) and the Rājavallabha (favourite of the king). A *Brahmottara* or grant to a pious Brahman was considered so sacred and inviolable that even the king could not enter or pitch his tent upon it at any time nor could any part of it be used for military operations by a Rānaka, nor could the police enter it even for detection of crime or punishment of offenders. The tenants of these estates were exempted from the payment of all other taxes or imposts for purposes of the State exchequer. Indirectly, it seems, all other lands were subject to these interferences and open to free pasturage. It is not however understood what worry or annoyance could be caused to the grantee of a *Brahmottara* estate by the chamberlain matrons of the royal household. It should be added that by this inscription the king granted lands to a young Brahman who had just returned from the preceptor's house after finishing his education and who was about to begin married life. The grant was made on the Bihu day on which the Brahman came to beg. Even now it is a custom among the Brahmans of Kamrup to go about begging on that auspicious day i.e. the *sankranti* of *Choitra*. The Kamauli grant of Vaidya

Deva, about 200 years after, was also made on this auspicious day.

After Balavarman III there is a gap covering nearly 100 years - the longest gap in the chronicle of the Kāmarupa kings from the fourth down to the twelfth century. It will not be possible to supply this gap until we discover an epigraphic record of a king intervening between Balavarman III and Ratnapala. In the first inscription of the latter the following occur :—

"After thus for several generations, kings of Naraka's dynasty had ruled the whole country the *Mlechhādhinatha*, owing to a turn of adverse fate, took possession of the kingdom. This was Sālastambha. In succession to him also there were kings, altogether twice ten (twenty) in number, who are well-known as Vigrahastambha and the rest."

"Seeing that the twentyfirst of them, the illustrious king, Tyāga Singha by name, has departed to heaven without leaving any of his race to succeed him, his subjects thinking it well that "*Bhauma*" (i.e. one of Naraka's race) should be appointed as their lord, chose Brahmapāla from amongst his kindred to be their king on account of his fitness to undertake the government of the country".

It is clear from the above quotation that Sālastambha's successors, in his own line, were altogether twenty in number and that therefore nineteen kings intervened between Sālastambha and Tyāga Singha who was the twentyfirst king of that line. Between Balavarman II and Prālambha there were, as we have already seen, probably two kings whose names have not been found. It would therefore appear that at least six kings, whose names are not found, intervened between Balavarman III and Tyāga Singha. With the help of the inscriptions discovered so far we can tentatively suggest the following list of the kings of Kāmarupa from the death of Bhāskaravarman till the accession of Brahmapāla which may have taken place during the last quarter of the tenth century :—

Name.		Approximate reign.
Avantivarman	...	650-655 A.D.
New dynasty begins.		
Sālastambha	...	655-675 A.D.
I		
Vijaya ...	...	675-685 „
Pālaka ...	...	685-700 „
Kumāra	...	700-715 „
Vajra Deva	...	715-730 „
Sri Harshavarma Deva		730-750 „
I		
Balavarman II	...	750-765 „

* * * * *

* * * * *

Chakra – Arathi (did not reign)

I

Prālambha	...	800-820	„
I			
Harjaravarman	...	820-835	„
I			
Vanamālavarman	...	835-860	„
I			
Jayamālavarman (Virabāhu)	...	860-875	„
I			
Balavarman III	...	875-890	„
* *	*	*	*
Tyāga Singha		970-985	„

New dynasty begins.

Brahmapāla	...	985	A.D.

CHAPTER VI.

Dynasty of Brahmapala.

As already stated in the previous chapter, according to the inscription of Ratnapāla, when Tyāga Singha died leaving no heir to succeed him the people elected Brahmapāla to be their king. We find here a parallel to the tradition that in order to remove the anarchy in Magadha and Gauda the people of those countries elected Gopāla, the first Pāla ruler of Magadha, as their king about the end of the eighth century. Such election by popular vote was clearly a myth. The fact is that both Gopāla in Magadha and Brahmapāla in Kāmarupa were actually adventurous upstarts who, finding the throne vacant, collected a following and proclaimed themselves as kings exactly as Bisu, the Koch, did in the beginning of the sixteenth century. As there was no one else strong enough to dispute the pretensions of Gopāla or Brahmapāla the people had no other alternative but to accept them as their rulers. After Brahmapāla became king it was perhaps given out that he was a king chosen by the people, like Gopāla, and, it seems that in imitation of the Pāla rulers of Magadha and Gauda, he assumed the surname Pāla. The writer of the Ratnapāla inscription, in order to make the story of popular election look more probable, added that Brahmapāla was a scion of the Bhagadatta dynasty and that is why the choice of the people fell upon him. It is stated in the Ratnapāla inscription that Brahmapāla was a warrior who could single-handed overcome his enemy in battle. He was evidently a powerful and resourceful leader; otherwise he could not have secured the throne. He was a young man when he became king, for it was after his accession that he married Kula Devi by whom he had a son named Ratnapāla. We do not know whether Brahmapāla had a long reign like his son but it appears that when Ratnapāla grew up Brahmapāla abdicated in his favour, probably to avoid a dispute relating to succession.

It seems that during Brahmapāla's reign Kāmarupa was attacked by Jātavarman, son of Vajravarman of the Varman dynasty which ruled probably in Eastern Magadha when the Pāla power began to wane. This invasion is mentioned in the Belava copper-plate inscription of Bhojavarma Deva (1), the grandson of Jātavarman, who thereby granted lands in the Paundra bhukti, the grant being issued from the victorious camp at Vikramapura. It is stated in verse 8 of this inscription that "seizing the great glory of Prithu son of Vena, espousing Virasri the daughter of Karna, extending his supremacy among the Angas, conquering the

(1) Epigraphia Indica vol. XII p. 37.

fortunes of Kāmarupa, putting to shame the strength of the arms of Divya, crippling the dignity of Gobardhan and giving away all his wealth to Brahmans he (Jātavarman) extended his own paramount suzerainty." Divya mentioned above has been identified to be the Kaivarta leader who successfully rebelled against the Pāla ruler. It appears that Jātavarman invaded Kāmarupa and defeated its king but could not annex the kingdom.* It is probable that after this defeat Brahmapāla abdicated in favour of his son Ratnāpala who appears to have removed the capital to Gauhati, on the banks of the Louhitya, and, after fortifying it, called it Durjayā or impregnable. It may be that Brahmapāla himself had removed the capital from Hāruppeswara to Gauhati and that his son Ratnapāla simply strengthened it by erecting necessary fortifications. Such strengthening of the defences of the capital was found to be necessary in view of the defeat sustained by his father.

Pandit Vidyāvinod supposes that when Sālastambha founded his dynasty he removed the capital to Hāruppeswara where all the kings of his line down to Tyāga Singha ruled. When the people elected Brahmapāla, a lineal descendant of Bhagadatta, as their king, he re-transferred the capital to Pragjyotishpur (Gauhati) or its neighbourhood. Ratnapāla after fortifying this city called it Sri-Durjayā. It is clearly stated that this city was on

* Pandit Vidyāvinod gives a different interpretation to the particular stanzā in the Belava inscription and holds that the supposed invasion of Kāmarupa by Jatavarman is really baseless.

the Brahmaputra. The lands granted by Ratnapāla's first inscription and by both of Indrapāla's inscriptions were, as stated in these inscriptions, on the *uttar kul* i.e. on the north bank of the river. From this specific mention of the *uttar kul* Vidyāvinod supposes that the capital was on the south bank of the river. Between Tezpur and Gauhati there is no other suitable site on the south bank of the river where a fortified city could be built. The identification of Śri-Durjayā with Gauhati is therefore almost inevitable.

We have two copper-plate inscriptions of Ratnapāla, known as the Bargaon and the Sualkuchi grants. It is satisfactory that both these grants state the regnal years in which they were recorded. The first grant was recorded on the *Vishnupadi Sankrānti* in the twentyfifth year of the king's reign. The second one was recorded in the following year. It is stated in these records that Ratnapāla was a warlike and powerful prince and that "by reason of the elephants pearls, carried forth by the impetus of the unrestrainable stream of blood running from the split foreheads of the elephants of his enemies* his, Ratnapāla's, battle field looked beautiful like a market-place strewn with the stores of merchants and ruby-coloured through the blood of the slain (2). A very glowing account is given of

* This fable of pearls, known as *Gaja-mukta,* being found in the frontal protuberances of certain elephants is referred to in the inscriptions of several old Hindu kings of the various countries of India.

(2) J. A. S. B. vol. LXvii (1898) p. 99.

the splendour and the strength of the fortifications of Ratnapāla's capital named Durjayā. It is stated that though the capital was "crowded with a dense forest, as it were, of arms of his brave soldiers who were hankering after the plunder of the camps of all his enemies, yet was it fit to be inhabited by wealthy people (merchants). In it the disc of the sun was hid from the view by the thousands of plastered turrets which are rendered still whiter by the nectar-like smiles of the love-drunk fair damsels standing on them. * * * * It is adorned by learned men, religious preceptors and poets who have made it their place of resort * * * * * * Like the cloth which protects the kings' broad chest, its boundaries were encompassed by a rampart, furnished with a fence strong like that used for the game-birds of the Sakas, fit to cause chagrin to the king of Gurjara, to give fever to the heads of the untameable elephants of the chief of Gauda (Gaudendra), to act like bitumen in the earth to the lord of Kerala, to strike awe into the Bāhikas and Taikas, to cause discomfiture to the master of the Deccan country (*dakshinatya*)* * * It is rendered beautiful by the river Louhitya * * * * Such is the town in which the Lord of Pragjyotisha took up his residence and which he called by the appropriate name of Durjayā. * * * * In that town, which emulated the residence of Vāsava, the King * * * * the Parameswara Parama-bhattāraka Mahārājadhirāja, the illustrious Ratnapālavarma Deva, who meditates at the feet of the Mahārājadhirāja, the illustrious Brahmapālavarma Deva, may he prosper." The above extract is from Hoernle's translation. Pandit

Vidyavinod has pointed out that on certain points Hoernle's interpretations are not quite correct.

The name of the poet who composed the verses of the inscription does not appear but the high literary merit of the composition is beyond question. The reference to Gurjara, Gauda and Kerala does not mean that Ratnapāla had actually any conflict with the kings of these countries, as supposed by Hoernle. It was simply meant to emphasize the strength and excellence of the fortifications. The inscription mentions that the king had certain copper-mines within his kingdom for it is said that "he delights in making his copper mines lucrative". These mines probably existed and still exist in the Garo or the Khasi Hills. In spite of what the court panegyrist has recorded, there is little doubt that about this time the Kāmarupa power was on the decline.

Ratnapāla had a long reign for about thirty years as his second grant was given in the twenty-sixth year of his reign. His son was Purandara Pāla. From some of the verses in the Indra Pāla inscription, found at Gauhati, Hoernle supposed that Purandara Pāla died during the life-time of his father Ratnapāla who was therefore succeeded by his grandson Indra Pāla (1). This supposition has been confirmed by the subsequent discovery of the inscription of Dharmapāla wherein it is stated that Pundarapāla died as *juvaraja*. In the Indrapāla inscription Purandarapāla is described as a poet (2). In this inscripion also the capital

(1) J. A. S. B. No. 2 (1897) pp. 128-132.
(2) Ibid.

is said to have been Śri Durjayā. It is also stated that Purandara Pāla "had the distinction of obtaining for wife the princess Durlabhā* * * who was descended from the royal races of the extensive kingdoms conquered by the victorious arms of Jāmadagnis son" (1). It is not possible to find from th is reference from what quarter princess Durlabhā came. Parasurāma is said to have overthrown all Kshattriya kings and so it can be surmised that Durlabhā was a Kshattriya princess, the daughter of some well-known king of northern India of that time, otherwise she would not have been so glorified. Vidyāvinod says that some Brahmans were settled near Parasurāma Kunda where a Hindu kingdom may have existed and Purandara Pāla may have married a princess of that kingdom. We do not think that this surmise is correct. It is stated that "when king Indrapāla sat on his throne the mosaic floor of his audience hall looked like a fruit-covered tree by reason of the strewn-about jewels that fell from the crowns of the princes as they voluntarily stood reverently bowing before him with joined hands" (2). It is also said that during his virtuous reign the earth was "greatly flourishing" and that he "had a residence of corresponding virtues, a town full of elephants, horses and jewels and impregnable to the attacks of any royal dynasty, whence it was named Śri Durjayā" (3).

---

(1) J. A. S. B, No 2 (1897) pp 128-132
(2) Ibid.
(3) Ibid.

We have two inscriptions of Indrapāla the first being recorded in the eighth year and the second in the twenty-first year of his reign. This shows that Indrapāla had also a fairly long reign. He was succeeded by his son Gopāla who ascended the throne probably about the middle of the eleventh century. In the first inscription of his grandson Dharmapāla it is stated that Gopala was a powerful prince who was also liberal in his gifts. His son Harshapāla succeeded him. It is recorded that the blood of his enemies killed by him in battle appeased the thirst of the Rākshasas (1). This indicates that Harshapāla was involved in war. In the *Vikramánka Charita* by Vihlan it is stated that the Chalukya prince, Vikramānka invaded Kāmarupa about this time. Harshapāla married Ratnā, a lady of high rank and had by her a son named Dharmapāla who has left two copper-plate inscriptions both of which have been published by Pandit Vidyāvinod in his "*Kamarupa S'āsanavali*". The first was recorded in the third regnal year and by this Dharmapāla granted lands to a Brahman, named Himanga, who appears to have been an expert in archery, and who was a native of village Krosanja in Sravasti. In the Silimpur stone-slab inscription of Prahāsa, deciphered by Mr. R. G. Basak, (2), which must be posterior in time to the Dharamapāla inscription, mention is made of the locality called Sravasti which Mr. Basak locates within Northern Bengal. Pandit Vidyāvinod

(1) Kamarupa Sasanavali pp. 150-158.
(2) Ibid

has attempted to prove that this locality was within Kāmarupa and that from this place some Brahmans migrated to Pundra (Northern Bengal)*. In the second inscription, the genealogy of Dharmapāla is drawn from Gopāla though in the first inscription it was drawn from Brahmapāla. We find from this inscription that the queen of Gopāla was named Nayanā. Another important fact found from this inscription is that the adoration of Śiva does not occur in it. The regnal year in which this incription was recorded is not stated but there is hardly any doubt that it was recorded towards the end of his reign for it contains an exhortation from the king himself which runs as follows:-

"Oh future kings, listen to this prayer of mine. Give up your false pride in your sovereignty which, like the flash of lightning, lasts only for a short while but do not give up *Dharma* which leads to eternal bliss."

This hankering for something eternal must have grown in his old age. The mention of "dharma"

* It is quite possible that the original home of the Brahmans to whom Dharmapāla granted land and that of the author of the Silimpur inscription were at Sravasti in Uttar Kosala referred to in Buddhist scriptures. Sravasti need not therefore be within either Kamarupa or Gauda. The Hindu kings used to grant lands even to persons living outside their dominions. In the tenth century a Ganga king of Orissa granted lands to a Kāmarupa Brahman and in the eighteenth century the Ahom king granted extensive estates in Assam to a Bengali Brahman of Navadwip.

is rather striking. As we shall see later, the Kāmarupa kings from Indrapāla to Dharmapāla were followers of the Tantrik tenet and about that period Kāmākshayā had become an important seat of Tantrik Buddhism. The *dharma* mentioned in this inscription very prabably referred to the "*Sahajia dharma*" or the Vajrayāna cult then prevalent in Kāmarupa. In both these inscriptions the name of the king as given in the seal is "Prāgjyotishādhipati Mahārājādhirāja Śri Dharmapāla Varma Deva" but although he is called "Lord of Pragjyotisha" it is stated in the second inscription, that he ruled at "Kāmarupanagar". In his first inscription his capital is not mentioned. Pandit Vidyāvinod supposes that before Dharmapāla had commenced his reign the capital of the kingdom had been shifted to Kamatāpur beyond the Brahmaputra valley. We have already stated in Chapter I that the capital of the kingdom was not removed from Prāgjyotishpur or Gauhati to Kamatāpur before the middle of the thirteenth century. As already stated, Bukhtiyar's disaster in Kamarupa in 1206 A. D. was recorded within the boundaries of Prāgjyotishpur in a rock inscription. The next Muslim invasions by Iwaz in 1226 A. D. and by Tughril Khan Malik Yuzbeg in 1255 A. D. seem to have proceeded as far as Gauhati and this is supported by the find at Gauhati. in 1880, of two coins, one of Iwaz dated 2nd Jumada 621 A. H. and another of Tughril minted at Lakhnauti dated Ramzan 653

Ananta Sâyi Vishnu, Asvakrânta.

A. H. (1). There is hardly any doubt therefore that the capital was at Gauhati or its immediate neighbourhood till at least 1255 A. D. If it was then at Kamatāpur the Muslim invasions would not have proceeded in the direction of Gauhati. Mr. Stapleton's supposition that both Iwaz and Tughril Khan Malik Yuzbeg were repulsed by the Kachari king of Prāgjyotishpur or Gauhati has no basis whatever (2). The Kachari aggressions did not evidently then advance westward further than the present district of Nowgong, for we find powerful Bhuyan chiefs holding Owguri, Luki, Pandu and Gauhati, on the south bank of the Brahmaputra, till the beginning of the sixteenth century. The ruins in Dimla Thana of the Rangpur district, described by Buchanan and referred to by Grierson in the Journal of the Asiatic Society of Bengal 1878, cannot, with any degree of certainty, be identified with "Kāmarupa-nagar" mentioned in the inscription. The city described by Buchanan was, as we shall see later, founded by another Dharmapāla, a king of Kamata, towards the beginning of the fourteenth century.

Our surmise is that the capital named Kāmarupa-nagar, the "city of Kāmrud" of the Muslim chroniclers, was at North-Gauhati near the temple of *Aswakranta*. The *Kamarupar Buranji* mentions the tradition that a king named Dharmapāla had his seat of government there. The modern town of North-Gauhati possesses temples, roads, bridges, fortifications and moats

(1). J. P. A. S. B. vol. VI (1910) pp. 621-622.
(2). Ibid.

which are clearly of pre-Ahom origin. There are two temples on the *Aswakrānta* hill. The upper temple contains the image of Vishnu lying on *Ananta-Sajyā*. It is one of the finest specimens of sculptural skill in Kāmarupa about the beginning of the twelfth century. The western part of the town is called Sil-Sāko because it still contains a small stone-built bridge over a stream. The eastern part is known as Raja-duar (king's gate), which shows that the Raja's palace was there. The second copper-plate of Dharmapāla was actually found in the village of Rangmahal about two miles to the north of Raja-duar. This is another indication that the capital was then at North-Gauhati. In Rājaduār itself exists the rock-inscription, dated 1127 Saka, proclaiming the destruction of the Turkish army of Mahammad Bukhtiyar. It is therefore extremely probable that North-Gauhati continued to be the capital from the time of Dharmapāla till about 1260 A.D. when the seat of goverment was transferred to Kamatāpur. Pandit Vidyāvinod's conjecture that the capital Kāmarupa-nagar was away from the river because the Brahmaputra is not mentioned in the inscription of Dharmapāla does not seem to be at all reasonable. We find from the *Darrang Rāj Vamsāvali* that the Koch king Viswa Singha stopped in North-Gauhati, near the *Aswakrānta* temple, for nearly a month and from a stone-slab inscriptioon found on the hill in Rāja-duār, abutting on the Brahmaputra, we find that this small hill was the abode of Śri Chandrabhārati, a well-known Kāmarupi poet of the sixteenth century. These facts go to show that

North-Gauhati was latterly the capital and that South-Gauhati or Prāgjyotishpur, subsequently called Śri-Durjayā, ceased to be the capital long before. It would therefore appear that North-Gauhati or Kāmarupa-nagar was the capital of Kāmarupa for about 160 years from *circa* 1100 A.D. to 1260 A.D.

Dharmapāla was succeeded probably by Jayapāla whose name we find from the Silimpur inscription mentioned above. It appears that there was a pious Brahman named Prahāsha in the Syamvaka village of Pundra who though persistently pressed by Jayapāla, a powerful king of Kāmarupa, refused to accept from the king the *tulapurusha* gift consisting of gold equal to the weight of the donor and also a gift of landed property. It appears that about the first part of the twelfth century, probably during the reign of Jayapāla, Rāma Pāla king of Gauda conquered Kāmarupa. This is mentioned inthe *Rāma Charita*, by Sandhyākara Nandi' wherein it is stated that a general of Rāmapāla named Māyana conquered Kāmarupa. Relying on R. D. Banerji's statement, in his paper on the "Palas of Bengal", to the effect that Rāmapāla was succeeded by his second son Kumāra Pāla about 1097 A. D., Pandit Vidyavinod states that Rāmapāla conquered Kāmarupa probably about 1095 A. D. when Dharmapāla was the king of Kāmarupa (1). We can not accept this, statement as correct. Of course the learned Pandit's theory is that after defeating Dharmapāla the king

(1) Kāmarupa Sasanavali p 41.

of Gauda snatched away only the south-westen part of Kāmarupa which was placed under the control of a vassal-king named Tingyadeva and that Dharmapāla and his successors continued to rule over the rest of Kāmarupa. In Chapter VIII we shall discuss this point more fully and attempt to prove that Pandit Vidyavinod's theory is incorrect. Here we shall only mention that the chronology of the Pāla rulers of Bengal is still uncertain. It has not been definitely proved that Kumārapāla succeeded Rāmapāla before the end of the eleventh century. On the other hand it is quite possible that Rāmapāla had a very long reign and that he was succeeded during the second quarter of the twelfth century. The Kamauli inscription, which must have been recorded very soon after Kumāra Pāla's death is, on palaeographical evidence, placed towards the middle of the twelfth century. On the other hand it is fairly certain that Kumāra Pāla had a very short reign (1). All these circumstances go to show that Rāmapāla reigned probably till 1130 A. D. and that his conquest of Kāmarupa took place about 1125 A. D. when Dharmapāla could not have been reigning. We are therefore of opinion that it was Jayapāla, the son of Dharmapāla, who was overthrown by Rāmapāla.

It will appear therefore that the names of all the kings of the dynasty of Brāhmapāla have been found from the inscriptions of Dharmapāla and the the Silimpur inscription referred to above. These kings ruled in due order of succession from about 985 A.D. till about 1125 A.D., when the last king

---

(1) Bangalar Itihash vol. I p 283

Jayapāla was overthrown, by the Pāla ruler of Bengal and a vassal named Tingyadeva was set up on the throne. The dynasty of Brahmapāla therefore ended with Jayapāla.

The following is the tentative chronology of the the kings of the dynasty of Brahmapāla :—

Name of king.		Approximate reign.
Brahmapāla	...	985-1000 A.D.
I		
Ratnapāla	...	1000-1030 „
I		
Purandarapāla (did not reign)		
I		
Indrapāla...	...	1030-1055 „
I		
Gopāla ...	...	1055-1075 „
I		
Harshapāla	...	1075-1090 „
I		
Dharmapāla	...	1090-1115 „
Jayapāla ...	...	1115-1125 „

CHAPTER VII

A REVIEW OF CULTURAL AND MATERIAL PROGRESS.

With Jayapāla, who was probably the son or grandson of Dharmapāla, the line of Kāmarupa kings, tracing descent from Bhagadatta, comes to an end. We may therefore now conveniently take stock and discuss how far Kāmarupa progressed materially and culturally during the rule of these kings from the fourth till the twelfth century A.D. The materials on which such a discussion may be based, with some degree of confidence, are however meagre. The account left by the Chinese pilgrim refers to conditions in the seventh century. The various copper-plate inscriptions however, though they were the works of panegyrists, afford some glimpse into the actual state of the country and the people practically throughout the whole period.

The most important development that took place in Northern India towards the close of the Upanishad period, not many centuries after the Mahābhārata war, was the rise of Gautama Buddha and his religion. Within a couple of centuries

Image of Buddha found at Gauhati.

after Buddha's *nirvāna* his religion spread far and wide. It is difficult to believe that Prāgjyotisha, which was so close to Uttar Kośala and Magadha, could remain free from Buddhistic influences, but though strange, we have it from Yuan Chwang's account that in the seventh century A.D. the people of Kāmarupa worshipped the *Devas* and did not believe in Buddhism. According to him, there were a few Buddhists in the country, but for fear of persecution they had to perform their devotional rites in secret. It seems that Yuan Chwang made an exaggerated statement, for, in his biography, Śilabhadra is said to have informed him, before he started for Kāmarupa, that the law of Buddha had not then widely extended in that country. This indicates that Buddhism was then prevailing in the kingdom but not to a wide extent. The king Bhāskaravarman was himself not a Buddhist though it is said that he treated accomplished *sramans* with respect. The eagerness and persistence with which he desired an interview with the Chinese Buddhist scholar in his own kingdom and his reluctance to part with the scholar show that he really had great respect for illustrious Buddhist professors. His Nidhanpur inscription begins, no doubt, with the adoration of his tutelary deity Śiva but, immediately after this adoration, he proclaims the victory of "Dharma, the sole friend of the Creation, the cause of prosperity in this and the next world, whose form is the good of others and which is unseen but whose existence is inferred from the results." Here we have a clear reference to the Law of Buddha. Vidyāvinod would ascribe this reference to Bhāskaravarman's association with Śri Harsha who, though not himself a Buddhist, was a patron of Buddhism and who was, to a considerable extent, influenced by his Buddhist sister Rājyaśri. This is not, however, probable for the inscription was recorded immediately after the conquest of Karnasuvarna, at least thirty years before Bhāskaravarman met either Yuan Chwang or Śri Harsha. Evidently the influence of Buddhism was felt in Kāmarupa long before Bhāskaravarman came to occupy the throne. According to the *Rajatarangini*, the Kāmarupa king of the fifth century, who was the father of Amritaprabhā, was himself a Buddhist as his religious preceptor was a Tibetan Buddhist.

The fact is that Buddhism spread into Kāmarupa at a very early age but it was not widely accepted as a faith by the people at large. Gait, in his History of Assam, writes:—"It was formerly thought that Buddhism had at one time great vogue in Assam, but this view seems to have been erroneous There is no trace of this religion in the old records and inscriptions." The above statement will not stand scrutiny for, as stated above, the Law of Buddha is mentioned in the inscription of Bhāskaravarman himself. Similar mentions are found in the inscriptions of Indrapāla and Dharmapāla. Indrapāla's first inscription mentions a *sāsana* or charter connected with the name of "Tathāgata" which cannot but mean Buddha. It seems that close to the lands granted by this king there existed a *chaitya* or *stupa*, over some relic of Buddha, in favour of which an endowment was made by a previous king.

We should refer here to the strong tradition current in Nepal and Tibet to the effect that the *mahāpari-nirvāna* of Buddha took place in Kusināra or Kusinagara, a town in Kāmarupa. In fact Waddell identifies it with the modern town of Sualkuchi, some nine miles to the west of Gauhati and eight miles to the south of the temple of *Hayagriva* which is still visited by Bhutanese Buddhists. Kusinagara was, however, the chief town of the clan of Mallas who cannot, by any means, be associated with any part of modern Assam. Waddell's identification is evidently wrong. Very likely Kusinagara or Kosinagara was a town on the east bank of the Kosi as it emerged from the Nepal hills. It was therefore probably a town, on the Nepal border, within the modern district of Purnea which was, in the ancient times, included within Prāgjyotisha. The Tibetan tradition was not therefore baseless. In his inscription, Bhaskaravarman is said to have revealed the light of Aryan religion (*Aryadharma*) in his kingdom by dispelling the accumulated darkness of the Kali age. We are not sure that here also we can detect a particular reference to the Law of Buddha. It may be that *Arya Dharma* meant the Buddhist or Brahmanic tenets as opposed to the tribal beliefs of the numerous non-Aryans who lived in the country. Bhāskaravarman and his predecessors were Śaivas and not Buddhists or Jainas and, being also regarded as good Kshattriyas, they were naturally looked upon as the patrons and protectors of the Brahmans. In the neighbouring Magadha empire the rulers, like the Mouryas and the Guptas, were either Buddhists or patrons of

Buddhism. The Mourya emperor Asoka, with his missionary zeal for the propagation of the Buddhist faith, must have done all in his power to popularise this tenet within his empire without going to the length of persecuting Brahmans. This is why a large number of Brahmans immigrated to Kāmarupa at an early period. As pointed out by Vidyāvinod, we find, in a single village in Kāmarupa, more than 200 families of Brahmans about 500 A.D.

The kings of the dynasty of Sālastambha, between the seventh and the tenth centuries, were perhaps more orthodox in their religious beliefs than their predecessors, the descendants of Pushyavarman. In the inscriptions of these kings we do not find the slightest trace of any reference to the Buddhist faith. These kings were the worshippers of their tutelary deities "Kāmeswara Mahā Gauri" mentioned in the inscription of Vanamāla. They had their capital much father up the Brahmaputra in modern Tezpur. They therefore found the necessity of having another shrine like Kāmākshyā near their capital. The second Kāmākshyā temple, on the Kāmakuta hill near Silghat, mentioned in the inscription of Vanamāla, was therefore founded. In this inscription mention is made of the numerous temples in the country and the sound of incantations proceeding from the various places where *Yajnas* were performed. Vanamāla himself rebuilt the large temple of Hātakeswara to which he dedicated a number of prostitutes evidently for service as *Devadāsis.* This system still persists in the Śiva temples of Hajo and Dubi in Kamrup and Neghriting in Upper, Assam, and it may have been

Terra cotta votive tablet with figure of Buddha.

part of the Tantrik system. Whatever that may be, although Brahmanic rites were widely prevalent amongst the populace there is no doubt that Buddhism also flourished, for it is mentioned in the "*Sankara Digvijaya*" that Sankarāchārya, the famous leader of the Brahmanic revival, in the beginning of the ninth century A.D., came to Kāmarupa in order to defeat Abhinava Gupta, the noted Buddhist scholar, in controversy (1). Abhinava Gupta probably belonged to Kāmarupa or at least flourished there in the ninth century. About the same time, or a little earlier, Kumārila Bhatta, another Brahmanic leader, flourished in India. It is believed by some that he was a native of Kāmarupa (2). The fact that both Abhinava Gupta and Kumārila Bhatta, two well-known leaders of two opposite schools, flourished about the same time in Kāmarupa, clearly shows that there were adherants of both Brahmanism and Buddhism in Kāmarupa during the rule of the earlier kings of the line of Sālastambha. Sculptured images on stones and terra-cotta plaques, which unmistakably represent Buddha and which can be assigned to the tenth or the eleventh century, have been found from exacavations at Gauhati. One of them is a distinct image of Buddha on a thin stone-slab, the figure exhibiting the *Abhaya mudrā*. The other is a terra-cotta votive tablet with the image of Buddha stamped on it. Below the figure is inscribed the well-known Mahāyāna creed in characters of the eleventh

(1) Sri Sankaracharya; His life and times by C. N, Krishnaswami Aiyar. Page 56·
2). Ibid p 26.

century. In this plaque Buddha is in the earth-touching attitude, *Bhumisparsā mudrā*. It is true that both of these images are of a portable nature and might easily have been imported from outside the kingdom by some Buddhists. Terra-cotta plaques with the stamped image of Buddha, exactly similar to the one found at Gauhati and, as a matter of fact, impressed with the same stamp, have been found in large numbers in Bengal and Bihar. Evidently these were sold at places of Buddhist pilgrimages but their occurrence in Gauhati shows that there were then Buddhists in Kāmarupa. Another important find from excavations in Gauhati is a large and heavy stone-slab containing the image of a deity with four faces and eight arms and a *Chaitya* above the head as tiara. The image is carved in the centre of the slab, all round being lotus-petals carved deep into the stone. One side of the slab is broken. The sitting pose of the deity is adamantine (*vajrāsana*). It is probable that this is the representation of *Mahāpratisarā*, a Buddhist Goddess of the period of Tantrik Buddhism. According to the *Sādhanamāla*, a Buddhist work, the *Mahāpratisarā* should have a *Chaitya* above the head. The image is however so corroded now that it is hardly possible to interpret it with confidence. In any case, the stone-slab on which the image is carved is certainly not portable.

When the Sālastambha dynasty was succeeded by the dynasty of Brahmapāla and the capital was removed to the vicinity of Gauhati the same tutelary deities, mentioned as "Mahā Gauri Kāmeswara" in the inscription of Indrapāla continued to be worshipped by the kings. Indrapāla's first inscription states that his grandfather Ratnapāla established numerous Śiva temples in the country and that during his reign the houses of Brahmans were full with riches presented by the king, the places where *Yajnas* were performed had numerous sacrificial altars and the sky was overcast with the smoke caused by numerous *homs*. It is said of Indrapāla himself that he was well-versed in the *Tantras*. It is clear therefore that Tantrikism had then been already introduced into the kingdom. This system, as an offshoot of Buddhism of the Mahāyāna school, developed about the ninth century under the Pāla rulers of Magadha. It was the Pāla king Dharmapāla who founded the Buddhist university at Vikramaśila, which became the famous centre of the Tantrik doctrines. From this centre Tantrikism probably spread into Kāmarupa and Tibet. Babu Nandalal Dey writes :—

"The improvement which Nāgārjuna introduced into original Buddhism in the first century A. D. and which was known by the name of Mahāyāna system, assumed a new phase on the revival of Brahmanical doctrines, during the early Gupta period and gradually developed into Tantrikism from the eighth century when the Pāla kings began to rule over Magadha and Gauda. The worship of the images of Buddha and Bodhisvattas with their female energies (Sakti) and other Buddhist Gods came into vogue, which, during the continuance of the rule of these monarchs, still further developed into mysticism and sorcery. The *mantra yogācharyas* maintained the popular propensity for magic rites and mystic practices by the performance of marvellous feats. Hinduism also imbibed the spirit of the time and the Buddhist Tantrik rites were absorbed in its system." (1).

This is how Tantrikism originated. It ultimately spread into Kāmarupa and established for itself a stronghold in Kāmākshyā. This disposes of Sir Edward Gait's supposition that Tantrikism originated in Assam. The Kāmarupa kings, probably after Brahmapāla, adopted Tantrikism as their tenet and, as a result of this royal patronage, Kāmākshyā soon became a renowned centre of Tantrik sacrifices, mysticism and sorcery.

That this system of mystic Buddhism, known as Vajrayāna and popularly called the "Sahajia cult", found its way into Kāmarupa as early as the tenth century, is corroborated from an unexpected source. It is found from Tibetan records that some of the eminent Buddhist professors in Tibet, of the tenth and the eleventh centuries, hailed from Kāmarupa. Giuseppe Tucci states, on the authority of two Tibetan works viz "Grub To'b" and the "Bka ababs bdun ldan" that the noted Buddhist *Siddha* Minanatha, who was looked upon in Tibet as an *avatār* of Avalokiteswara, was a fisherman from Kāmarupa (2). The statement of Mahāmohopādhāya Pandit Haraprasad Sastri that Minanatha was a native of Bengal belonging to the

---

(1) J. P. A. S. B. (New Series) vol. X 1914 page 346.
(2) J. P. A. S. B (New Series) vol. XXVI, 1930. No. 1 pp. 133-141,

"Nath" or weaver caste is evidently incorrect (1). It is also found from the same Tibetan records that Rahula, another Buddhist teacher in Nepal, was a Sudra from Kāmarupa. It is said that he was a disciple of Nāgārjuna who should not, however, be confused with the famous preacher of the Mahāyāna. The preceptor of Rahula was perhaps the Nāgārjuna mentioned by Alberuni who stated that Nāgārjuna flourished about 100 years before his time. Thus both Nāgārjuna and Rahula can be placed about the middle of the tenth century. Nāgārjuna was also a physician and alchemist. In the Kāmarupi Ayurvedic pharmacopoeia there are still certain specific remedies which are associated with the name of Nāgarjuna.* Besides Minanātha and Rahula, two other Buddhist teachers mentioned in Tibetan records viz. Mohidhar and Dārik also very probably belonged to Kāmarupa. Minanātha is supposed to have been the author of a work known as *Akulaviratantra* and he is men-

(1) "*Bauddha Gān O Dohā*" by M. M. Pandit H. P. Sastri.
We give below a *Dohā* composed by Minanātha:-
"*Kahanti guru paramārthara bāt*
Karma kuranga samādhika pātth
Kamala bikasila kahiha na jamarā
Kamala madhu pibibi dhoke na bhomorā."
This *Doha* appears to be in mixed Kamarupi-Maithili dialect.

* The late M. M. Pandit Haraprasad Sastri found the M. S. of a medical work entitled *yoga-Sataka* (hundred prescriptions) in the Nepal Durbar Library. These prescriptions are attributed to Nagarjuna. The Pandit is however of opinion that this Nagarjuna is not the same person mentioned by Alberuni. He has not however given any reasons for his opinion.

tioned in the *Sabaratantra* as one of the twenty-four *Kāpālika siddhas*(1).

The fact that Minanātha, one of the 24 *Kāpālika siddhas*, hailed from Assam leads one to suppose that the very revolting religious practices associated with the *Kāpālikas*, perhaps to some extent exaggerated by their opponents, were at one time in vogue in Kāmarupa, at least among the lower classes of society, such as the fishermen.* What connection these *Kāpālikas* had with the votaries of the *Sahajia* cult we do not know. There is however evidence to show that the *Kāpālika* sect existed as early as the time of Asanga and Harivarman about the fourth century A. D. Evidently both of these sects were off-shoots of Tantrik Buddhism and both practised similar rites. Abhinava Gupta, to defeat whom Sankarāchārya came all the way to Kāmarupa, was the author of two well-known works on *Tantra* viz, the *Tantrasāra* and the *Tantrāloka*. Evidently, in the ninth century, Abhinava Gupta had a great following in Kāmarupa and that is why Sankarāchārya found it necessary to fight him. These *Tantriks* have of course been painted in the blackest colours by the Brahman revivalists of an earlier age and by the Vaisnava reformers of a subsequent period, but a considerable mass of *Tantrik* literature has now become accessible to scholars some of whom do not seem to subscribe to the sweeping condemna-

---

(1) J. P. A. S. B. vol. XXVI, 1930, No, pp 133-141.

* The late Rai Bahadur Gunabhiram Barua was of opinion that the Kaibartas of the Assam valley were Buddhists. They are now, almost to a man, strict Vaisnavas of the shool started by Sri Sankar Deva.

tion of *Tantrikism* as a tenet. Here is what Giuseppe Tucci, a competent authority, has got to say on the subject :—

"Very little attention has been paid up till now to Tantrik literature; and yet, apart from some exceptions, the Tantras contain almost nothing which can justify the sweeping judgment of some scholars who maintain that they represent the most degenerate form of Indian speculation. On the other hand, after a careful study, I cannot help seeing in them one of the highest expressions of Indian mysticism, which may appear to us rather strange in its outward form, chiefly because we do not always understand the symbolical language in which they are written" (1).

The probability is that the esoteric teachings of the tenet were high and sublime but they were actually comprehensible only to a few, called *Siddhas*, whereas the common folk were mystified by the feats of sorcery performed by the lower order of the preachers who could thus trade on the credulity of the common people and compel them to submit to their demands. It is therefore well that these esoteric teachers and their practices were supressed by the Brahmans and the Vaisnavas, of a later period, not so much with the help of the ruling kings but chiefly by appeal to the common people themselves.

The influence of Kāmarupi Buddhist preachers in Tibet incidently proves the close cultural connection between Tibet and Kāmarupa in the early

(1) J. P. A. S. B. vol. XXVI pp 133-141.

ages. We find the Tibetan Buddhist scholar Stunpa acting as preceptor to a Kāmarupa king, probably Balavarman I, in the early part of the fifth century. The image of Buddha found at Gauhati, exhibiting the *Abhaya mudra*, with its distinctly Mongolian physiognomy and a thick shawl covering the whole body, down to the ankles, seems to be unmistakably of Tibetan origin.

It will appear from what we have stated above that several noted Buddhist scholars, as well as critics of the Buddhist doctrines, flourished in Kāmarupa between the eighth and the tenth centuries. We find from Yuan Chwang's biography that during his stay in Nalanda a learned pundit of Kāmarupa went to engage in a controversy with the Buddhist scholars and professors assembled there. According to the account of the Chinese pilgrim, Bhāskaravarman was a lover of learning and Kāmarupa was a seat of learning. He found that during the first half of the seventh century students from other parts of India came to Kāmarupa for study. It has been recently pointed out that Viśākha Datta, the author of the well-known drama *Mudrarākshasam*, who flourished towards the latter part of the seventh century, very probably belonged to that part of Kāmarupa which lay between the Teesta and the Kausika (1). It is reasonable to suppose that he belonged to the colony of Nagar Brahmans settled in the Chandrapuri *vishaya*. This is indicated by his surname Datta. It is not therefore at all strange that Kāmarupi pundits were

(1) J. P. A. S. B. vol XXVI pp 241-245.

Ruins of Pragjyotishpur, Panel on plinth

honoured in other parts of India also. In the copper-plate inscription of Anantavarman, the Ganga king of Kalinga (*Circa* 922 A.D.) we find the mention of a Kāmarupi pandit, named Vishnu-somāchārya, to whom Anantavarman granted lands (1). This Brahman belonged to the Paraśara *gotra* and his native village was Srangatika in Kāmarupa. It is not possible now to identify this village in Assam or Northern Bengal with any degree of certainty.* The inscriptions of Vanamāla and Ratnapāla, while describing their capitals, specially mention that they were abodes of many learned men, as these kings were patrons of learning. The *Kālika Purāna,* a well-known work, gives the Sanskritized names of most of the rivers and hills of eastern and western Assam. It gives a full account of the Naraka legend and the old city of Prāgjyotishpur. It dwells upon the special merit and sanctity of the shrine of Kāmākshyā. There is hardly any doubt that this work, like perhaps the *Yogini Tantra*, was compiled in Kāmarupa probably at a time when the kings claiming descent from Naraka were ruling, when the capital was in the neighbourhood of the old city of Prāgjyotishpur and the shrine of Kāmākshyā and when Tantrikism was the prevailing tenet. We can therefore tentatively assign this work to the eleventh century when the kings of the dynasty of Brahmapāla, who

---

(1) R. D. Banerji's History of Orissa, vol. I. pp. 233-241.

* The Kālikā purāna makes mention of the existence of a *linga* in Sringataka which Rai Bahadur A. C. Agarwala identifies with Singri in Darrang below Tezpur. (Abahan vol III No 4).

claimed descent from Naraka and particularly distinguished themselves from the previous *mlechha* dynasty, were ruling. In the *Kālika Purāna* the *mantra* given to consecrate the sword meant for the human sacrifice runs as follows :—

"*Asir visasana Khadgastikhnadhāro durāsadah Srigarbho Vijayaschaiba Dharmapāla namastute.*"

The sword is here eulogised as Dharmapāla meaning "protector of the faith". In our opinion, however, it is possible to detect here a reference to king Dharmapāla of the Brahmapāla dynasty. It would not therefore be quite unreasonable to suppose that the *Kalikā Purāna* was compiled during his reign and perhaps under his auspices.*

In the seventh century Yuan Chwang found that the language spoken by the people of Kāmarupa differed only a little from that spoken in mid-India. This shows that the language then spoken in Kāmarupa was a Sanskritic dialect. It was probably an eastern variety of Prākrit bearing close affinity to Maithili and it was no doubt the parent of modern Kāmarupi or Assamese language. The Chinese traveller's account also makes it clear that, even at such an early age, the people in general had adopted an Aryan language and that therefore Aryans had settled in the kingdom and diffused their culture many centuries before his visit. The language used in the *dohas*, by the Buddhists of Kāmarupa in the ninth or the tenth century, was not necessarily the actual spoken language. These *dohās* were com-

---

* According to Pandit Jogesh Chandra Rai Vidyanidhi, the Kālika Purāna was compiled in Assam about the tenth century (Bharatvarsha, Baisakh 1337 B. S.).

Image of Bodh-Janardana in Gauhati.

posed in a language which was perhaps the *lingua franca* in Eastern India at that time.

We find from the inscription of Vanamāla that, towards the middle of the ninth century, he re-erected the "lofty (like a peak of the Himalaya) white temple of Hātaka Śiva which had fallen down." Probably the temple had been destroyed by an earthquake. It is evident that this temple was rebuilt with bricks and stones and was white-washed. The inscription of Balavarman III states that Vanamāla erected a huge palace consisting of many rooms and decorated by carvings. Again in the Ratnapāla inscription we find it mentioned that in his capital at Śri Durjayā, towards the middle of the eleventh century, "the disc of the sun was hid from view by the thousands of plastered turrets." The Indrapāla inscription states that Ratnapāla constructed numerous white temples of Śiva throughout the kingdom. These references make it clear that architecture had reached a high state of perfection during the rule of these kings and also earlier. As a matter of fact, architectural remains, going back to the pre-Ahom and the pre-Koch period, exist to this day. Although no regular archaeological exploration has yet been undertaken in Assam the existing remains are by no means inconsiderable. In sites of old cities like Gauhati, Tezpur, Silghat and Bishnath, one can notice scattered remains in abundance.

That both the builders and the sculptors of ancient Kāmarupa reached a high standard can be judged from the few remains that have so far come to light without any regular exploration. The modern town of Gauhati, which represents the site of old Prāgjyotishpur, was probably sacked and destroyed after the death of Bhāskaravarman when Sālastambha usurped the throne. It ceased to be the capital for more than three hundred years during which period perhaps even the ruins largely disappeared. It is not known definitely whether the kings of the dynasty of Brahmapāla used it as their capital. Latterly the Kacharis perhaps occupied it for a time and the Muslim invaders also carried on raids up to this town. Subsequently the Muhammadans occupied it for a considerable time and they were dislodged by the Ahoms after a long period of bloody conflicts during which much devastation must have been done. The town was practically re-built after British occupation. Some 50 years ago, the foundations of an old stone and brick enclosure wall in the eastern part of this town were dug up in order to find out stones to be broken into road-metal. Numerous carved and chiseled stones were broken into fragments to provide road-metal. Some were preserved, not by the authorities, but by individuals taking interest in relics of antiquities. Since the establishment of the Kāmarupa Anusandhan Society, some of these scattered relics have been collected and placed in the small museum of the Society. These collections include some pre-Ahom sculptured images of deities, chiselled octagonal or hexagonal stone pillars, carved stone pedestals of pillars and finely carved panels containing figures of elephant-heads *en face*, lion-heads and human heads, used to decorate the outer side of the stone plinths of palaces or temples. The elephant-head *en face* is a peculiarity of Prāgjyotisha as the kings invariably used the same emblem in the metal seals of their copper-plates. The rock-cut images of Vishnu and Ganeśa found in or near Gauhati similarly go back to an early age.

The shrine of Pāndu contains five rock-cut figures four of which represent Ganeśa and one represents a female deity, probably Durga. Two more figures cut in the open rock below, facing the Brahmaputra river, represent, according to Mr. Dikshit, the sun-god and Indra respectively (1). Numerous cuttings on rock are to be seen also on the western slope of the Kāmākshyā hill. These include miniatures of temples of the *sikhara* type with small *lingas* enshrined in them and also rock-cut niches containing *lingas* and figures or Ganeśa. On the west side of the Kāmākshyā temple is a modern temple, known as Ghantākarna, into the basement of which stone fragments of older temples have been built. One of these fragments, as described by Mr. Dikshit, "is a beautifully carved frieze in which the band represents a series of garlands and the lower scroll-work, in which some very spirited representations of animals occur. Only four animal figures of the series viz a buffalo, a deer, a lion and a tiger are extant, but the quality of the art manifested in them is unsurpassed in Assam" (2). This is also undoubtedly a pre-Ahom piece of sculptured art. Mr. R. D. Banerji

(1). **Annual Report of the Archaeological Survey of India, 1923-24, pp 80-81.**

(2). **Annual Report of the Archaeological Survey of**

thinks that these carvings belong to the seventh or the eighth century A. D. (1). The ruins existing in or near Tezpur are much more extensive and varied in character. The late Dr. Bloch conjectured that the modern civil stations of Gauhati and Tezpur stood upon large mounds "which contain the remains of two ancient cities." In 1906, while foundations were being dug for additions to the Deputy Commissioner's office in Tezpur, the excavators came upon the remains of an ancient stone building. A large number of carved and sculptured stones were discovered. The majority of them were transferred to the compounds of the European officers and the tea-planters club for the purpose of decoration. Some of them were subsequently brought to the Cole Park and arranged there. The late Mr. R. D. Banerji, Superintendent, Eastern Circle, Archaeological Survey of India, wrote as follows in the Annual Report for the year 1924-25 :—

"On examination of the remains in the park at Tezpur and those preserved in the Planters' Association or Club at the same place I find that the carvings belong to three different periods of history and therefore must have belonged, at least, to three separate buildings. The most remarkable sculptures of the first group are two shafts of pillars at the entrance to the Planters' Club and a heavy lintel of a stone door-frame now lying in the public park. The shaft of one of these pillars is sixteen-sided, the upper end being ornamented with a broad band having *kirtimukhas* at the top and the

Ruins of Hārappeswara, stone pillar of Gupta type.

lower with dentils. Over this band the shaft is round and appears to be lathe-turned like the upper parts ot the Western Chalukyan columns ot the Bombay Presidency. In the second pillar the upper part of the shaft is dodecagonal and near the top is divided into three raised horizontal bands two of which contain *kirtimukhas* and the third a series of diamond-shaped rosettes. In style, both of them belong to the same period and appear to have come from one and the same building. The lintel of the stone door-frame in the public park also belongs to the same period and most probably to the same building. It is divided into two different parts. The upper part represents five miniature temples with the phallic emblem of Śiva in each of them. In the lower part we see a continuation of the ornamentation on the jambs, viz., two vertical bands containing meandering creepers and two others consisting entirely of rosettes which turn an angle and are continued on the soffit of the lintel. In the centre of the lower part of the lintel is a small niche containing a miniature image of Ganeśa. It appears from the nature of the carvings that the temple to which these three architectural specimens belong was erected late in the tenth century A. D. The length of the lintel is 6′ 10″ and the breath 1′ 5½″.

"The second group of sculptures at Tezpur consists of specimens from a massive temple on the ruins of which the office of the Deputy Commissioner has been built. On each side of the entrance of the Planter's Club at Tezpur lie the door-sill and the lintel of the principal entrance to this enormous temple. The size of the lintel enables us to determine the size of the door-frame and consequently of the principal entrance to the sanctum. The enormous lintel is 10′ 3″ in length and 1′ 8″ in breath. There are three raised panels on it, one in the centre and one on each side and each of them is divided into a large niche in the centre with a smaller one on either side. The panel on the left contains a standing figure of Brahmā in the central niche with an attendant on each side. The central panel is occupied by a figure of Surya with two attendants while the panel on the extreme right contains a standing figure of Śiva with an attendant in each of the side niches. The space between these raised panels is divided into six niches, three to the left of the central panel and three to the right. They contain six divine figures which cannot be identified. All the niches are separated from each other by a round pilaster 2′ in height, the height of the lintel itself being 2′ 7½″. According to the general practice in Hindu temples, the central niche or panel of the lintel of the stone door-frame of the sanctum is generally occupied by the presiding deity of the temple. It appears certain, therefore, that this gigantic temple was dedicated to Surya or the Sun-god. The sill of this door-frame is also of gigantic dimensions and shows a vase in the centre flanked by two lions *satatant.* Each end is occupied by a niche containing a male and a female and flanked by a smaller and narrower niche on a recessed corner, containing a single human figure. It is a pity that the jambs of this enormous door-frame have not been discovered as yet. The large jamb in the public park appears to belong to a much later period. It is impossible

Ruins of Hāruppeswara. Plinth mouldings.

therefore to deduce the height of the door-frame correctly, but it is obvious from the length of the lintel and the sill that the height of this door-frame could not have been less than 15′. If the height of the stone door-frame of the main entrance to the sanctum was 15′ then the height of the interior of the chamber must have been 20′ to 25′, leaving us to imagine the total height of the spire or *s'ikhara* of the original temple, which must have been considerably over 100′. The majority of the carved stones in the public park at Tezpur are taken from the plinth mouldings and string-courses of the gigantic temple, the door-frames of which have been described above. The string-sourses were ornamented with *kirtimukhas* of various shapes and sizes and sunken panels containing ornamental rosettes and meandering creepers. Some of them are evidently portions of enormous capitals which were held together by metal clamps or dowels. In the centre of some of these pieces there is a projecting niche flanked by round pilasters containing divine figures. In one of these niches we find a fat female squatting on the ground, holding a piece of cloth over her head, while a female stands to her left with her hands clasped in adoration. The second specimen of the same type contains the figure of a goddess holding a lyre in her hands, evidently Sarasvati, the goddess of learning. A third specimen contains the well-known group of *Kamalatmika* or *Gajalakshmi*, more commonly known in Bengal and Assam as *Kamale-Kamini* in which two elephants pour water over the head of a goddes from vases held in their trunks. A fourth specimen contains figures of Śiva and Durga seated in the well-known conventional posture so common in images of this particular type in northern India. The outlines of the plinth mouldings show that the mediaeval architects of Assam employed the same motifs and figures as those in other provinces of northern India. Some of these ornaments appear in relief as diamond-shaped and circular rosettes, set in between arabesque work of a type known to us from the temples of Orissa. The most remarkable specimen in the collection in the public park at Tezpur, however, is a slab taken from the upper part of the plinth mouldings. It is divided into a number of sunken panels by means of circular pilasters, each containing a male or female, two females or two males. Beginning from the right we find a man fighting with a lion, a male playing on a flute and a female dancing by his side, two males playing on conch shells, a male playing on a drum and a female dancing by his side, a female playing on a lyre and another dancing to her right, a male playing on a drum and another dancing to his left. This slab apparently formed part of a series of similar panels all round the lower edge of the walls of the sanctum. Another slab bears on it a conventional representation of the Chaitya-window pattern, so common in the temples of Central India, especially those in the Rewa State and at Khajuraho. The interior of the sunken panels is entirely covered with geometrical patterns with a half rosette in the centre. The second group of sculptures at Tezpur belongs to a temple erected in the twelfth century A. D. if not later. The size of the stones indicates that the temple was very large in size and provided with a very tall spire. There are two specimens

General view of Bamuni Hill Ruins, Tezpur.

in the public park at Tezpur which appear to belong to another temple of some later date. One of these is a high door-jamb and the second a slab bearing three sunken panels occupied by very crude human or divine figures. The entire collection contains only a single specimen carved in the round, a lion, presumably on an elephant. The conventional representation of the lion shows that the inhabitants of the Assam valley were not very familiar with the king of beasts."

As remarked by Mr. Banerji "Assam is the only province of India the history of the architecture and sculpture of which is still practically unknown." It is for this reason that we have made a lengthy quotation from the report of a competent authoriry on the subject. We are, however, in doubt whether Mr. Banerji's conjecture that the ruins in Tezpur town represent only temples is correct. The remains of the stone building dug up in the Kutchery compound may be of the palace of Vanamāla which he erected in the ninth century. We cannot, however, agree with Mr. Banerji that any of the buildings mentioned by him was erected in the twelfth century for, towards the end of the tenth century, the capital Hāruppeswara was, in all probability, abandoned by Brahmapāla. The buildings in Tezpur must therefore belong to the ninth century. Further, the lofty temple the ruins of which he has described in the quotation given above and which, he conjectures was a sun-temple, may be the Himalaya-like temple of Hātaka Sulin which Vanamāla is said to have reerected.

In his report for the year 1925-26 Mr. Banerji gives a full description of the Bamuni Hill ruins to the east of Tezpur town. In his opinion the remains belong to a group of seven shrines. He writes :—

"Six of these shrines are situated in a large rectangular enclosure, namely, one in each of its four corners and two large ones in the centre, while the seventh stands to the east. The pavements inside the *garbhagrihas* of both of the larger shrines in the middle of the enclosure are still intact. One of these central temples was originally smaller in size than the other. The larger temple faces the north and an *antarala* with a circular sculptured door-step intervenes between its sanctum and its *mandapa*, which must have been gigantic in size. The shaft of a pillar seen in the *debris* measures 10′ 8″ in length and 1′ 8″ in diameter. I may also mention a cross-shaped bracket which measures 4′ 6″ x 4′ 9″ and a huge lintel ornamented with horned *kirttimukhas* which measures 6′ 8″ in length and 1′ 8″ in breadth. An image of *Nataraja* measuring 2′ 1″ in height and 1′ 6″ in breadth, with one head and six hands was discovered among the ruins. Another lintel measures 12′ 1″ x 3′ 6″ x 2′ 5″. The door-jambs of the larger temple are lying on the top of the ruins and measure 5′ 4″ in length and 2′ 4″ in breadth. Each of them is decorated with a raised band on each side with a row of miniature temples superimposed in the centre. The band on the left jamb bears a meandering creeper pattern and that on the right a row of rosettes alternately square and round. There are three miniature shrines in each horizontal row in the centre. There is a large panel bordered by two round

Temple door-frame in Dah Parbatia.

pilasters with a trefoil arch on the top in the centre and an exactly similar panel or recessed corner on each side. The smaller panels contain male or female attendant figurines. The central panels contain the figures of the Man-lion, Parasurāma, Balarāma, Boar and Rāmachandra incarnations of Vishnu. Many of the the faces of the square brackets bear oblong panels with bas-reliefs. One of them bears the figure of a male and a female dancing side by side."

The ruins discovered at Parbatia, to the west of Tezpur town, are far more interesting. The following is Mr. Banerji's description of these ruins :—

"Close to the modern civil station of Tezpur is the small village of Dah Parbatia which possesses the unique distinction of having within its limits the ruins of the oldest temple in Assam. The ruins consist of the remains of a brick-built temple of Śiva, of the Ahom period, erected upon the ruins of a stone temple of the later Gupta period, *circa* sixth century A. D. The former collapsed, during the earthquake of 1897, revealing the stone door-frame of the older structure. At some subsequent date the local villagers built a crude hut on the mound, which had collapsed at the time of my visit. The mound is nearly 20' above the surrounding ground and is entirely covered with large rubber trees and small undergrowth. The door-frame stands in front of a large block of stone with a square cavity in its centre. Most probably the older *linga* was fixed in this hole. The carving on the door-frame is characteristic of the style of the early Gupta schools of sculpture, of which so many examples have been discovered at various sites excavated by Sir John Marshall in northern India. The carving on the jambs consists of high reliefs in the lower part and four different vertical bands of carving in the upper. In the lower part of each of the jambs is the figure of a female deity whose divine nature is indicated by the halo behind her head. Each of the goddesses stands with a garland in her hands in an elegan posture and these two figures appear to represent *Gangā* and *Yamunā*, so common in door jambs oj ancient Gupta and mediaeval temples. These two larger figures are attended, in each of the jambs, by a number of smaller ones. At the bottom of the jamb on the right are two female figures, one standing with a *chamara* and the other kneeling in front, with a flat receptacle containing flowers. A third female figure is seen with a *chāmara* behind or to the right of the main figure. To the left of the halo we find a *nagi* kneeling and to the right two geese flying towards the main figure. The lower part of the jamb on the left is not so well preserved as that on the right. Here we find a female standing with an indistinct object to the left and another to the right or in front of the main figure, the lower part of which is damaged. On this jamb also is the figure of a *naga* kneeling to the right of the halo of the main figure and two geese flying to the left of it. The upper part of each of these jambs is separated into four long narrow vertical bands two of which are continued on the lintel. The first of these begins from the head of the *naga* or of the *nagi* and consists of a meandering creeper with extremely beautiful ornamental foliage in the inter-spaces and the second of a straight vertical stem

Enlarged view of Gangā in door-frame

from which issue a number of lotus leaves and other conventional flowers. Two dwarfish figures are observed at the bottom holding on to the stem. The third band is made up of four super-imposed panels containing human figures standing on oblong bosses bearing ornamental foliage on their surfaces. At the top, each of these bands ends in a vase with ornamental foliage hanging from its corner. A pilaster, square in section, rises from the vase and ends in a cruciform capital, with a sprawling *gana* on each of its arms. The fourth band consists of a vertical row of ornamental rosettes. As in the case of the Gupta temples at Bhumra in the Nagod State, Nachna-Kuthara in the Ajaigadh State and at Deogarh in the Jhansi district, the lintel is larger in size than the door-frame, extending a little on each side of the jambs. Two of the inner bands of carving on the jambs are continued as horizontal bands at the bottom of the lintel and exhibit in the centre in high relief a beautiful flying male figure holding a garland in its hands. Above these two ornamental bands is another band in higher relief containing a number of Chaitya-windows so common in the Gupta temples at Bhumra and Deogarh. In this case there are five Chaitya-windows in all, arranged in a row on the surface of the lintel Three of these windows are large while two are comparatively smaller in size. The one on the extreme right contains the figure of a male seated on a throne, with four hands, two of which are broken. One of the left hands holds a *ḍamaru*, the peculiar small drum of Śiva while the space below the throne shows the waves of the sea. The window between this one and the central one contains a horse-headed male figure, with two hands, kneeling. The central Chaitya-window is the largest of all and has a *suparna*, the mythical deity half man and half bird, on either side. The Chaitya-window itself is occupied by a figure of Śiva, in the form of *Lakulisa*, seated with a rope tied round his leg. A female is holding a cup to his left while another stands to the right. The window between the central one and that on the extreme left contains the figure of a man seated and playing on a flute while over his head is seen the hood of a snake. That on the extreme left contains in its medallion a beautiful image of Surya seated cross-legged holding lotus flowers in both of his hands. The attendant to the left holds a pen and an ink-pot while that on the right holds a staff of the orthodox description. The door jambs are 5′ 3″ in height and 1′ 4″ in breadth while the lintel measures 3′ 9″ in length and 1′ 3″ in breadth. The artist's sense of proportion, the beautiful symmetry of the figures and ornamental devices and the excellence of execution tend to prove that this door lintel belongs to the same period as the great schools of sculpture which existed at Pataliputra and Benares in the fifth and sixth centuries A. D."

The temple at Parbatia is therefore not only the oldest but the finest piece of architectural work in Kāmarupa. This temple must have been built by a predecessor of Bhāskaravarman in the fifth or the sixth century A.D. During the clearance of the ruins of this temple a number of terracotta plaques, showing a seated human figure in each, were discovered. According to Mr. Banerji the moulding of the torso and the general technique

Enlarged wiew of Jamuna in door-frame.

proves beyond doubt that these plaques cannot be later in date than the sixth century A. D. Two of these plaques reveal the existence of a modified form of the acanthus *motif* in Assam in this early age. This device has been noticed in some of the Gupta temples of other parts of northern India notably at Bhumra and Nachna Kuthara. Another striking feature of this piece of work is the pose of the figures of Gangā and Jamunā which seems to be characteristically Greek while in their anatomical correctness these figures resemble Hellenic art more than anything else.

Relics of ancient architecture and sculpture are not confined to Gauhati and Tezpur. They are to be found in many other places. Two images were discovered on the Golaghat - Dimapur road. One of them is an image of Vishnu which is now preserved in the museum of the Kamarupa Anusandhan Samiti. With regard to this image Mr. K. N. Dikshit writes :—

"It is a very fine example of the ninth century art of Assam and is inscribed in characters similar to those of the Harjara inscription from Tezpur. The right hands and the feet of the image have broken off, and the halo behind the head is lost. The left upper hand holds the conch and the left lower the *gadā*. Vishnu has all the usual ornaments, the *kaustubha* and *srīvatsa* symbols, the sacred thread and the long cable-like garland reaching to the knees (*vanamālā*). The expression of the face and the treatment of the lower lip and the crown are characteristic of the late Gupta sculpture. The inscription is engraved on the right side of the image and consists of four lines in very corrupt

Sanskrit verse" (1).

Ruins of pre-Ahom edifices have been found in Bishnath and also in Negriting. In the last named place the Ahom temple was actually built on the mound containing the ancient stone-built temple. Both in Umananda and Aswakranta in Gauhati the Ahom temples were built with stones and carved images belonging to more ancient temples. The Ananta-Sāyi Vishnu of Aswakranta is a piece of of sculpture of very high merit. It belongs probably to the tenth or the eleventh century. Another very fine piece of sculpture, now deposited in the museum of the Kamarupa Anusandhan Samiti, is an image of Vishnu of the *Yogaswami* variety sculptured on black schist. The image exhibits the *Dhyāna mudrā* and is surrounded by *āvarana devatās* such as Durga, Ganeśa and Kārtikeya with the winged Garuda below it. With regard to this image Mr. K. N. Dikshit writes to us that "the presence of Ganeśa and Mahishamardini on the right leads to the inference that the idea was to depict Vishnu in the centre of the five gods (*Panchadevata*). The deities on the left one should have expected to be Śiva and Surya, but actually they are different. The upper figure is apparently in the attitude of Hanuman or some attendant of Vishnu while the lower one resembles an ascetic seated cross-legged. It is likely that the figure represents the donor as a devotee." There is a collection of stone images and other architectural fragments preserved at the entrance of the Sub-

(1) **Annual Report of the Archaeological Survey of India, 1923-24 p 82.**

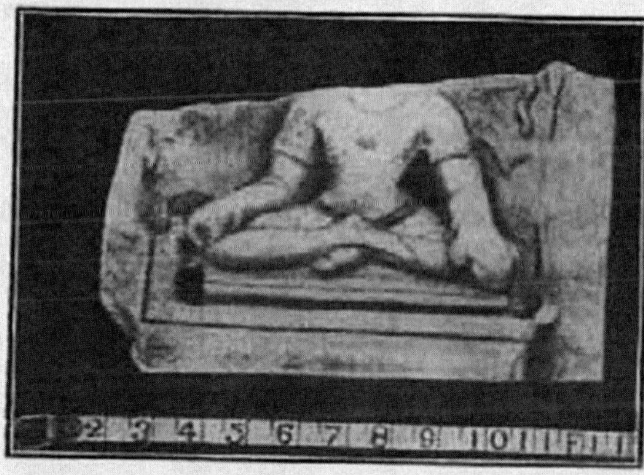

Broken terra-cotta plaque found in Parbatia

(By kind permission of the Archeological Survey of India

divisional officer's residence in Sibsagar. These are believed to be the remains of a Vishnu temple, in the neighbourhood, dating approximately from the tenth to the eleventh century A. D. According to Mr. Dikshit "the sculptures follow in the main the artistic traditions of the school represented by the Tezpur and Bamuni Hill temples of Central Assam, which are assigned to the ninth and tenth centuries". Very probably the ancient temple near Sibsagar was constructed by the Kāmarupa kings of the tenth or the eleventh century and it is thus evident that even till the eleventh century the Kāmarupa kings exercised their rule as far as the easternmost corner of the Assam valley. Mr. Dikshit also remarks that "the affinities of Assamese art would seem to lie more with the schools of Bihar and Orissa than with the contemporary Pāla art of Bengal. This is not unnatural as of the streams of influence that have moulded the culture of Assam, the strongest current has always been from North Bihar and Mid-India" (1). The cultural affinities between Mithila and Kāmarupa have already been alluded to by us.

Another instance of the architectural and engineering skill of the people of Kāmarupa in ancient times was the construction of stone bridges over rivers. There is still a small stone bridge in the western part of North Gauhati which is called *Sil-sāko*. The other *Sil-sāko* (stone bridge) was over a channel of the Barnadi and it was this bridge over which Mahammad-I-Bukhtiyar and his Turkish

(1) Annual Report of the Archaeological Survey of India, 1927-28 pp. 112-113.

cavalry passed in the year 1206 A. D. A description of the bridge, which was destroyed by the great earthquake of 1897, will be given in a subsequent chapter.

It appears that this bridge was constructed without lime and mortar and such construction was no doubt necessitated by the heavy rainfall in the country and the luxuriant vegetation which attacks all masonry structures in which mortar is used. Hannay, who in 1851 saw and measured the bridge, wrote as follows :—

"From the great care taken in the chiselling, squaring and fitting up of the component parts of the whole, as well as the great size and weight, the work is one of great strength and solidity. And this accounts for the good state of preservation in which we find it in the present day; for with the exception of the masonry of the abutment at each end, in which large trees have taken root and displaced the stones, the rest of the structure may be said to be entire. From a fracture in one of the pillars I observed that the upper blocks were kept in their places by means of iron pins firmly wedged into the lower ones; four apparently through the centre and one on each side of the square of the shaft, and although not visible, other portions of the work may be iron-clamped; the slabs of the platform were marked with clamping holes and on the edge of the outside slabs are three square holes (3 inches square) which were no doubt intended for the wooden supports of a balustrade. Several frieze-carved blocks are also lying near the end abutment from which I imagine the entrance of each may have been ornamented or these may have been

Image of Vishnu found in Gauhati.

gateways."

"The design and style of architecture of this bridge evidently belongs to a remote period in the annals of Kamrup and, in its original structure at least, must be co-eval with the erection of the ancient Brahmanical temples the remains of which are found so widely scattered throughout the length and breadth of Assam; the works of its former Brahmanical kings, a race long ago extinct in the annals of modern Hinduism and of whom the present race in Assam know nothing"(1).

Both sculptural and architectural skill degenerated during the Ahom period as, until the Ahom kings were thoroughly Hinduized, the art lacked royal support and encouragement. The result was that when in the seventeenth and the eighteenth centuries the Ahom kings set themselves to rebuilding the Hindu temples the Assamese sculptors of the day, known as *Silakutis*, were hardly equal to the task. Their sculpture was distinctly inferior. The finer images that we now see mounted on some of these post-Ahom temples were actually recovered from old ruins. In some instances the Ahom kings did not disturb the mound of ruins at all but erected an inferior brick structure on the top of it, the scattered old stones being commonly used for steps leading up to the mound. There is clear evidence to prove that quite a good number of carved and sculptured stones, chiselled bases, columns and capitals belonging to an older age found scattered or recovered from old ruins were

---

(1) J. A. S. B. No. iv, 1851, pp 290-294.

utilized by architects of more recent times in reconstructing temples demolished either by the Muhammadan invaders or by earthquakes. Old bricks also have been similarly utilized. Such old bricks and also pottery, belonging to a period much earlier than the advent of the Koch and the Ahom rulers, can also be met with here and there. The collection of pottery in the museum of the Kāmarupa Anusandhan Samiti, recovered from excavations in Gauhati town, includes certain specimens which exhibit the ceramic art of a bygone age - may be a very old age, possibly pre-Aryan - but here also lies a field of study entirely unexplored. Remains of military fortifications like *Garhs* and of works of public utility such as embanked roads and tanks, belonging to the pre-Ahom period, are still in existence. The large rectangular tank in Gauhati, known as the Digholi tank, is clearly of pre-Ahom origin for the Ahoms, who constructed numerous tanks in the Sibsagar district, had a much more scientific system of constructing large reservoirs of drinking water. The Digholi tank in Gauhati is believed to date back to the time of Bhagadatta for, it is said, the tournament of archery, arranged in connection with the marriage of Bhagadatta's daughter Bhānumati, was held on a platform erected over this tank. It is said that a fish was tied aloft at the end of a long pole and the great archer Karna looking at the image on the water aimed overhead and pierced the eye of the fish with his arrow. He thus won the tournament and obtained the hand of Bhānumati but, at his request, she was married to Duryodhana, the eldest of the Kauravas. It is on account of this relationship that Bhagadatta

Standing image of Vishnu from Deopani

sided with Duryodhana in the Mahabharata war. The *Hajarapukhri* in Tezpur is a large tank excavated by Harjaravarman in the ninth century.

Masonry buildings, roads and fortifications constructed by the kings of Kāmarupa were not confined to modern Assam. They existed also in that part of modern Bengal which was included in the old kingdom of Kāmarupa. One can find in the accounts of Buchanan Hamilton and Glazier and also in the contributions to the Journal of the Asiatic Society of Bengal, in the last century, many references to cities, temples, roads and fortifications erected by these kings long before the rise of Viswa Singha the first Koch king. In his notes on the Rangpur district, Mr. Grierson, in 1876-77, mentioned the existence, till that date, of a vast dyke or an embanked road or *Garh* extending right across the district from east to west which in his opinion was built to resist Muhammadan invasions (1). We get no mention of such a fortification having been constructed in the Rangpur district by the Koch rajas. This *garh* must have therefore been built by the kings of Kāmarupa probably after Bukhtiyar's invasion.

We have already alluded to the development of arts and industries during the time of Bhāskaravarman, the extensive use of iron in making weapons of war and armours for men and even elephants and the building of large war-boats which constituted an important arm during the attack on Karnasuvarna both by land and water. Even till the time of the Koch and the Ahom rulers the

(1) J.A.S.B.(1877) p. 186.

soldiers of Assam were proficient in naval warfare and, on many occasions, defeats sustained in naval engagements compelled the Muslim invaders to retreat. Harjaravarman's rock-inscription, in the early part of the ninth century, shows that the boats maintained by the king were numerous and, even in so wide a river as the Brahmaputra, regulation of boat traffic was found to be necessary in order to prevent collisions between the royal barges and the boats of fishermen. Vanamāla's inscription states that the royal boats were beautifully carved, painted and decorated and also fitted with musical instruments. Iron was plentiful as in the adjacent hills iron-ore could be had in abundance and iron-smelting by a crude process was known. Till very recent times the Khasis of Assam used to smelt iron from ore after this process. Of the more precious metals, gold and copper could be obtained within the kingdom itself. From time immemorial, till very recent times, gold-washing had been practised in the rivers of Assam. The Subansiri (Suvarna-sri) derives its name from the gold that it carries. Even the water of the Lauhitya (Brahmaputra) was known to contain gold for we find a clear mention of it in the inscription of Vanamāla wherein it is stated that the river carried the gold-dust caused by the friction of huge gold-bearing boulders of the Kailāsa mountain. The Muhammadan historians tell us that the temple, where Mahammad-i-Bukhtiyar and the remnants of his forces took refuge, being surrounded by the Kamarupa troops, contained a huge image of solid gold weighing, according to the Riyaz, one thousand maunds (1). Jayapala, the last king of the dynasty of Brahmapala, offered, according to the Silimpur inscription deciphered by Mr. Basak, to make a gift of gold equal to his own weight to a learned Brahman over and above 900 gold coins. It is evident therefore that gold was, by no means, a rare metal in the kingdom in the old days. Incidentally, the reference in the Silimpur inscription proves that the Kāmarupa kings used to mint gold coins though unfortunately no such coins have yet been discovered and though we have found coins minted by the Koch and the Ahom kings of the subsequent period. The inscription of Ratnapāla mentions the existence of a copper-mine within the kingdom which the king worked with profit. Evidently copper was used for coinage also. Harjaravarman's ordinance, inscribed on the rock, prescribed a penalty of 100 cowries for infringement of the regulations. This shows that the cowri was a legal tender but it does not mean that metal coins were not then in circulation. In the vicinity of Sadiya existed a temple having a roof made of copper-sheets and this temple was dedicated to the goddess Durga called *Tāmeswari māi.* This temple was erected by the pre-Ahom Chutia kings.

Rice was then, as now, the staple crop. The extent of the lands, granted by the various inscriptions, was stated in terms of the yield of paddy. Yuan Chwang noticed that cocoa-nut and jack trees were numerous. As a matter of fact cocoanut thrives within the present districts of Goalpara and

(1) Riyaz-us-Salatin, Abdus Samad's translation, p 67.

Kamrup. As regards the cultivation of arcca nut and betel leaf in Kāmarupa, we find a mention not only in the Nowgong inscription of Balavarman III but also in the Aphshad inscription of Adityasena (*circa* 672 A. D.) wherein the betel-plants being in full bloom on the banks of the Lauhitya is stated. The Nowgong inscription describes the areca-nut trees within Prāgjyotishpur being wrapped by the betel-creepers (pān), a system of growing pān which persists till today. Pragjyotishpur was, even in the ancient times, noted for its betel-nut groves which subsequently gave the name Guā-hāti (Gauhati) to this town. The presents sent by Bhāskaravarman to Śri Harsha, about 606 A. D. included sugar in the form of liquid molasses in earthern pots. This indicates that sugarcane was cultivated even in the most ancient times. The other more important products of the kingdom as stated by Yuan Chwang, and also mentioned in some of the inscriptions, were *Aguru* or āgar-essence, musk, silk-fabrics and elephants.

There is evidence to show that from the earliest times the people of Kāmarupa traded with the people of other parts of India. This trade was carried on by a class of people called *Sadāgars* and the main trade routes were the river Brahmaputra and the various navigable tributaries feeding it. It appears that the *Sadagars* of Kāmarupa carried their merchandise in large boats down the Brahmaputra and reached the sea after skirting round the Garo Hills. They crossed this sea and traded in sea-ports like Tāmralipti. The bardic tales relating to Behula mention that *Chand Sadāgar*, whose *mer-ghor* in Chaygaon, built of stones, existed till recent times, used to trade in sea-going boats. It appears that the Kalitas of Assam were then the *Sadagars* and the gold coins or rather pieces with which they used to buy goods were known as *Kaltis*. The name of this coin is mentioned in the "Periplus of the Erythrian sea" a Greek account of the first century A. D. wherein it is supposed that a gold-mine existed then in this part of India. As a matter of fact, the gold was obtained by washing in the Brahmaputra, Subansiri and other rivers.

In one of the aphorisms of Dāk, who is placed about the eighth century A. D, mention is made of the profitable trade with the people of Lankā. Probably this Lankā is not to be identified with Ceylon but with the country on the Burma coast which Yuan Chwang named Kāmalankā and which, according to him, lay to the south-east of Samatata on a bay of the sea. Perhaps traders from Champā, Kāmarupa and Vanga visited this coast for purposes of trade.

CHAPTER VIII

THE LATER KAMARUPA KINGS.

The Kamauli grant of Vaidya Deva deciphered by Venis, which on palaeographical evidence has been placed about 1142 A. D, records that Vaidya Deva was the favourite minister of Kumārapāla king of Gauda, that Vaidyadeva's father Bodhideva was the minister of Rāmapāla and that Vaidyadeva was not only a capable minister but also an efficient general for it is stated that in southern Bengal he won a naval battle over a certain enemy. It is also recorded that "in the direction of the east", the "respected King" Tingyadeva having rebelled the lord of Gauda (Kumārapāla) appointed the illustrious Vaidyadeva as the king of that country (1). The powerful Vaidyadeva, obeying the order of his master, after a few days hurried marches, defeated Tingyadeva in battle and became himself king." It is stated that the battle was fierce, the number of killed was large and that the enemy

(1) Epigraphia Indica vol. II p 347

king was slain. The inscription then narrates the various qualities of Vaidyadeva and states that he was a devout worshipper of Vishnu. By this grant, recorded on the *Vishuva sankrānti* of *Choitra*, in the fourth year of his reign, Vaidyadeva donated to a Brahman named Sridhara, lands included in the *bhukti* of Prāgjyotisha, *Mandala* of Kāmarupa, *vishaya* of Bada and villages Śanti Bada and Mandāra. The grant was issued from the victorious camp of Hangsakonchi and Vaidyadeva is described as "Mahārājadhirāja Parameswara Paramabhattāraka" (1). It seems that Tingyadeva, who was a vassal of the Pāla rulers, finding the Pāla King engaged in warfare with an invader in southern Bengal, rebelled and therefore Vaidyadeva had to be despatched in haste to subdue the rebel king. Tingyadeva put up a desperate fight but having been defeated and slain in battle Vaidyadeva became himself the king. It appears that, soon after, he threw off the allegiance to the Pāla ruler and became independant.

Pandit Padmanath Bhattacharya Vidyayinod thinks that Rāmapāla could not conquer the whole of Kāmarupa but wrested from the Kāmarupa king a large slice of territory towards the south-west, over which he installed a vassal-king who was designated as *nripati*. This ruler was Tingyadeva who, having rebelled after the death of Rāmapāla, was crushed by Vaidyadeva, the minister and general of Rāmapāla's son Kumāra Pāla. Vaidyadeva therefore, by the Kamauli grant, donated

(1) Epigraphia Indica vol. II p. 347.

lands within this slice of territory the eastern boundary of which was probably a large river (1). Pandit Vidyavinod strengthens his theory by pointing out that, in the Kamauli inscription, Tingyadeva is not mentioned as the ruler of Kāmarupa or Prāgjyotisha but he is described as the "ruler in the direction of the east". There is no doubt some force in the contention of Pandit Vidyavinod whose researches into the history of ancient Kāmarupa are so well-known and whose theories are not to be lightly set aside. In this matter, however, the Pandit has evidently fallen into an error. He says that the slice of territory ceded to Rāmapāla was sufficiently large, for its ruler was called *nripati* or *nareswara*. If this was a fact then nearly the whole of the tract which subsequently got the name of Kāmata, including Rangpur, part of Bogra and Cooch-Behar, to the east of Karatoyā, had to be ceded. On the other hand, the Pandit locates Kāmarupanagar, the capital mentioned in Dharmapāla's second inscription, near Karatoyā and places the conquest of Kāmarupa by Rāmapāla about 1095 A. D. which is also the approximate date of Dharmapāla's first inscription (2). Now if about the date of his first inscription Dharmapāla was dispossessed of the western part of his kingdom, which contained his capital, how is it that his second grant, recorded towards the end of his long reign, was issued from the same capital? As we have already stated, Pandit Vidyavinod seems to have antedated Rāmapāla's invasion of Kāmarupa by

(1) Kamarupa Sasanavali page 40.
(2) Ibid P 41, footnote (4).

nearly twentyfive years. We do not think that any part of Kāmarupa was conquered by any one during Dharmapāla's reign. It was probably during the reign of his successor Jayapāla that Rāmapāla conquered Kāmarupa. Vidyavinod's theory that Dharmapāla and Jayapāla were ruling in the eastern part of Kāmarupa simultaneously with Tingyadeva and Vaidyadeva, who ruled over the ceded western part of the kingdom, is perhaps incorrect. We find no mention of such an intervening kingdom, between Gauda and Kāmarupa, in the beginning of the next century when Bukhtiyar's invasion took place. At that time the kingdom, to the east of Gauda, was "Kamrud" and the ruler of this kingdom was the "Rae of Kamrud" This kingdom then had the river Karatoyā as its boundary.**

The lands donated by Vaidyadeva were within Kāmarupa *mandala* and Prāgjyotisha *bhukti*. It

---

** Both Gait and Vidyavinod appear to have overlooked the fact that till the middle of the thirteenth century when Minhaj wrote his account, the *Tabaquat-i-Nasiri*, Kamatā or Kamatāpur was unknown and the name of the kingdom was Kamrud, its capital "Kamarupanagar" being called the "City of Kamrud". Later Muslim historians, like the author of the *Riyaz*, only make mention of "Kamru-Kamata" as if both were synonymous terms because the seat of government was then at Kamatāpur and Kamatā became the name of the whole of the western portion of the old kingdom of Kāmarupa. Kamatāpur could not possibly have been the capital of Dharmapāla in the beginning of the twelfth century or nearly 150 years before the *Tabaquat-i-Nasiri* was written. "Kangur", as mentioned in the Dharmamangal, may have been an abreviation "Kamatapur" but it could not have been the same as "Kamarupanagar".

seems that when Rāmapāla conquered and annexed the whole of Prāgjyotisha that kingdom became a *bhukti* within Gauda. The *mandala* of Kāmarupa, within the Prāgjyotisha *bhukti*, probably referred to the area which now constitutes the present district of Kamrup. Vaidyadeva's victorious camp, Hangsakonchi, from which he issued his grant, appears to have been within the modern district of Kamrup. The suffix Konchi, Kunchi or Kuchi occurs in the names of numerous villages in this district, e.g. Sualkuchi, Kamarkuchi, Ranakuchi, Patacharkuchi, Vyahkuchi, Kahikuchi, Majkuchi, Dongarkuchi etc. Such names are rare even in the contiguous districts of Goalpara, Darrang and Nowgong. Evidently Hangsakonchi is the Sanskritized form of Hāhkuchi. Kuchi means a bundle. A bundle or collection of dwelling houses is a village or Kuchi. There is hardly any doubt that Hāhkuchi was a village in modern Kamrup and therefore Vaidyadeva had his camp or headquarters within that district. The lands granted could not therefore have been anywhere in modern Bengal as supposed by Vidyavinod. We are therefore forced to the conclusion that Vaidyadeva was the king of the whole of Kāmarupa though probably the eastern districts of the Assam Valley were then outside Kāmarupa. Tingyadeva, who was probably not a scion of the Pāla line but a local feudatory chief of repute, was established in Kāmarupa as a vassal ruler and he, no doubt, had his capital at North Gauhati or Kāmarupanagar founded by Dharmapāla. Vaidyadeva had evidently his headquarters at Hāhkuchi for some time. There are even now remains of a fort in northern Kamrup known as

Vaidyar Garh (fort of Vaidya). Local tradition no doubt ascribes that fort to Arimatta who, as we shall show later, was probably a king of Kamatā ruling two centuries later. It is quite possible that this fort was originally built by Vaidyadeva and therefore it was named *Vaidyar Garh.* Subsequently Arimatta, while fighting with Fingua Koar, of the line of Durlabhnārāyan, repaired or rebuilt this fort and occupied it.

Tingyadeva did not probably rule, as a vassal-ruler, for more than five or six years at the longest. He rebelled as soon as Kumāra Pāla ascended the throne. We can therefore suppose that he was overthrown by Vaidyadeva about 1131 A. D. and that Vaidyadeva's Kamauli grant was issued about 1135 A. D. According to R. D. Banerji, Kumāra Pāla had a very short reign, not exceeding two years and his immediate successor Gopala III was also assassinated after a brief reign (1). Vaidyadeva therefore found it very convenient to throw off the yoke of the Pāla rulers four years after the overthrow of Tingyadeva. R. D. Banerji thinks that Vaidyadeva asserted his independence after the death of Gopala III (2).

During the reign of Madanapāla, who succeeded Gopala III, the Sena king Vijayasena conquered practically the whole of Gauda and became the immediate neighbour of the Kāmarupa king. This conquest is mentioned in the Deopara inscription of Vijayasena wherein a reference is made to the king of Kāmarupa (*Gaudendra madrabat apākrita*

---

(1) Bangalar Itihash vol. 1. p. 285.
(2) Ibid p. 284.

Kāmarupa bhupam). This has been taken by some scholars to mean that Vijayasena conquered Kāmarupa. Pandit Vidyavinod, however, surmises that the word *apākrita* indicates that the Kāmarupa king having encroached within the limits of Gauda Vijayasena drove him out (1). Mr. C. V. Vaidya interprets the stanza to mean that Vijayasena actually subdued the king of Gauda who had troubled the king of Kāmarupa (2). Mr. Vaidya's interpretation may be correct. In any case, it was not perhaps anything more than a skirmish on the frontier. About this time, towards the middle of the twelfth century, perhaps Vaidyadeva was ruling in Kāmarupa. He probably ruled till 1250 A. D. R. D. Banerji, however, states that Vijayasena died about the beginning of the twelfth century and was succeeded by his son Vallālasena (3). On the other hand, in the *Gauda Rājamāla*, the reign of Vallālasena is shown as 1159-1169 A. D. This seems to be more correct because Vallālasena's son Lakshman Sena, the Rae Lakshmania of the *Tabaquat-i-Nasiri*, was an aged king when Mahammad-i-Bukhtiyar invaded Bengal in 1202 A. D. R. D. Banerji seems to have antedated the death of Vijayasena by fifty years. Vaidyadeva was therefore very probably a contemporary of Vijayasena.

From his Madhainagar inscription it appears that Lakshman Sena invaded Kāmarupa and de-

(1) Kamarupa Sasanavali p. 42, foot note.
(2) History of Mediaeval India, p. 240.
(3) Bangalar Itihash vol. 1 p. 291.

feated its king (1). This must have taken place about the end of the third quarter of the twelfth century when a successor of Vaidyadeva was probably ruling. We do not know who succeeded Vaidyadeva but we know that, towards the close of the twelfth or the beginning of the thirteenth century, there ruled in Kāmarupa a virile king who is not named but simply called "Rae of Kamrud" in the account of Minhaj. This Rāja of Kāmarupa, who evidently had a long reign, caused the destruction of the entire army of Mahammad Ibn Bukhtiyar in the year 1206 A. D. Before we take up that narrative in the next chapter we should mention that, some 45 years ago, a copper-plate inscription was discovered in Tezpur and it is known as the Assam plate of Vallabhadeva. It was edited and published by Keilhorn. This inscription relates to a grant of land made by a ruler named Vallabhadeva in the year Saka 1107 corresponding to 1185 A. D. It is not stated over what kingdom Vallabhadeva ruled but the genealogy mentioned therein is shown below :—

Bhāskara
I
Rāyari Deva
I
Udaya Karna
I
Vallabha Devā (1185 A. D.)

Evidently these Kings could not have been rulers of Kāmarupa for the simple reason that

(4) J. A. S. B. vol. V.

there is no room for them between Vaidyadeva and 1185 A. D., the date of Vallabha Deva's inscription. Our impression is that they were, like Tingya Deva, feudatory chiefs perhaps under the later Kāmarupa Kings. This supposition is strengthened by the fact that of the seven villages granted by the inscription two bear Kāmarupa names. They are Devuni-Konchi and Sangsrahi-Konchika. Further, according to Kielhorn, the characters of the inscription belong to a variety of the northern alphabet used about the twelfth century in the most eastern parts of northern India. There is mention in the inscription of Rāyāri Deva being a valiant fighter. It is stated that "at the gorgeous festival of battle which was fearful on account of the presence of the lordly elephants of Vanga he made the enemy abandon the practice of arms". It is quite possible that Rāyāri Deva fought on the side of the Kāmarupa king during the hostilities on the frontier with Vyayasena, the Sena king of Vanga. As we shall see later, one Purusottam, a feudatory chief under the Kamatā king, in the early part of the fourteenth century, similarly granted lands to Brahmans by a copper-plate inscription. If Vallabha Deva and his ancestors had been kings of Kāmarupa that fact would have been prominently set forth in the inscription.

Vaidya Deva must have been followed by two other kings after whom came Prithu who was probably the king ruling when Mahammad-i-Bukhtiyar invaded Kāmarupa. We find his name indirectly from the Muslim historians as well as from the account of Buchanan Hamilton. Minhaj, the author of the *Tabakat-i-Nasiri*, refers to him as Bartu

(Britu) and Sir Wolsely Haig, in the Cambridge History of India vol. III, supposes that he was no other than the king of Kāmarupa who repulsed not only Bukhtiyar in 1206 A. D. but also Hisam-ud-din Iwaj (Sultan Ghiyas-ud-din) in 1227 and was ultimately over-thrown by Nasir-ud-din, the son of Iltumish in 1228 A. D. As we shall show in the next chapter, Prithu was undoubtedly a king of Kāmarupa and very probably he was a descendant of Vaidya Deva. After he was defeated and slain probably Nasir-ud-din set up his son or any one else on the throne and exacted a promise from him to pay tribute. The hold of the Muhammadans on Bengal, at that time, was not very secure and so it was not possible for Nasir-ud-din to annex the kingdom of Kāmarupa and administer it directly. After Prithu, probably two of his successors ruled at North-Gauhati before the capital was removed to Kamatāpur. When Malik Yuzbeg, otherwise known as Sultan Mughis-ud-din, invaded Kāmarupa and advanced as far as Gauhati in 1254-55 the king of Kāmarupa was perhaps Sandhyā who is mentioned in the *Guru Charitra* by Ramcharan Thakur. It was this king who defeated Sultan Mughis-ud-din and destroyed his army. Soon after, he removed the capital to Kamatāpur in the neighbourhood of which his predecessor Prithu had already erected extensive fortifications.

The following is the approximate chronology

of the Kāmarupa kings after the extinction of the Pāla dynasty :—

Name of king.		*Probable extent of reign.*
Tingya Deva	...	1125-1131 A. D.
Vaidya Deva	...	1131-1150 „
* *		* * *
Prithu ...	...	1200-1228 „
* *		* * *
Sandhyā...	...	1250

CHAPTER IX

THE MUHAMMADAN INVASIONS.

The closing years of the twelfth century presented a turning point in the history of northern and eastern India. The Muhammadans who had gained the Punjab attempted to conquer the whole of northern India. The most important and powerful Hindu kingdoms of northern India at this time were Delhi and Ajmere of the Chauhan Rajputs under Prithvi Raj, the Chālukya kingdom of Guzerat ruled over by Bhim, the Chandela kingdom of Bundelkhand the ruler of which was Paramardideva and the Gāhadvāla kingdom of Kanauj under Jaychānd. Let it be said to the credit of Muhammad Bin Sam, their leader and of the rank and file of his troops, that their dash and perseverance made them masters of practically the whole of northern India within the short period of ten years beginning from 1190 A. D. In 1186 it was the Hindu king of Jhammu who invited Muhammad to make his second invasion of the Punjab (1). After settling himself in the Punjab Muhammad, instead of making only plundering raids, like Mahmud of Ghazni, resolved upon the regular conquest of India. His first blow was to fall upon Prithvi Rāj or Rai Pithaura, as the Muslim historians called him. Muhammad captured Bhatinda and placed Quazi Ziauddin in command of it. Hearing that Prithvi Rāj was advancing to meet him he turned to meet the Hindu king. The two armies met on the field of Tārouri or Tirouri in the winter of 1190-91. The Muslims were over-powered and both their wings were driven from the field. In sheer desperation Muhammad led a furious cavalry charge against the Hindu centre and personally encountered the Raja's brother, Govinda Rai. Muhammad shattered his teeth with his spear but Govinda Rai drove his lance through Muhammad's arm (2). A young Turk then leapt upon Muhammad's horse and, sitting behind him, prevented him from falling. The Muslim army then fled and Muhammad returned to Ghazni discomfitted. Prithvi Rāj then advanced upon Bhatinda and recovered the place though Ziauddin held out for a long time (3). It took little more than a year for Muhammad to organize and equip a fresh army to enable him to avenge his defeat. This was ample time during which the Hindu Rajās of northern India could have formed a confederacy in order to resist the common enemy but each Raja was envious of the

(1) Cambridge History of India, vol. III p. 39.
(2) Ibid p 40.
(3) Ibid p 40.

other and instead of coming to the assistance of Prithvi Rāj the other Rajas preferred to watch and witness his downfall, little thinking that they themselves would fall one by one. As a matter of fact, each one of the contemporary kings had been humbled by Prithvi Rāj during a period of internecine war. His most powerful rival was the Gāhadvāla king Jaychānd. This fratricidal war, with the enemy at the gate, was the main cause of the downfall of Hindu India for when Muhammad of Ghor attacked the Hindu kings, one by one, they were all exhausted by previous fighting and although they all fought valiantly they failed to resist the Muslims. If, however, they had combined and offered united resistance to Muhammad of Ghor very probably history would have recorded a different tale. In 1192 Muhammad again invaded India and found Prithvi Rāj encamped on the same field of Tarouri. Muhammad, this time, by his clever tactics, outwitted the Hindus who were at last completely routed. Both Prithvi Rāj and his brother, Govinda Rāi, were slain. This victory gave Muhammad the whole of northern India up to the gates of Delhi. After this Ajmere was also taken and Muhammad generously appointed the son of Prithvi Rāj as governor of Ajmere (1). By the end of 1192 Muhammad's trusted general, Qutb-ud-din Aibak, captured Delhi from the Chauhan Rajputs. Meanwhile a Turkish leader under Aibak, named Muhammad Bin Bukhtiyar led a plundering raid to Bihar and Tirhut. He

(1) Cambridge History of India vol III p. 41.

attacked Odantapuri, destroyed the great monastery there and put to death the Buddhist monks who had taken arms to protect their sacred place. After this both Bin Sam and Aibak attacked Jaychānd, the Gāhadvāla king of Kanauj, who had looked on unconcerned when his old rival, Prithvi Rāj, was being destroyed. The two armies met on the banks of the Jumna. After a severe fight the Muslims were on the point of giving way when a fortunately aimed arrow hit Jaychānd on the eye and he fell dead on his elephant, whereupon the Hindus broke and fled and were pursued with great slaughter. Thence the Muhammadans marched to Benares where they destroyed several temples. Muhammad then returned to Ghazni leaving Aibak in India as his viceroy. In 1195 Guzerat was invaded and the Hindu commander, Kunwar Pal, was defeated and slain (1). The king, Bhimpal, escaped and, after the Muhammadans withdrew, again made preparations for a fight. In 1197 Bhim attacked Aibak near Ajmere, and defeated him (2). Later in the year however re-inforcements arrived from Ghazni and with these Aibak marched upon Guzerat and attacked Bhim's army. The Hindus obstinately resisted till midday when they broke and fled. About 15,000 Hindus were slain and about 20,000 were captured (3). None of the other Hindu Rajas came to the assistance of Bhim. Three hundred years before the Christian era, the small Hindu states of the Punjab were, one by one,

(1) Ibid p 43.
(2) Ibid p44.
(3) Ibid p 44.

subdued by Alexander. If these states had then joined the Paurava king and fought together on the banks of the Jhelum a different tale would have been recorded in history. Fifteen hundred years after, history repeated itself. Within less then ten years the chief Hindu kings were overthrown one by one and the whole of northern India, from the Sutlej to the confines of Bengal, lay prostrate at the feet of the Muhammadan invaders. According to Mr. Vaidya the principal causes accounting for the defeat of the Hindu kings, in quick succession, one after the other, were internecine fighting, absence of a common national feeling, rigidification of caste, weakness in cavalry and undue importance given to the elephant corps as an arm of war (1). We would add to these the valour, dash and strength of the Turks and Afghans and the undoubted superior military talents of some of their generals. During the last two years of the twelfth century Magadha was occupied. After conquering Magadha Muhammad Bin Bukhtiyar led an expedition into Bengal in 1202. According to the Mussalman historians, Muhammad Bin Bukhtiyar, with only seventeen followers, took the city of Nuddea by surprise. The reigning king, Rai Lakshmania, hurriedly fled to Vikrampur leaving his palace and the city to be plundered by the invaders.* The only two Hindu kingdoms in Eastern India which successfully resisted the

---

(1) Downfall of Hindu India by C.V. Vaidya pp. 360-372.

* Bukhtiyar evidently led a marauding expedition into Nuddea. It appears that even after the retreat of Lakshman Sen his sons ruled over a part of lower

Muslim invaders for a considerable time were Orissa or Jajnagar and Kāmarupa. The kings of Orissa repeatedly attacked and defeated the Muslims and included a part of southern Bengal within their dominions. In Kāmarupa several successive Muhammadan invasions, beginning with Muhammad-i-Bukhtiyar's ill-fated enterprise in 1205-06, were repulsed by the Hindu kings before the rise of the Koch power in western Kāmarupa and the Ahom power in eastern Kamrupa. The hostilities between the Muhammadans and the Ahoms continued during the sixteenth and the seventeenth centuries and at length the whole of the western part of Kamarupa, as far the Manas river, had to be given up to the Mughuls, the Ahoms retaining only the rest of the Assam Valley to the east of the Manas.

As we have noticed in the last chapter, the chronology the Kāmarupa kings can be traced to the middle of the twelfth century if we take the Vaidyadeva grant as the last epigraphic record relating to these kings. The period of the history of Kamarupa from the beginning of the thirteenth till about the middle of the fifteenth century is however comparatively dark. We shall try to piece together history, as far as possible, by the aid of the lights shed by the Muslim chronicles, the Ahom Burunjis, such local records as the *Guru-*

Bengal for a considerable time though with much difficulty being pressed not only by the Muhammadans but also by the kings of Orissa and the Mags of the Arracan coast.

chāritra (1) and reliable traditions recorded by Buchanan-Hamilton more than 100 year ago. These records however very rarely mention the names of the kings, nor is it clear where they ruled. The Muslim chronicles, though on the whole trustworthy, cannot be relied on with regard to all particulars.

The first Muhammadan host to enter Kāmarupa was led by Muhammad, son of Bukhtiyar, in the year 1205-06 A. D. Muhammad was a Turk of the Khilji tribe who came into prominence as a military leader under Qutb-ud-din, the viceroy under Muhammad of Ghor. Muhammad Ibn Bukhtiyar became governor of Bihar and thence he invaded Bengal in 1202 A. D. By a rapid movement he suddenly appeared in Nuddea with only a few mounted soldiers and surrounded the palace of Rae Lakshmania, the Bengali king, who hurriedly escaped, first perhaps to Lakshanāvati and thence to Vikrampur in east Bengal. Muhammad followed him as far as Lakshanāvati which he found to be the capital town. This city was originally named Rāmāvati, after Rāmapāla the Pāla king, and subsequently Lakshman Sena, Rae Lakshmania of the Muslim historians, renamed it Lakshnāvati. Since Muslim occupation the city came to be known as Gaur. Muhammad Bin Bukhtiyar, instead of following the Bengali king to Vikrampur, established himself at Lakhnauti which became his capital. He also assumed the honorific name Ikhtiyar-ud-din. Three years later he decided upon further conquests

(1) The biography of Sri Sankar Deva, the Vaisnava reformer of Assam.

and equipped an army of mounted soldiers. The Mussalman historians have recorded that his objective was Tibet, Turkistan or China, beyond the Himalayas. Towards the end of the year 1205 A. D. he marched from Devkot, within the modern district of Dinajpur, at the head of 10 or 12 thousand horsemen. It appears that a Mech chieftain, whom Muhammad had converted into Islam and who was known as Ali Mech, guided the army. Muhammad proceeded with his army to a town called Burdhankot on the banks of a river which was called Begamati and which in magnitude, depth and breadth is said to have been three times more than the Ganges (1). Thence he followed the course of the river northwards for ten days until he came to a place where he found the river spanned by a stone bridge consisting of more than 20 arches. He then crossed the river and entered Kāmarupa (2). It is said that the king of Kāmarupa,* who was evidently informed previously of Muhammad's intentions, sent the following message :—"It is not proper at

(1) Tabaquat-i-Nasiri, Translation by Raverty, p. 561. Minhaj writes:-

"They relate after this manner, that in ancient times' shah Gushtasib returned from the country of Chin and came towards Kamrud and by that route got into Hindusthan and founded that city (Burdhankot)."

(2) Ibid p. 561

* Gait writes that at this time the ruler of Kāmarupa bore the title Kāmeswara but this is not correct. The earliest muslim account of this expedition is that given in the Tabaquat-i-Nasiri wherein the ruler of Kāmarupa is called the "Rae of Kamrud" and not Kameswara. On this point the later Muslim accounts should not be depended upon. The Rajas of Kamata, a century later, bore the little Kameswara,

this time to march into the country of Tibbat, and it is necessary to return, and to make ample preparations, when in the coming year I, who am the Rae of Kamrud, agree that I will embody my own forces and will precede the Muhammadan troops and will cause that territory to be acquired" (1). Muhammad disregarded this advice and continued the march until he emerged into a plain which was well-cultivated and thickly populated and in the midst of which stood a strong fortress. The Turks started plundering the villages whereupon the inhabitants of the country joined the garrison in the fort and offered stubborn resistance. Muhammad was soon forced to fight a defensive battle. Throughout the day he held his ground in spite of very heavy losses. At length he got information that the enemy was being re-inforced from another fortified town, 15 miles off, which was named Kararpatan or Karampatan and which was inhabited by Brahmans (Hindus) and Nunis. As a matter of fact, a horde of Mongol horsemen emerged to oppose the invaders. Muhammad then held a council of war and decided on immediate retirement. This retreat was disastrous. The road in the rear of the invaders had been blocked and all supplies had been cut off. The Raja of Kāmarupa attacked the retreating army. Large numbers were killed or captured. After enduring great hardship and privation Muhammad, with the remnant of his forces, reached the river only to find that two arches of the bridge had been destroyed and the river was unfordable. He then took shelter in a Hindu tem-

---

(1) *Tabaquat-i-Nasiri* p 564.

ple in the vicinity which contained a huge image of gold (1). The Rāja besieged him and threw up a bamboo palisade all round the temple.* The Turks then grew desperate and, breaking through the palisade, made for the river. A few of them tried a ford and, having found the river fordable to a certain!distance, shouted to the others to follow. Then all rushed into the river headlong. Hundreds were carried away by the rapid stream and these found a watery grave. Only Mahammad and a few of the best-mounted soldiers, with much difficulty, reached the opposite bank. Mahammad passed through Koonch or Kuch Behar and thence he returned to Gaur and in 1206 A. D. he died of grief and mortification. Some authorities assert hat he was murdered by one Ali Mardan. This

---

(1) Ibid p. 569. Minhaj. wrote:-

"They pointed out an idol temple, in the vicinity of that place, of exceeding height, strength and sublimity and very handsome and in it numerons idols, both of gold and silver, were deposited and one great idol so large that its weight was, by conjecture, upwards of two or three thousand *mans* of beaten gold."

* The nearest existing Hindu temple is the Siva temple of Gopeswār about 4 miles from the site of the *Sil-sako* as the crow flies. There may have been a temple nearer to the brige. Captain Dālton writing in the Journal of the Asiatic Society of Bengal (No.1 of 1855) stated that there were ruins of no less than eighteen temples "just outside the fortifications of the ancient city and not far from the great stone bridge." He, however, supposed that the temple where Bukhtiyar took shelter was the famous temple of Hajo which is lower down the stream spanned by the bridge. He, conjectured that the Muhammadans were compelled to "proceed lower down the stream in search of a ford". The Hajo temple still exists and it is certainly more well-known than the Gopeswar temple, but it is not nearer to the bridge.

is the story, in brief, depicted by the Muslim historians.

The earliest Muslim account of this ill-fated expedition is contained in the *Tabaquat-i-Nasiri* the author of which, Minhaj-ud-din gathered the story, some 35 years after the disaster, from one Matammad-ud-Dawlah "a trusted vassal of Mahammad Ibn Bukhtiyar". It is not stated whether this trusted vassal was one of those who marched with Mahammad into Tibet or Kāmarupa. In Kāmarupa there is an epigraphic record of this expedition. It is a rock-inscription in North-Gauhati which was, about this time, the capital of the kingdom and which we have identified with "Kāmarupanagar" mentioned in the second inscription of Dharmapāla. This rock-inscription reads as follows :—

S'āke turaga jugmeśa madhumāsa trayodaśe.
Kāmarupam samāgatya Turuskāh Khyayamāyayuh.

"On the thirteenth of Choitra, in the year Saka 1127, the Turks coming into Kāmarupa were destroyed".

Now it is clear from the Muslim account as well as the rock-inscription that the Muhammadan host had entered Kāmarupa and was destroyed there, but it is not clear whether Mahammad's objective was Tibet itself or China via Tibet or Kāmarupa. Further, it is not clear from the Muslim records what river he crossed and how far into Kāmarupa he had advanced.* It is however

* According to the *Tabuquat-i-Nasiri*, the river crossed was Begamati. Accordin to the *Riyazus Salatin* it

reasonable to suppose that his objective was not Kāmarupa but China, for in the rock-inscription it is not stated that the Turks had invaded Kāmarupa. They simply had "come into Kāmarupa" (*Kāmarupam samāgatya*). If it was a hostile invasion into Kāmarupa itself the text of the inscription would have been different. Our conjecture is that Mahammad followed the course of the river Teesta and nearing the hills crossed it by fording. There he was told that a more direct route to China lay to the further east. He therefore travelled eastward within Kāmarupa over the high road leading from Jalpaiguri to eastern Assam. On this road he crossed the stone bridge to the north-west of Gauhati. This bridge then spanned the Barnadi river which, running through the present abandoned bed known as Puspabhadrā, fell into the Brahmaputra several miles below its present confluence.* Bukhtiyar then followed the course of this river towards the north and reached the foot hills near about Kumrikata on the Bhutan border which is due north of Gauhati. This Kumrikata is probably the place mentioned as Kararpatan or Karampatan in the *Tabaquat-i-Nasiri*. Near about this place or in the interior of the hills, the Bhutanese outpost and the Mongol horsemen opposed Bukhtiyar so strenuously that he had to fall back on the main road.

was known as Namakdi while according to the *Tarikh-i Ferista* the river was Timkari. Probably Namakdi was the Bodo name of the river.

* It has been ascertained locally that the river at the point where it was spanned by the stone-bridge was known in old times as Najuli meaning a combination of nine streamlets.

The Rāja of Kāmarupa had, during Bukhtiyar's march towards the hills, removed the flat stones of the platform and rendered the bridge impassable. He also blocked the road in the rear of Bukhtiyar and cut off supplies. He thought that he was justified in doing so as Mahammad Bukhtiyar had disregarded his advice, his soldiers had plundered villages for supplies and had advanced almost up to his capital. Mahammad, on getting information that his communications were threatened and the Rāja had turned hostile, hastily fell back and found himself caught in a trap. The Rājā's troops surrounded him when he took shelter in a neighbouring Hindu temple. In sheer desperation he and his horsemen galloped into the river and, in as attempt to ford it, all except a small remnant died. This took place on the date mentioned in the rock-inscription which exactly tallies with the date given by the Muslim historians. This memorable event was recorded in the rock-inscription on the eastern extremity of North-Gauhati, the then capital of the kingdom. Only the occurrence and the date were recorded. The script is of the thirteenth century. It is not stated who destroyed the Turks or how they met with destruction. Evidently the Kāmarupa king did not consider that a glorious deed had been done, but military considerations demanded the destruction of the foreign host so near the capital and the occurence was so memorable that it was thought worth while to record it. We have no doubt that it was the stone bridge, over a channel of the Barnadi, over which Mahammad passed in the year 1205-06 A. D. This bridge was destroyed by the great earthquake of 1897. The stumps of the piers and the abutments on both sides however still exist.

A drawing of this bridge by Captain Dalton was published by Hannay in the Journal of the Asiatic Society for the year 1851. Hannay wrote as follows :—

"This bridge, a remnant of ancient times in Kamrup, is situated about 8 miles N. W. of North Gauhati, on the high alley which, no doubt, formed at one time the principal line of land communication with ancient Gauhati (Prāgjyotisha) and western Kamrup, * * * * The structure is of solid masonry, built without lime or mortar, of the same massive and enduring material (gneiss and granite) found in the neighbouring hills, and which appears to have been used so largely in the construction of the more ancient temples of central and lower Assam. There are no arches - the superstructure being a platform with a slight curve 140 ft. long and 8 ft. in breadth composed of slabs of stone six feet nine inches long and ten inches thick, numbering five in the whole breadth, resting on an understructure of sixteen pillars, three in a row, equally divided by three large solid buttresses; with a half buttress projecting from a circular mass of masonry forming the abutments at each end of the road, there being, in the whole, 21 passages for the water. The accounts by Muhammadan writers of the earliest conquests of Kamrup by the subordinates of the Moslem kings appear to be mixed up with so much of the fabulous that it is quite impossible to place much reliance on them as historical records. If, however, we could suppose that the expedition of 1205-06, as above quoted, came in

The Silsāko as it existed in 1851

(By kind permission of the Asiatic Society of Bengal)

sight of the Brahmaputra at Rangamati, crossed the Mānas and marched through northern Kamrup, the possession of which would oblige the Rājā to submit, it is not improbable that this is the stone bridge over which Bactiyar Khilji and his Tartar cavalry passed, previous to entering the outworks of the ancient city of Gauhati (or Prāgjyotisha), the bridge being but a short distance from the line of hills bounding Gauhati on the North N. W. and west, on which are still visible its lines of defences extending for many miles on each side from the N. W. gate of entrance or pass through the hills.

The Muhammadan general is also said to have been obliged to retreat from an advanced position (perhaps Charduar) hearing that the Rājā of Kamrup had dismantled the stone bridge on his rear; now it is quite evident, from the marks on the stones of the platform, that they had been taken off and replaced somewhat irregularly."

The reasons which have led us to reach the conclusions stated above may be summarised as follows :—

1. As stated by Sir Wolseley Haig, the vague accounts of the Muslim historians, ignorant of geography and preserved in corrupted texts, cannot be relied upon. It is stated by Minhaj that in ancient times Shah Gustasib, on his way from China, first entered Kāmarupa and through that route reached Hindustan (1). Mahammad Bin Bukhtiyar therefore wanted to reach China by the same route. The Muslim historians believed, without the least

(1) *Tabaquat-i-Nasiri* p 561.

hesitation, the story that Gustasib actually came into India from China by way of the "City of Kamrud" and that he left in that city twelve hundred "hoards" of treasure which subsequently fell into the hands of Sultan Mughis-ud-din, *alias* Ikhtiyar-ud-din Malik Yuzbeg, when he occupied the capital of Kāmarupa temporarily in the year 1254-55 (1). Evidently Mahammad Bin Bukhtiyar also believed that the route to China lay through the "City of Kamrud".

2. If, as stated above, China and not Tibet was the real objective of Mahammad he must have been informed when he reached the foot hills that the more direct route to China lay through the north-eastern corner of Assam. He had therefore to traverse the Assam valley, north of the Brahmaputra, by the old highway and pass over the stone bridge 8 miles to the north west of the Kāmarupa capital which was called "Kāmarupa Nagar" or the "City of Kāmrup."

3. Mahammad had no idea of the difficulties of a march through the hostile hilly country and the Rāja of Kāmarupa properly warned him that much more ample preparations were to be made for transport and supplies before forcing a passage through the hills. Mahammad disregarded this advice but still the Rāja refrained from attacking him until he had actually approached the outer defences of the capital when military considerations dictated that a foreign armed host, so near the capital, must be destroyed by any means fair or foul.

---

(1) *Tabaquat-i-Nasiri* p 764.

4. If Mahammad simply passed through the north-western corner of Kāmarupa, i.e. the Jalpaiguri district, to reach Sikhim the Rāja would not have attacked the retreating Turks. No stone bridge over the Teesta or the Karatoya is known to have ever existed and it is not at all likely that a river on the boundary of the kingdom would have been spanned by a stone bridge. The river when it debouched from the hills was no doubt fordable in the winter and therefore a bridge at such a point was unnecessary.

5. Towards the end of the twelfth century and earlier the Bhutias were in possession of the Dooars. In northern Bengal a Bhutia (Kamboja) dynasty ruled for some time after the Pāla power declined. Mahammad must have encountered stiff resistance from the Bhutias on every point along the Bhutan border. In north Kamrup, on the Bhutan border, which was no doubt the open cultivated country referred to in the *Tabaquat-i-Nasiri*, there were Bhutia forts to guard the frontier and one of them was perhaps at Kumrikata which is spelt as Karampatan. As this town is said to have contained a Brahman or Hindu population it could not have been anywhere in Sikhim, Bhutan or Tibet. Besides, it is stated by Minhaj. that a large number of Bhutia ponies called *Tangan* were daily sold in this town. Even now Bhutia ponies are called *Tangna* in Kamrup and the cold weather mart for Bhutia ponies is at Daranga which is quite close to Kumrikata. A horde of Mongol or Bhutia horsemen and the Bhutanese soldiers in the forts checked Mahammad who had therefore to fall back

on the road within the territories of the Rāja of Kāmarupa. The Rāja of Kāmarupa then turned hostile and caught him in a trap as already described.

6. According to the account of Minhaj the soldiers of the fort and the surrounding country, who so fiercely opposed Bukhtiyar, all looked like Turks i.e. they had Mongoloid features and their offensive and defensive arms consisted of long bows and arrows, pieces of the spear bamboo and cuirasses, body armour, shields and helmets all made of slips of bamboos fastened and stitched overlapping each other. This war-outfit seems to have belonged to the Mongoloid people living in the plains and the foot-hills rather than the inhabitants of Tibet or upper Bhutan.

7. The bridge crossed by Mahammad was no doubt the one described by Hannay who in 1851 found the large stone slabs of the platform irregularly replaced after they had been removed in order to block Mahammad's passage. There was no other stone bridge, within the kingdom, of similar dimensions, of which any mention can be found. According to local traditions, Mahammad Bin Bukhtiyar crossed this bridge. The *Kamarupar Buranji*, a historical *puthi* collected by the Assam Government and published by the Departm ent of Historical and Antiquarian Studies, states that Bukhtiyar Khilji advanced as far as Kāmpith i.e. that portion of Kāmarupa which lies between the Sonkosh river and Duimuniśila above Tezpur. North Gauhati is in the centre of Kāmpith.

8. Raverty has adduced several reasons to

prove that it was not the Silsāko, described by Hannay, which Bukhtiyar crossed over but his arguments are not convincing. He himself says that so large a river as the one described by Minhaj could not have been spanned by a bridge of "over twenty arches". According to his own supposition the river referred to was the Teesta and the bridge over it was within Sikhim. If so, it is not understood how the Kāmarupi Hindus could go there to destroy the bridge or how there could be a Hindu temple on the opposite side of the river. Raverty's conclusions are entirely wrong for it is clear from the Muslim accounts that the bridge was within the territories of the Raja of Kāmarupa. It is absurd to suppose that at this period the kingdom of Kāmarupa included any part of Bhutan, Sikhim or Nepal. Minhaj makes the astounding statement that between Kāmarupa and Tirhut there were no less than thirtyfive mountain passes (1).

9. It is stated in the *Tabaquat-i-Nasiri* that Ali Mech guided the Muslim army as far as the bridge and that when Mahammad with a few followers crossed the river, on his return, Ali Mech again met him and guided him back to Devkot. This shows that the "Kuch" and "Mej" (Mech) country was to the west of the river. In other words, the river spanned by the bridge was to the east of Kuch Bihar. It could not therefore have been either the Teesta or the Dharla which are to the west of the "Kuch" country. On the other hand, Kuch Bihar was always within Kāmarupa.

---

(1) *Tabaquat-i-Nasiri* p 568.

So the statement of Minhaj that the river crossed formed the boundary of the kingdom cannot be true.

10. Raverty thinks that the removal of the flat stones of the platform could not have prevented the Turks from crossing over the bridge as wood and bamboos must have been plentiful in the locality and the Muslim soldiers could easily throw up a temporary bridge as the piers were not destroyed. It should not however be forgotten that the Kāmarupi troops, who surrounded the Turks, were not idle spectators. They must have been raining arrows and other missiles at the Turks all the time and the Turks themselves and their horses were all in a famished condition. It is stated by Minhaj that the Muslim troops were fatigued and knocked up by the march and a large number were martyred and disabled on the the first day of the fight. Further, "when they retreated, throughout the whole route, not a blade of grass nor a stick of firewood remained as the inhabitants had set fire to the whole of it and burnt it; * * * * * During these fifteen days not a pound of food nor a blade of grass did the cattle and horses obtain; and all the men were killing their horses and eating them". This being the position one can easily imagine that the Turks were really reduced to great straits and became desperate when they reached the bridge-head.

It is therefore abundantly clear that Bukhtiyar's host had actually penetrated into Kāmarupa and were destroyed not far from the Kāmarupa capital. As Sir W. Haig puts it, this was the greatest disaster that had yet befallen the Muslim arms in India (1).

A contributor to the Journal of the Asiatic Society of Bengal, writing in 1840, held the view that Bukhtiyar must have entered Assam through Sylhet and, crossing the Khasi and Garo Hills range, north of Sylhet, invaded Kāmarupa. He wrote :—

"Muhammad Bukhtiyar was the Governor of Bihar and in 1203 A. D. entered Bengal, and having rapidly overcome that country, he immediately turned his forces against Kamrup, which adpears to have been then a powerful kingdom and worthy of his arms" (2).

The theory of Bukhtiyar crossing the Khasi Hills is perhaps untenable but the view that he actually came into the heart of Kamrupa is no doubt correct.

Mr. S. N. Bhattacharya, in his recent book "Mughal North-East Frontier policy", admits that the "place of discovery of this inscription, its date as well as its phraseology raise a natural presumption that the first Muslim host penetrated into the heart of Kamarupa and reached the vicinity of Gauhati where they were thoroughly worsted". He however thinks that "in view of the testimony of the contemporary Muslim chronicler and the peculiar political conditions of Bengal and the Brahmaputra Valley of the early thirteenth century

(1) Cambridge History of India vol III p 50
(2) J,A.S.B. vol, IX pp 838-840,

the presumption appears rather untenable." It has already been stated that Minhaj gathered the story 35 years after the occurrence. A more competent authority, Raverti, found that even Minhaj was not to be trusted with regard to a Muslim reverse. Mr. Bhattacharya has not explained what "peculiar political condition of Bengal and the Brahmaputra valley" at that period prevented Bukhtiyar from marching into Kāmarupa. Did not Hisamuddin Iwaz proceed as far as Gauhati, twenty years after and was he not repulsed?*

As stated by Raverty the hold of Iltumish over Bengal was very partial. Since the time the Khilji Maliks had set him on the throne at Lakhnauti, Hisamuddin Iwaz paid scant regard for Iltumish. Iwaz occupied the throne in the year 1211 A. D.

---

* The latest contribution on the subject is a paper on "Mahammad Bukhtiyar's invasion of Tibet: A revaluation of the text of *Tabakat-i-Nasiri* as in Raverty's Translation" by Mr. Nalinikanta Bhattasali, M.A. The contribution is being shortly published. After we had sent this book to the press, Mr. Stapleton informed us that Mr. Bhattasali had written such a paper. At our request Mr. Bhattasali kindly favoured us with a typewritten copy of his paper. We cannot therefore quote from that important and authoritative paper, in *extenso*, in our text which we would have otherwise done. We must therefore refer to that paper in this foot note.

It is rather striking that Mr. Bhattasali has come to practically the same conclusions as we have reached. These are:—

(1) The large river named as Begamati, Bangmati, or Nangmati and which was also called the "Samund", was no other than the Brahmaputra in front of Rangamati. (The early Muslim historians, who named Prithu as Bartu or Britu, Jagannath or Puri as Sankanat and Raja Ganesh as Raja Kans, could certainly have named Rangamati as Bangmati).

and ruled till 1226 A. D. During these years Iltumish had to invade Bengal on several occasions to assert his authority. In his *Tabaquat-i-Nasiri* Minhaj writes that "the august Sultan Shamsuddin-wa-ud-Duniya Iltumish, on several occasions, sent forces from the capital Dehli towards Lakhnauti" (1). Iwaz minted coins in his own name and one such coin struck by him in 621 A. H. (1224 A. D.) was found at Gauhati in 1880. Iltumish could not tolerate the insubordination of Iwaz any longer and in 1225 A. D. marched into Bengal. Iwaz then prudently submitted to Iltumish and paid him tribute (2). After Iltumish had withdrawn Iwaz again rebelled and occupied Bihar which Iltumish

(2) From Rangamati Ali Mech guided Mahammad Bukhtiyar along the north bank of the Brahmaputra, within the kingdom of Kamarupa, as far as the stone-bridge.

(3) It was the *Silāko* described by Hannay which the Turkish army of Bukhtiyar crossed.

(4) After crossing the bridge Mahammad turned northward towards the hills, via Rangiya and Tambulpur. After crossing the first line of hills he probably reached as far as Karu-gompa which may be the Kararpatan or Karampatan mentioned by Minhaj.

(5) Being strenuously opposed by the hillmen Mahammad retired with heavy loss and coming back to the bridge found two arches of it destroyed. The disaster then took place as described by Minhaj.

Mr. Bhattasali thinks that a temple nearer than the present temple of Gopeswara seems to be indicated. It is possible that a temple nearer to the bridgewas then existing. It should however be noted that a distance of 5 miles, over a well-maintained road, is nothing to an army of mounted soldiers.

(1) *Tabaquat-i-Nasiri* pp 590-591.

(2) Ibid p 593.

had left in charge of Malik Izzudin Jani (1). Then in the year 1227 A. D. Nasir-ud-din Muhammad, the eldest son of Iltumish, again invaded Bengal learning that Iwaz was then away in an expedition into "Bang and Kamrud" (2). As soon as Iwaz received information of the invasion by Nasiruddin and the occupation of his capital he hurried back from Kāmarupa, but as stated by Raverty, "whether part of or all his army returned with him is doubtful" (3). This was the second Muslim host to enter Kāmarupa. According to Minhaj Iwaz led his army from Lakhnauti towards the territory of "Bang and Kamrud". This indicates that the line of advance was along the Brahmaputra from the direction of Rangpur or Mymensing or, as conjectured by Gait, Iwaz advanced up the Brahmaputra by boats. Minhaj does not say that this expedition was successful or that Iwaz could even invest the Kāmarupa capital. The fact is that, as stated by Gait, he was defeated and driven back. During his hasty retreat he suffered such heavy losses that he was unable to resist Nasir-ud-din at Gaur. He was completely defeated and put to death. Nasir-ud-din then ruled over Bengal as his father's deputy for about two years.

During this short rule Nasir-ud-din, as stated by Sir Wolseley Haig, attacked and defeated a Hindu Raja named Bartu or Britu (Prithu) (4). Minhaj makes the following reference to Britu :—

" The accursed Bartu (Britu) beneath whose

---

(1) *Tabaquat-i-Nasiri* p 594.
(2) Ibid p 594.
(3) Ibid p 594. Foot note.
(4) Cambridge History of India vol III p 54.

sword above a hundred and twenty thousand Mussalmans had attained martyrdom he (Nasiruddin) overthrew and sent to hell ; and the refractory infidels, who were in different parts of the country of Awadh, he reduced and overcame and brought a considerable number under obedience ".

From the above reference one is led to think that Nasiruddin subdued the Hindu chief, called Bartu, while he was in Oudh prior to his invasion into Bengal and that Bartu was a Raja somewhere in Oudh.* The account of Minhaj is not however chronologically arranged and, besides, history is silent as to any Hindu king of Oudh who had, about this time, destroyed such a large Mussalman army. Sir Wolseley Haig supposes that this Britu (Prithu) was no other than the Hindu king of Kāmarupa " who had until that time defeated the Muslims on every occasion on which they had attacked him" (1). The feeling of bitterness with

---

* Raverty writes:—
"Who this Hindu chief was we have no means of discovering, I fear, as other subsequent writers do not notice these events at all. He is styled in some of the best copies as above, which is probably meant for Prithu".

(1) Cambridge History of India vol III p 54.
The quotation below will show the sequence of events:—
"After the retirement of Iltumish from Bengal in 1225 Iwaz rebelled, expelled the king's governor from Bihar and illtreated those who had aknowleged his authority. The governor fled to Oudh and in 1227 Mahmud, the son of Iltumish, invaded Bengal from that province to punish the rebel. Iwaz being absent on an expedition, he occupied Lakhnauti without opposition and when Iwaz returned he defeated him, captured him, put him to death and imprisoned the Khalji nobles who had formed a confederacy to oppose the Suzerainty of Delhi."
"Mahmud now governed Bengal as his father's deputy

which Minhaj refers to Britu suggests that it was he who 22 years before had destroyed the forces of Mahammad Bukhtiyar and had subsequently driven back the host of Iwaz inflicting severe losses. The supposition of Sir Wolseley Haig is therefore correct. In the *Yogini Tantra*, which must have been compiled in the early part of the sixteenth century, it is recorded that a Śaiva king named Jalpeswar ruled over Kāmarupa and that it was he who built the Śiva temple of Julpesh in Jalpaiguri. The author of the *Kāmarupar Buranji*, a historical *puthi*, states that Prithu was the other name of Jalpeswar. Not knowing that Jalpeswar and Prithu were indentical Buchanan, alluding to the so called prophesies in the *Yogini Tantra*, wrote as follows :—

"After him (Nāga Śankar), but at what intervals is not mentioned, would be a Rāja named Jalpeswar, who would still further encourage that (*linga*) worship and who would build the celebrated temple of Jalpis. Very considerable ruins are at no great distance from that place, as will be hereafter described, but they are ascribed to a *Prithu Rāja* who may however have been a person of the same family".

and made the most of an opportunity which was closed by his early death in April 1229, for he defeated and slew Raja Britu, possibly the Raja of Kamrup, who had, until that time, defeated the Muslims on every occasion on which they had attacked him."

It is therefore clear that Nasiruddin Mahmud attacked and defeated the Hindu Raja Britu after overthrowing Iwaz and some time before his death, probably in the year 1228 A.D.

"This Prithu Rāja, from the size of his capital and the numerous works raised in the vicinity by various dependants and connections of the Court, must have governed a large extent of the country and for a considerable period of time. Although he is, in some measure, an object of worship among the neighbouring Hindus, they have few traditions concerning the place from whence he came nor at what period he lived; and I heard it only mentioned by one old man that he governed before the time of the dynasty which will be next mentioned."*

Glazier refers to Prithu as an important king of Kāmarupa who had constructed extensive fortifications in the present district of Jalpaiguri (1). It is very probable that this Prithu Rāja was the king of Kāmarupa who caused the destruction of Bukhtiyar's forces in 1206 A. D., who, in 1227 A. D., repulsed Ghiyasuddin Iwaz inflicting severe losses and who, probably in the following year, was overthrown by Nasiruddin, son of Iltumish. It is related by Buchanan that, according to traditions, when an army of untouchables entered his capital he, for fear of having his purity sullied, threw himself into a tank and died. The capital of Prithu was in North-Gauhati in the vicinity of

* Buchanan Manuscripts, published by the Department of Historical Studies in Assam. The dynasty next mentioned by Buchanan is the one of Dharmapāla whose sister-in-law was Mainamati the mother of Gopichandra. We are unable to connect this Dharmapāla with any line of kings ruling in Kāmarupa or Kamata. The next dynasty mentioned is that founded by Niladhvaj.

(1) Report on the District of Rangpur page, 8.

which he repulsed both Bukhtiyar and Iwaz. The extensive fortifications in Jalpaiguri, referred to by Glazier, were no doubt erected by him after Bukhtiyar's invasion by that route in order to be in a position to offer stronger resistance to an invader at the entrance to his kingdom.

It appears that although Prithu was overthrown and killed Nasiruddin could not get a hold over Kāmarupa. Probably he placed a successor on the throne and, on promise of annual tribute from him, retired from Kāmarupa. It is not known who succeeded Prithu but it seems that after the Muhammadans had left the country the Raja gradually assumed independence. The next invasion by Malik Yuzbeg was undertaken evidently because the then Raja of Kāmarupa, stopped payment of the tribute.

This invasion was in the year 1254-55 corresponding to Heziri 655. Minhaj, in his *Tabaquat-i-Nasiri* gives the following account of the invasion :—

"After he (Malik Yuzbeg) returned from Awadh to Lakhanawati, he determined upon marching into Kamrud, and transported an army across the river Beg-mati. As the Rae of Kamrud had not the power to resist him, he retired precipitately some whither. Malik Yuz-Bak took the City of Kamrud and possessed himself of countless wealth and treasure, to such extent, that the amount and weight thereof cannot be contained within the area of record."

"The author, at the time he was sojourning at Lakhnawati, had heard from travellers whose statements are to be relied upon, that from the reign of Gushtasib, Shah of Ajam, who had invaded Chin, and had come towards Hindustan by that route (by way of Kamrud), twelve hundred hoards of treasure, all sealed, which were (there deposited), and any portion of which wealth and treasures not one of the Raes had availed himself of, the whole fell into the hands of the Musalman troops. The reading of the Khutbah, and Friday religious service were instituted in Kamrud, and signs of the people of Islam appeared there. But of what avail was all this, when the whole, from phrensy, he gave to the winds? for the wise have said that "the seeking to perform overmuch work hath never turned out fortunate for the seeker."

"After Kamrud was taken (possession of), so they related, several times the Rae sent confidential persons (to Malik Yuz-Bak), saying: "Thou hast subdued this territory, and no Malik of the Musalman people ever before obtained such success. Now do thou return, and replace me upon the throne, and I will send to thee tribute every year so many bags of gold, and so many elephants, and I will continue the Khutbah unchanged, and the Musalman stamped coin as established."

"Malik Yuz-Bak did not become willing to agree to this in any way; and the Rae gave command that all his train, and the peasantry, should go to Malik Yuz-Bak, and get him to pledge his right hand (for their safety), and buy up all the grain procurable in (the city and country of?) Kamrud, at whatever price he might require, so that the Musalman troops might have no provisions left. They did so accordingly, and bought up from them all the produce that was obtainable at heavy rate."

"Depending on the cultivated state and flourishing condition of the country, Malik Yuz-Bak did not lay up any stores of grain; and, when the time of the spring harvest came round, the Rae, with the whole of his subjects, rose, and opened the water dykes all around, and brought Malik Yuz-Bak and the troops of Islam to a state of helplessness, in such wise, that they were near perishing through destitution. They now took counsel together, and came to the conclusion that it was necessary to retreat, otherwise they would die of starvation".

"They accordingly set out from Kamrud with the intention of proceening towards Lakhanawati. The route through the plain (country) was flooded with water, and occupied by the Hindus. The Musalmans obtained a guide to bring them out of that country by conducting them towards the skirt of the mountains. After they had proceeded some few stages, they got entangled among passes and defiles, and narrow roads, and both their front and rear was seized by the Hindus. In a narrow place a fight took place in front of the leading rank between two elephants; the force fell into confusion, the Hindus came upon them from every side, and Musalman and Hindu mingled pell mell together. Suddenly an arrow struck Malik Yuz-Bak, who was mounted on an elephant, in the breast, and he fell, and was made prisoner; and all his children, family, and dependents, and the whole of his force, were made captive."

"When they carried Malik Yuz-Bak before the Rae, he made a request that they would bring his son to him ; and, when they brought his son to him, he placed his face to the face of his son, and yielded his soul to God. The Almighty's mercy be upon him !"

As the army was "transported across the river Begamati" clearly there was no stone bridge over this river as stated by Minhaj in his account of Bukhtiyar's invasion fifty years before. Raverty says that the Kāmarupa capital at this time was Kamatapur but he is wrong. Three coins minted by Malik Yuzbeg at Lakhnauti, in Ramjan 653 A. H, were found at Gauhati in 1880 (1). This proves almost conclusively that the "City of Kamrud" occupied by Malik Yuzbeg was North-Gauhati or its immediate vicinity which Dharmapāla had named "Kāmarupanagar" or the "City of Kamrup".* Stapleton rightly conjectures that the three coins discovered at Gauhati "represent a loot captured from the Mussalmans" but his other supposition that the Rae of Kamrud who defeated Malik Yuzbeg *alias* Sultan Mughis-ud-din was the

(1) J.A.S.B. (1910) P. 621.

* If, as conjectured by Mr Bhattasali, Begamati or Bangmati really meant the Brahmaputra in front of Rangamati, it would appear that Malik Yuzbeg's advance was in the direction of Gauhati and not Kamatapur which was not then the capital. If Malik Yuzbeg, advancing from the direction of Rangpur, crossed the Brahmaputra at Rangamati his march was against the old capital Gauhati which he temporarily occupied. This is more probable because his coins have been found at Gauhati and his retreat was along the Khasi and Garo Hills on the south of the Brahmaputra. When Malik Yuzbeg occupied Gauhati the Raja's palace was on the north bank of the river. On the flight of the Raja he may have occupied the Raja's palace also.

Kachari Raja of Gauhati is incorrect.

According to the Mussalman historian, Malik Yuzbeg, in order to avoid the flooded country, was retreating along the slopes of the hills and it was in a defile that he was surrounded and defeated by the troops of the Raja. This shows that he was retreating from Gauhati along the foot of the Khasi Hills and the Garo Hills in the direction of Mymensing. There could not have been any hilly country intervening between Kamatapur and the seat of the Muhammadan Sultan of Bengal. Consequently Malik Yuzbeg could not have attacked Kamatapur. As already stated, it was after the repulse of this expedition that the seat of Government was transferred westwards.

After the repulse of Malik Yuzbeg, *alias* Sultan Mughis-ud-din, Kāmarupa enjoyed freedom from serious foreign aggressions for a period of more than two hundred years until the closing years of the fifteenth century. There were however occasional Muslim raids, particularly from the direction of Mymensing, during this period and though chronologically they should be mentioned later we shall, for the sake of convenience, enumerate them in this chapter.

There was probably another expedion into Kāmarupa about 1321-22 A. D. undertaken by Sultan Ghiyas-ud-din. That he subjugated the northern part of Mymensing, east of the Brahmaputra, which had from the early times been included within Kāmarupa, is beyond doubt for a coin minted by him at Kasba Ghiyaspur, within this tract, has been found. The find of another coin of this Sultan dated 721 A. H, within the district of

Nowgong, however may raise the presumption that he invaded Assam as far as Nowgong. There is, however, no mention of this expedition in the Muslim chronicles. In any case, it was perhaps nothing more than a marauding raid which was probably repulsed by the Kacharis who had then occupied the Nowgong district. The Kāmarupa capital was then at Kamatapur and the Gauhati region was then probably under a local Bhuyan chief.

We need hardly refer to the supposed invasion of Assam by Muhammad Bin Tughlak referred to only in the *Alamgirnamah.* The find of his coins in the Mymensing district cannot raise any presumption that he invaded Kāmarupa. This expedition into Kāmarupa did not take place at all though it is true that 1337-38 A. D. Muhammad Tughlak attempted a march into Tibet through Nagarkot or Kangra and this ended in a disaster (1). The author of the *Alamgirnamah* perhaps thought that the only way to Tibet lay through Assam.

The next invasion of Kāmarupa by Sikandar Shah in 1357 A. D. is mentioned both by R. D. Banerji (2). and by P. N. Bhattacharya (3). The authority for this statement is a silver coin bearing the name of Sikandar Shah minted at "Chawalistan urf (*alias*) Kamru" and dated 759 A. H. (4). This invasion is not mentioned by any of the Muslim historians. Mr. Stapleton's surmise

(1) Cambridge History of India, vol III, pp 154-155,
(2) Bangalar Itihash, vol. II, p 32.
(3) Moghul North Eastern Frontier Policy, p 63.
(4) Catalogue of coins in the Indian Museum vol II. p 152.

that Sikandar's activities were confined to the north of Mymensing, east of the Brahmaputra, which constituted a part of Kāmarupa and that the coin was minted in that part of Mymensing appears to be correct and we can dismiss as unfounded Mr. Bhattacharya's theory that Sikandar advanced as far as the Barnadi. Mr. Bhattacharya argues that Sikandar's invasion in 1357 was opportune as at that time the Rāja of Kamata was involved in war with the Ahom king Sukhrangpha. As a matter of fact Sukhrangpha ascended the throne in 1332 and the plot against him by his half brother Chao Pulai was hatched soon after the accession. The Kamata Rāja's invasion of the Ahom territories to help his relative, Chao Pulai, therefore must have taken place before 1340 A. D. or long before the alleged invasion of Sikandar in 1357 A. D. The statement that at that time the Kamata king was otherwise engaged and could not therefore offer resistance to Sikandar is incorrect. On the other hand it appears that Illiyas Shah died at the end of 758 A. H. and was succeeded by his son Sikandar Shah. Before his death Illiyas Shah had heard of the preparations made by the Emperor Firoz Tughlak for his second expedition into Bengal and being alarmed at this news, Illiyas had sent envoys with presents to Delhi towards the end of 758 A. H. (1). Sikandar Shah on ascending the throne had therefore to make preparations for resisting the invasion of Firoz Tughlak. It is not at all likely that immediately after ascending the throne he started on

(1) Coins and chronology of the Early Independent Sultans of Bengal by N.K.Bhattasali, p 44.

an expedition into the interior of distant Kāmarupa. As a matter of fact, Firoz Tughlak started on his second expedition to Lakhnauti in 760 A. H. and in the same year compelled Sikandar to retire to Ekdala fort which was invested by Firoz. All these circumstances go to show that the alleged conquest of Kamru, as recorded in the coin of 759 A. H., was an empty boast. It appears that whenever they effected a lodgment in east Mymensing these Sultans boasted of the conquest of Kamru and minted coins. Even Sylhet was considered a part of Kamru.*

Mr. Bhattacharya's other theory that in 1394 A. D. Ghiyasuddin Azam Shah invaded Kāmarupa seems to be equally untenable. Mr. Bhattasali has shown that Sikandar Shah lived till October 1393 A. D. (1). Ghiyasuddin who had revolted against his father was busy fighting with his father till the end of 1393 A. D. It is not at all likely that in the following year, instead of consolidating his position in Bengal, he set out on an invasion into Kāmarupa. The Muslim historians make no mention of such an invasion. Neither R. D. Banerji

* Ibn Batuta who visited Bengal during 1346-47 A.D. wrote in his narrative that he came to the "mountains of Kamru" to visit a saint named Shaikh Jalaluddin Al-Tabrizi. It is now recognized by historians that this Jalaluddin was no other than the famous Shah Jalal of Sylhet who died about 1346 A. D. shortly after Ibn Batuta visited him. It will appear therefore that the country to the east of Mymensing was called "Kamru" irrespective of the territories actually within the kingdom of Kāmarupa.

(1) Coins and chronology of the Early Independent Sultans of Bengal, p 71

nor Mr. Bhattasali make any such mention. It is however true that the Muslims invaded Kamata some time after 1397 A D and prior to 1407 A D and that they were driven out with the help of the forces pespatched by the Ahom king Sudangpha. We shall refer to this matter in the next chapter.

Next we come to the conflict between the king of Kāmatapur and Sultan Barbak Shah of Bengal said to have taken place about 1473-74 A. D. or about a hundred years after the alleged invasion by Sikandar. The story is based on what is stated in a Persian manuscript, the *Risalat-Ush-Shuhada.* According to this account Barbak's army having been repeatedly defeated by Kāmeswar (Kamateswar) the king of Kāmarupa, whose name is not given, Barbak selected a holy man named Ishmail Ghazi, and appointed him as his commander. The powerful king of Kāmarupa advanced and met Ishmail Ghazi's forces near Santosh in the modern district of Dinajpur. After a sanguinary battle the king of Kāmarupa completely defeated the Muslim commander and destroyed practically the whole of his army. The Muslim commander then made peace overtures which the king of Kāmarupa rejected. Warfare was therefore continued and this time, it is said, Ishmail brought into play his supernatural powers which over-awed the Kāmarupa king so much that he was compelled not only to submit to the Muslim commander but also to accept the Islamic faith.

The Persian M. S. entitled *Risalat-Ush-Shuhada* was found by Mr. G. H. Damant, I. C. S. in the possession of a fakir in charge of Ishmail Ghazi Durgah at Kanta Duar and he published the text of the M. S. with a sketch, in English, of its contents in the J. A. S. B. for the year 1874. The author of this M. S. was one Pir Muhammad Shattari who recorded this account in 1633 A. D. as it was related to him by three Mussalmans, viz, Shaikh Kabir, Shaikh Latif and Shaikh Masud who were then the keepers of Ismail Ghazi's tomb. This account was therefore written more than a century and a half after the death of Ishmail Ghazi.

It is stated in this account that the Sultan first sent Ishmail as commander of the army against Raja Gajapati of Orissa who had previously defeated the Sultan's troops. Ishmail succeeded in defeating Gajapati who was taken prisoner and beheaded. The Sultan next deputed Ishmail to subdue the Raja of Kāmarupa who had repeatedly repulsed the Muslim forces and who was known as Kāmeswar. According to the M. S. Kāmeswar was "one of the greatest heroes of his time and possessed good military talents". The first battle was fought "on the field of Santosh within the borders of Islam" which shows that it was the Rāja of Kāmarupa who was the aggressor. Ishmail was completely defeated and his army was annihilated. It is stated that the only survivors were Ishmail, his nephew Muhammad Shah and twelve paiks. Ishmail subsequently reinforced himself and is said to have garrisoned his troops on a piece of high land, surrounded on all sides by water, and that the piece of high land was actually raised above water by God on the prayer of Ishmail! From this place Ishmail is said to have sent the following message to the Rāja of Kāmarupa :-

"Sultan Barbak has appointed me to receive your submission, you must present yourself before me, ready equipped for a journey, in order that I may take you to the Sultan and recommend him to grant you your life and restore to you your kingdom and preserve your standard. If you do otherwise, you must suffer the consequences".
The envoy came to the Raja and delivered the letter. After reading it the Raja "became violently enraged" and replied to the envoy in the following terms :—

"I save your life because it is not my custom to slay envoys ; however tell Shah Ishmail to meet me on the field of battle. I order him to meet me there. Tell him that I am not that Gajapati whom he has conquered and whose kingdom he has subdued. Let Ishmail remember what befell his first army. When all his zealous comrades have fallen, what can he do with his single arm?"

On receiving this reply Ishmail advanced and a battle took place. Both sides fought till darkness but the issue was indecisive. On the cessation of fighting, taking advantage of the darkness, Ishmail disguised himself and riding stole into the Raja's camp unnoticed and penetrated into the apartment where the "Raja and the Rani were lying asleep in each other's arms". He did not kill them, as he might easily have done, but fastened their hair together, and unsheathing a sword, which was lying near the Raja, he placed the blade across their breasts. Having done this he rode back to his camp. Next morning the Raja and the Rani awoke and were surprised to find themselves in such a predicament. At first they thought it was the work of some evil spirit but when horse's foot-marks on the courtyard were discovered the Raja came to the conclusion that some one on horseback had trespassed into his camp. He then kept strict watch but on the next morning also he found the sword in the same position over himself and his queen. The same thing happened on the third night also. The Raja then became thoroughly alarmed and believed that Ishmail was possessed of supernatural powers. He therefore sent a messenger to Ishmail wishing to come and pay respects if his life was secure. Ishmail replied assuring safety. The Raja then came bringing with him tribute and rich presents and fell prostrate before Ishmail. He also ate some food given out of Ishmail's mouth thus making himself a Muslim. As a reward for his voluntary submission Ishmail conferred on him the title of "*Bara Larwā*" (great fighter). He sent information to his Sultan that Kāmeswar had voluntarily submitted and paid tribute. The Sultan was overcome with joy and showered presents on Ishmail.

After this, according to this account, Bhandasi Rai, the Hindu governor of Ghoraghat, represented to the Sultan that the alleged voluntary submission of Kāmeswar was a fraud and that Ishmail had really formed an alliance with the Raja of Kāmarupa in order to set up an independent kingdom for himself. The Sultan, believing the information to be true despatched an armed force against Ishmail who repulsed the Sultan's forces several times but at last submitted. He was then beheaded by order of the Sultan on Friday, the 14th Shaban 878 A. H.

This is the story narrated in the Persian M. S. Stripped of all legend it seems that Ishmail concluded a truce with the Raja of Kāmarupa to whom he had to cede some territory, probably in Ghoraghat. We find that the Kāmarupa king, Nilambar, built a road from Kamatāpur to Ghoraghat and erected a fort at Ghoraghat.

The whole story about the alleged conflict between Ishmail Ghazi and the Raja of Kamatāpur and the beheading of Ishmail under orders of Sultan Barbak is probably a myth for we find that Ishmail Ghazi, as general of Alauddin Hussein Shah, invaded Orissa in 1509 A. D. He sacked Puri and destroyed temples there. The king of Orissa then hurried from the south and Ishmail retreated. The Orissa king, Pratapa Rudra, pursued him and defeated him on the bank of the Ganges within the district of Hugli. (Banerji's History of Orissa, vol. I p. 325-326). The kings of Orissa were no doubt known as "Gajapati", but the story that Ishmail defeated the king of Orissa, took him as prisoner and beheaded him is entirely false for it is found that in 1510 A. D. Pratapa Rudra recorded his Kavali grant wherein it is stated that he defeated the king of Gaur. Pratapa Rudra, who was a contemporary of Sri Chaitanya, died in 1540 A. D. after a long reign.

It would therefore seem to be probable that if Sultan Barbak had any conflict at all with the Raja of Kamatāpur his general was not Ishmail Ghazi but some one else who was defeated by the Raja. Ishmail Ghazi may have, as general of Alauddin Hussein Shah, attacked Nilambar, the king of

Kamatapur towards the end of the fifteenth century before his expedition into Orissa. Pir Muhammad Shattari, the author of the *Risalat-Ush-Shuhada* evidently confused dates and introduced a legend in his book.

It will appear from the above that the various Muslim invasions, from the beginning of the thirteenth century, failed to overthrow the line of Hindu kings reigning either at Gauhati or at Kamatapur. All these invasions, except those undertaken by Bukhtiyar, Nasiruddin and Malik Yuzbeg *alias* Sultan Mughisuddin, were only raids which left no permanent impression. Bukhtiyar and Malik Yuzbeg were severely defeated and their armies annihilated. Even Nasiruddin's success against Prithu was a temporary success. Since the defeat sustained by Malik Yuzbeg in 1255 A.D. Kāmarupa enjoyed freedom from serious foreign aggressions for a period of more than 200 years, until the end of the fifteenth century. During the first fifty years of this period the seat of government was shifted to Kamatapur and in Kāmarupa proper Bhuyan chiefs were established at various places as wardens of marches. It is true that these chiefs owed only nominal allegiance to the Kamata kings and that they often fought against one another but when a foreign foe appeared they combined and offered united resistance.

CHAPTER X.

THE KINGS OF KAMATA.

During the long period of peace and freedom from external aggressions many changes took place in the internal condition of the kingdom. It seems that during this period the Kacharis became powerful and advanced towards the west up to the boundary of the present district of Kamrup. Owing to the extension of the Kachari power the Kāmarupa kings were, it seems, compelled to remove their capital from Gauhati further west to Kamatapur. Since then they were known as the kings of Kamatā and the kingdom included only the Goalpara and the Kamrup districts of the modern Assam Valley besides a portion of northern Bengal and a portion of Mymensing to the east of the Brahmaputra then flowing through that district.*

* The name Kāmta or Kamatā may have been derived from Kāmadā, Kāmā or Kāntā which were the various

The Ahoms entered Assam from the north-east during the first part of the thirteenth century. About 1253 A. D. Sukāphā, the leader of the Ahom invaders, had firmly established himself at Charaideo (1). During the reign of his successor the Kacharis on the south bank of the Brahmaputra were forced to retire to the west of the Dikhu river. Sukhāngphā, the great grandson of Sukāphā ruled from 1293 A. D. to 1332 A.D. (2). During his reign the Ahoms pushed so far to the west as to come into conflict with the Raja of Kamatā who then ruled over the western part of the old kingdom of Kāmarupa. On the north bank of the Brahmaputra the country seems to have been ruled by a line of Chutia kings and also by some Bhuyans who were ultimately subdued by the Ahoms.

---

names of the deity known as Kāmākshyā as stated in the Kālikā Puran. According to Vidyavinod, "Kāmeswara Mahā Gouri" worshipped by the kings of Harjara's line in Hāruppeswara and "Mahā Gouri Kāmeswara" worshipped by the kings of the Brahmapāla dynasty at Sri Durjayā were the same idols which were removed to Kamatāpur by the later kings and these then got the names "Kamateswar" and "Kamateswari" or "Kānteswar" and "Kānteswari". Nearly a century and a quarter ago Buchanan saw the ruins of Kamatāpur and recorded that the idol or the *vigraha* of Kamateswari was not actually desecrated by the Mussalmans but, according to local tradition current at that time, it concealed itself during the Muslim occupation and re-appeared during the regime of the Hinduized Koch kings of Kamarupa. Buchanan noticed a small heap where the temple of Kamateswari stood and other ruins to the west which indicated the existence of another temple dedicated to another deity. This was probably the temple of Kamateswar.

(1) Gait's History of Assam. p. 78.
(2) Ibid. p. 80.

During the latter part of the thirteenth and the beginning of the fourteenth century, it appears that the Chutias on the north and the Kacharis on the south intervened between the Ahoms and the Kamatā kings. As already stated, the Ahom king Sukhāngphā made war against the Kamatā king probably towards the end of the thirteenth century. Hostilities continued for several years. At length the Raja of Kamatā was obliged to sue for peace, which he did, by giving his daughter or sister named Rajani to the Ahom king. The five villages given by the Kamatā king as dowry with princess Rajani included one called Patilā-dohā which is still a populated village in the Barpeta subdivision of the Kamrup district. This indicates that the kingdom of Kamatā then extended as far as the present district of Kamrup towards the east.*

Sukhāngphā had, by this princess, a son named Chao Pulai who was old enough to be appointed as the Sāring raja on his father's death in 1332. It is therefore evident that peace between Sukhāngphā and the Kamatā king was concluded about the beginning of the fourteenth century. On the death of Sukhāngphā his eldest son, Sukhrāngphā, ascended the throne. Soon after, his half-brother Chao Pulai, the son of the Kamatā princess, hatched a conspiracy against him(1). When the plot was detected Chao Pulai fled to Kamatā. The king of Kamatā thereafter marched into the

---

* It should however be noted that Patla-Doh was also the name of a locality in Ghoraghat Pargana between the Karatoya and the Brahmaputra and therefore within the kingdom of Kamarupa.

(1) Gait's History of Assam p 81.

Ahom kingdom as far as Sāring. Sukhhrāngphā did not dare to oppose the Kamatā king but, opening negotiations, became reconciled with Chao Pulai. Thereupon the Kamatā king withdrew his forces. This took place about 1340 A. D.

Gait says that, if the Bāro-Bhuyan accounts can be relied upon, Durlabhnārāyan, the king of Kamatā, who settled the Brahmans and the Kayasthas including Chandibar, the great-great-grandfather of Śri Śankar Deva, in Kāmarupa, would seem to have ruled towards the end of the thirteenth century (1). It is stated that Durlabhnārāyan had hostilities with one Dharmanārāyan who styled himself as Gaudeswar. When peace was concluded Dharmanārāyan presented seven families of Brahmans and seven families of Kayasthas to Durlabhnārāyan who settled them within his kingdom. Kayastha Chandibar was the ablest of all these immigrants and he was settled in the easternmost part of the kingdom which was then subject to raids by the Bhutias. It is stated in the *Guru Charitra* that he repulsed the Bhutia raids with only a handful of men.

The *Guru Charitra* by Ramcharan Thakur, who was the nephew of Śri Madhava Deva and who must have written towards the end of the sixteenth century, gives a rather confused account of Durlabhnārāyan. According to this account there was a king named Sandhya who became the Gaudeswara. His son was Sindhu Rai who became a *Rāja-rājeswara* i.e. paramount over other kings. Sindhu Rāi was succeeded by his

(1) Gait's History of Assam p 81.

son Rup (Rupnarāyān ?) whose fame spread to other countries. The son and successor of Rup was Singhadhvaj, whose minister was a Kayastha named Pratāpadhvaj, son of Lāharia. Pratāpadhvaj killed Singhadhvaj and became himself the king. He had a son named Durlabhnārāyan by his queen Parvāvati. It is stated that Durlabhnārāyan,, as Gaudeswara secured a kingdom after some time, but it is also mentioned that a cousin (*belegiā bhāi*) of Durlabhnārāyan named Dharmapāla *alias* Dharmanārāyan was the Kāmeswara. Now we have it from the contemporary Muhammadan accounts that the kings of Kamāta, in the fourteenth and the fifteenth centuries, were called Kāmeswara. So we can suppose that Dharmapāla *alias* Dharmanārāyan was the king of Kamatā or Kāmarupa. As a matter of fact, Ramcharan Thakur calls him also Kamateswara. It is stated in the *Guru Charitra* that all the Bhuyans were subordinate to Dharmapāla. The Goddess Kāmākshyā having cursed him he left his kingdom and went to another country. Then there was anarchy and the Bhuyans became supreme in every village in the northern territories. Durlabhnārāyan, who is styled Gaudeswara, established his headquarters at a place called Garia after bunding a river with the help of Chandibar and this place was nine hours' journey from Cooch Behar. It is said that Dharmapāla had his headquarters in Ghoraghat in Rangpur and that he had a son named Tāmradhvaj. Afterwards there was a long-standing war between Durlabhnārāyan and Dharmapāla *alias* Dharmanārāyan. At length peace was established and the Gaudeswara presented to the Kamateswara the fourteen families of Brahmans and Kayasthas. It would thus appear that, according to this account, it was Durlabhnārāyna the Gaudeswara, who presented the Brahmans and the Kayasthas to Dharmanārāyan, the Kamateswara or, in other words, the popular tradition that Dharmanārāyan presented the families of the Bhuyans is reversed.

It is not clear from this account where Sandhyā and his successors ruled, but it is clear that Dharmanārāyan *alias* Dharmapāla was the king of Kamatā. This is corroborated by the reference to Kāmākshyā, Cooch Behar and Ghoraghat, all places within the kingdom of Kāmarupa. Now it is not probable that Durlabhnārāyan's father ruled over one kingdom and his relative Dharmanārāyan ruled over Kamatā. Our supposition is that Sandhyā and his successors were all kings of Kamatā. Very likely they styled themselves also as Gaudeswara as a part of Gauda was within their kingdom or the title was then considered to be more high-sounding. The mention that Sandhyā became the the Gaudeswara indicates that it was he who shifted the capital from Kāmarupa-nagar to Kamatāpur and commenced using the title Gaudeswara. His great-grandson Singhadhvaj was killed by the minister Pratāpadhvaj who occupied the throne. From Ramcharan Thakur's account we may conjecture that when Pratāpadhvaj died Dharmanārayan, his nephew, usurped the thorne and styled himselt as Kāmeswara. In order to provide for a possible contingency in future, he built a new city near Dimla in the Rangpur district and this is the city described by Buchanan.* He removed the seat of government to this city. This removal is referred to in the *Guru Charitra* as being due to the curse of the Goddess Kāmākshyā. After the removal of the headquarters to the new city in Rangpur the Bhuyan chiefs in the northern and eastern part of the kingdom raised their heads for a time. Durlabhnārāyan then, finding an opportunity, seized a part of the northern territories and established his headquarters at Garia. This led to hostilities between the two cousins but at length peace was concluded and, it seems, the kingdom was divided, the northern and the eastern part with Kamatāpur going to Durlabhnārāyan and Dharmanārāyan retaining the territories to the south including perhaps Rangpur and Mymensing. It is clearly stated that after the meeting in which the treaty was concluded Dharmanārāyan proceeded to Ghoraghat where his son Tāmradhvaj received him. Hema Saraswati, a contemporary writer, makes Durlabhnārāyan the king of "Kamatā mandala". It is stated by Kaviratna Sara-

* Buchanan wrote:—

"About two miles from a bend in the Tista, a little below Dimla, in the Rangpur district, are the remains of a fortified city, said to have bewn built by Raja Dharmapala, the first king of the Pal dynasty in Kamarupa." Buchanan was wrong because Dharmapāla, of the dynasty of Brahmapâla, was not the first king of that dynasty. The founder of the city near Dimla had evidently no connection with the Pala kings of Kamarupa.

swati, another contemporary writer, in his *Jayadratha Vadha*, that his father, Chakrapāni Kayastha, was a petty revenue officer under Durlabhnārāyan in Chota-Sila, now a village in the Barpeta Sub-division. The kingdom of Durlabhnārāyan therefore included the present Assam districts of Kamrup and Goalpara, the State of Cooch Behar and the Bengal district of Jalpaiguri. It is probable that after this division of territories Durlabhnārāyan became the Kāmeswara and Dharmanārāyan styled himself as Gaudeswara.

In order to fix the chronology of these kings we have to proceed from the birth date of Śri Śankar Deva. We know that Śri Śankar Deva was born in the year 1371 Śaka, equivalent to 1449 A.D. His great-great-grandfather Chandibar was the contemporary of Durlabhnārāyan. We can therefore place Durlabhnārāyan's reign about the second quarter of the fourteenth century and that of Sandhyā about the middle of the thirteenth century.

Durlabhnārāyan was an important king of Kamatā. He was a patron of learning. During his reign some Kāmarupi poets flourished. They were Hema Saraswati, Kaviratna Saraswati and Hāribor Bipra. They all wrote in Assamese verse. According to Ramcharan Thakur's account Durlabhnārāyan had seven queens. He was succeeded by his son Indranārāyan who, according to Kaviratna Saraswati, was a devout Vaisnava. It is not known how long Indranārāyan ruled or who succeeded him. Neither do we know anything definitely as to what became of Dharmanārāyan and his son Tāmradhvaj. Kaviratna Saraswati wrote in his *Jayadratha Vadha*, that through the blessings of Śiva Indranārāyan would be the "Pancha Gaudeswara" i.e. king over all the five Gaudas. Evidently Kaviratna Saraswati died during the reign of Indranārāyan. As we shall see later, very probably, Indranārāyan did not enjoy a long reign. He was probably defeated and killed by an usurper and that the line to which he belonged ended with him. The following chronology of the Kamatā kings down to Indranārāyan can thus be tentatively suggested:-

Sandhyā	1250-1270 A.D.
I	
Sindhu	1270-1285 "
I	
Rup	1285-1300 "
I	
Singhadhvaj	1300-1305 "
Pratāpadhvaj	1305-1325 "
Dharmanārāyan	1325-1330 "
Durlabhnārāyan	1330-1350 "
I	
Indranārāyan	1350-1365 "

It was very likely Sandhyā, the king of Kāmarupa, who after defeating Tughril Khan Malik Yuzbeg, also known as Sultan Mughis-ud-din, in 1255 A.D., removed the seat of government to Kamatāpur about 1260 A. D. This removal was probably necessitated by the menace of the Kacharis and also by the fact that Gauhati was then easily accessible to raiding Muslim invaders from the direction of Sonargaon. Pratāpadhvaj was perhaps the Kamatā king who concluded peace with the Ahom king by giving to the latter his daughter Rajani in marriage. Durlabhnārāyan was evidently the Kamatā king who subsequently marched into the Ahom kingdom as far as Sāring.

It is possible to glean from the *Guru Charitra* and other records that about this time, and probably earlier, the Bhuyans who were mostly Kayasthas and Kalitas, but who included also Brahmans and Ganaks, were the leaders of the populace. They were the feudal barons under the later kings of Kāmarupa. As the overlordship of the degenerate kings was not however strong these Bhuyans often fought with one another and sometimes combined against a common foe. From the Raut Kuchi grant of one of these Bhuyans viz, Purusottam Dasa, recorded in the year 1251 Saka corresponding to 1329 A. D., we find that lands were given by him to a Brahman in Raut Kuchi, not far from Nalbari. It is stated in this grant that Purusottam's grandfather, Vāsudeva, was the right hand of the king of Kāmarupa and that he always marched at the head of a thousand swordsmen on the side of the king (1). He might have been a contemporary of Sandhyā or his son Sindhu. His son was Jayadeva who is described as the "lotus of his own race and who posseessed the characteristic qualities of the Aryans" (2). This reference indicates that Jayadeva Das

(1) Social History of Kamarupa. vol I p 247.
(2) Ibid p 247.

was either a Kayastha or a Kalita Bhuyan. "From him was born the illustrious Purusottama who on account of his great wealth was matchless and was like the *Kalpa* tree on earth. By dint of the valour of his arms and heroism he had defeated the rival kings (chiefs?) and obtained the glory of sovereignty" (1). It is clear from the above extract that Purusottam subjugated several other Bhuyans and the Kamatā king had to recognize him as a vassal king over a specified tract rather than as an ordinary feudal baron. History tells us that even at a much later period, during the rule of the Koch kings, feudatory local chiefs of Rani, Luki, Dimorua, Rangjuli and Soosung (in Mymensing) were designated as Rajas.

Relying on the *Gurucharitra* by Ramcharan Thakur and the works of contemporary writers like Hema Saraswati and Kaviratna Saraswati we can trace the history of the Kamatā kings down to the middle of the fourteenth century after which the history of the kingdom is most uncertain. We know that Durlabhanārāyan was succeeded by his son Indranārāyan but we do not know for certain who succeeded the latter. From the Ahom Buranjis it is found that towards the end of the fourteenth century the Kamatā king again came into conflict with the Ahom king Sudāngphā. It appears that one Tao Sulai, who was paramour of Sudāngphā's queen, fled to Kamatā and when the Ahom king demanded his return the Raja of Kamatā refused to give him up

(1) Ibid p 8.24

(1). Sudāngphā then despatched an expedition into Kamatā under the Bargohain. The Raja of Kamatā was, in the meantime, attacked by the Muhammadans. He therefore submitted to the Ahom king and sought his aid to drive out the Muslim invaders. Sudāngphā ordered the Bargohain to help the Kamatā Raja. The combined forces of the Kamatā Raja and the Bargohain defeated the Muslims and drove them out of Kamatā. The Raja, being pleased, gave his daughter Bhājani in marriage to Sudāngphā with a suitable dowry consisting of horses, elephants, ornaments and servants. This must have taken place about the end of the fourteenth or the beginning of the fifteenth century, for Sadāngphā died in 1407 A. D. This Raja of Kamatā was no doubt a successor of Indranārāyan*. Gait has not mentioned the assistance

(1) Gait's History of Assam p 84.

* With regard to the two Kamata princesses Rajani and Bhajani the several *Buranjis* do not agree. According to the *Deodhai Buranji* Rajani was married to Sukhangpha who reigned from 1293 A D. This is the version accepted by Gait and it seems to be the correct one. The *Deodhai Buranji* however makes Rajani the sister of the Kamata king whose daughter was Bhajani. It is stated that Rajani intervened and persuaded her brother to give his daughter Bhajani to Sudangpha. This is not probable because it is not at all likely that princess Rajani whose son Chao Pulai was a grown up man in 1332 A D lived till Sudangpha became king in 1397 A D. On the other hand, the *Bahgoria Burayohain Buranji* makes the incorrect statement that Rajani and Bhajani were two daughters of the Kamatā king and that they were both given in marriage to Sukhrangpha and that a subsequent Ahom king Sudangpha got another princess from Kamata. It is also said in this *Buranji* that to this princess was given as dowry the estates known as Sherpur, Karaibari, Dashkaunia, Bahirbund and Bhitarband which are all localities in the

given by the Ahoms to the Kamatā Raja but this is mentioned in the Assamese Buranji called "*Suarganārāyān Mahārājār Akshyāna*" wherein it is stated that the Bargohain drove out the Muslim invaders and cleared the country as far as the Karatoyā.*

According to the account given in the M. S. of an Assamese Buranji known as the "*Swarganārāyan Mahārājâr Janma Charitra*" a king of Kamatā became very friendly with the Sultan of Bengal who gave his daughter to the Kamatā Raja. This princess was very beautiful and was named Susuddhi. It appears that after having been Hinduized she became the chief queen of the Raja. The other queen was Sulochanā by whom the Raja had a son named Durlabhendra. Suśudhi fell

---

present districts of Rangpur and Mymensing.

According to the *Deodhai Buranji* the father of Rajani was named Sekhang while the father of Bhajani was named Manik. It seems that the author of the *Buranji* misplaced the names. It is more probable that the father of Bhajani was named Sekhang, perhaps the Ahom rendering of the Hindu name Śukarang, (Śukaranka), the son of Arimatta who, as we shall show later, was probably the king of Kamatā about this time. Gajanka, Sukaranka and Mriganka used to be popularly called Gajang, Sukarang and Mrigang. Manik was probably the name of the minister of Singhadhvaj who having killed the king and usurped the throne assumed the highsounding name Pratapadhvaj.

* This is supported also by the *Deodhai Buranji* and the *Bahçoria Bura Gohain Buranji*. In the former it is stated that Sudangpha ordered the Bargohain in these terms:— "Kamateswara has asked for our assistance to fight the Muslims. You better go and support him and if he gives a princess bring her with you." The statements of Blochman and Prinsep, refered to in the footnote to page 84 of Gait's History of Assam, are thus confirmed.

in love with Chandrasekhara a son of Nilāmbar who was the Raja's priest. Chandrasekhara used to visit the queen at night secretly. This was detected and Chandrasekhara was put in chains. Suśudhi, who was known also as *Gaurmā* (Princess of Gaur), was disgraced, turned out of the palace and made to live in a hut attended only by a maid servant. She then managed to send information to her father. In the meantime the Raja had caused the secret murder of Kesava Rai, the son of Satānanda, the chief gate keeper, on the suspicion that he assisted Chandrasekhara to enter the palace at night in order to hold intrigue with the queen. A part of the flesh of Kesava was cooked and his father was invited to dinner. He came and unwittingly ate of his son's flesh. When at length he came to know the real fact he fled to the Sultan and urged him to invade Kamatā. At length the Sultan despatced Turbak with an army with orders to rescue *Gaurmā* and seize the Raja. At this the Raja fled to the Ahom kingdom and sought the aid of the Ahom king· This was in 1401 Saka. When the Kamatā king left his kingdom Suśudhi invited the Kachari king to come and take her away. The Kachari king sent men who carried *Gourmā* away. He made her his chief queen. This was in 1405 Saka equivalent to 1483 A. D. Turbak came to Kamatā but did not find *Gourmā* there. He learned that she had been taken away by the Kachari king. On getting this information the Sultan sent Meet Manik to the assistance of Turbak. They invaded the Kachari kingdom and about the same time the Ahoms also attacked the Kacharis. The Ahoms killed the Kachari king and captured *Gourmā* with her baby the issue of the Kachari Raja. She was presented, to the Ahom king who, enamoured of her beauty, took her as his wife. Then the Ahoms continued war with Turbak for several years. They were not at first successful but at length the Bargohain visited Turbak in his camp on the false pretence of tendering submission and assassinated him. The Muslims were then defeated. At Kamatā Durlabhendra, the son of Sulochanā became king. He was killed by Fingua, a kinsman. Fingua defeated and killed Arimatta but Arimatta's son Ratna Singha defeated and killed Fingua. He then became king of Gauhati as well as Kamatāpur. He spared Suchāruchand, the son of Durlabhendra. The Ahom king then drove away Ratna Singha and placed Sachāruchand, on the throne of Kamatā.

The above account does not appear to be reliable because Turbak's invasion took place about 1532 when the Koch king Viswa Singha was ruling in Kāmarupa, whereas this account anetdates that invasion by nearly 50 years. The line of Kamatā kings came to an end after the sack of Kamatāpur by Sultan Alauddin Hussein Shah, towards the end of the fifteenth century. There is hardly any doubt that Durlabhanārāyan continued to rule till about the middle of the fourteenth century and that he was succeeded by his son Indranārāyan. On this point the testimony of a contemporary poet is much more reliable than a Buranji writen some centuries after. The story of *Gourmā* alias Suśudhi therefore appears to be a legend to which no historical importance can be attached. No such story is mentioned in the Ahom Buranji translated by Rai Sahib G. C. Barua. Durlabhendra Nārāyan was perhaps the same as Indranārāyan. It appears that the names of Durlabhnārāyan and his son Indranārāyan have been wrongly combined in Durlabhendranārāyan. Suchāruchand might have been the name of Indranārāyan's son. It seems that after Indranārāyan, the regular line ended and an era of upstarts and adventurers followed. Indranārāyan himself might have been deposed by such an adventurer. We are inclined to think that this usurper was no other than Arimatta *alias* Gajānka who, for a time, was contested by Fingua, a member of the family of Durlabhanārāyan. At length Fingua was vanquished and slain. Arimatta was succeeded by his son Ratnasingha *alias* Sukarānka who, in his turn, was succeeded by Sutarānka whose son was Mrigānka. It is said that Mrigānka, who was ruler over the whole kingdom as far as the Karatoyā, died without leaving any issue.

There are numerous conflicting legends concerning Arimatta. He is supposed to have been the son of a queen begotten on her by the river-god. The *Kâmarupar Buranji* makes him the descendant of Dharmapāla. This Dharmpāla may have been the same person known as Dharmanārāyan *alias* Dharmapāla. We know that Tāmradhvaj was the son of Dharmanārāyan. Arimatta may have been the son of Tāmradhvaj and therefore a nephew of Indranārāyan. One of the traditions mentioned by Gait makes him a descendant of one Tāmradhvaj. (1). According to Wade's account compiled in 1800 A. D., either from traditions or from written records, Arimatta defeated and killed the Raja of Kamatāpur named Durlabhendra and succeeded to the kingdom.* Then he killed Fingua Koar, a nephew of Durlabhendra and overthrew Rāmchandra, a local chief, who ruled somewhere in the modern district of Darrang.

---

(1) Gait's History of Assam, p 18, Footnote.

* According to traditions, incorporated in Wade's account, Durlabhendra, whom Arimatta slew, was the Raja of Behar (Cooch-Behar) and was known as Kamaleswara (perhaps Kamateswara or Kāmeswara). Having secured the throne of Durlabhendra Arimatta marched into Kamarupa and established his headquarters at Vaidyargarh where he erected a fort. Thence he removed to Pratappur, near Bishnath, and established his capital there. Sukaranka, the son of Arimatta, reigned there and died at Aswakranta in North-Gauhati. His son Sutaranka also reigned at Pratappur but Mriganka, the son of Sutaranka, was the king over the whole of Kamarupa as far as the Karatoya river on the west. It is also stated that Arimatta and his three successors ruled from 1238 A.D. to 1478 A.D. It is further added that when Mriganka died without a male issue the line of Arimatta became extinct and then the Bara-Bhuyans *commenced a new dynasty* of kings who became Rajas of the country.

This account would give 240 years for the reign of four monarchs which cannot obviously be accepted. When Mriganka died a new dynasty of kings originating from the Bhuyans began to rule. As we shall show later, this dynasty was the Khān dynasty founded by Niladhvaj which came to an end about 1498 A.D. Mriganka therefore died about 1440 A.D. and Arimata usurped the throne of Kamata about 1365 A.D., thus allowing 75 years for the reign of four kings of Arimatta's line. Anyway, this account makes Arimatta a king of Kamata though antedated, perhaps, by a century. It, however,

He was succeeded by Sukarānka, Sutarānka and. Mrigānka. When Mrigānka died without any issue the Bhuyans commenced a new dynasty and ruled the country and during their rule Hussein Shah invaded Kāmarupa. The probability is that Arimatta, who was probably the grandson of Dharmapāla *alias* Dharmanārāyan, usurped the throne of Kamatā either after the death of Indranārāyan or by deposing and killing him and that he subsequently subdued the local chiefs in eastern Kāmarupa who had previously thrown off the yoke of the Kāmata rule. He founded a dynasty in Kamatā which ended with Mrigānka before the middle of the fifteenth century. Another dynasty then ruled the kingdom and it was during the reign of a king of this dynasty that Hussein Shah invaded Kāmarupa about 1498 A. D. The tradition current in Assam that Arimatta killed his own father can perhaps be explained by the supposition that he deposed and killed Indranārāyan who was his uncle.

Curiously enough, we find the name of Arimatta

makes Pratappur the headquarters of all the kings of Arimatta's line. This is not quite probable because, as will be shown in chapter XI, the powerful Chutia kings were then ruling in north-eastern Assam. It is quite possible that Arimatta had his capital, for some time at least, in the modern Assam valley and that is why traditions about him are still extant in the Assam valley but his successors Sukaranka, Sutaranka and Mriganka are more or less unknown in the Assam valley. They were kings of Kamata who had but little influence over eastern Assam, though they were the western neighbours of the Chutia kings on the north and the Kacharis on the south of the Brahmaputra.

sought to be confirmed from another unexpected quarter. It is stated in the Kashmere chronicle that king Jayapida, grandson of Muktapida Lalitaditya, who overthrew Yasovarman of Kanauj in the eighth century, came as far as Pundravardhana and led an expedition against a neighbouring king of Nepal named Arimuri.* A writer in the Calcutta Review (1867) identified this Arimuri with Arimatta and thus placed him towards the close of the eighth century A. D. The following is a quotation from the Calcutta Review:—

"The Cashmerian prince advancing into the country, found Arimuri posted with his forces on the bank of a river. Excited with the hope of a speedy triumph, he plunged into the stream, but found, when it was too late, that he could not stem the current. Many of his soldiers followed him into the water and were drowned, and he, powerless to defend himself, was captured by a party of Arimuri's men who launched out into the torrent on inflated skins. He was confined in a strong castle on the banks of "Gondhica", the same river, in all probability, as the Gandak which, at that time, formed the western boundary of Kamarupa; whilst the remnant of his army returned in dismay to Cashmere. The tidings of this discomfiture and of the captivity of the king spread consternation throughout Cashmere. The ministers immediately met for deliberation, when one Deva Sarma undertook to effect the deliberation of the monarch.

---

* According to one account published by Gait, in his Report on Historical Research, Arimatta conquered a part of Nepal.

Proceeding with a considerable force into Assam and encamping his men on the banks of the river opposite to where the fort stood which held his master captive, he himself repaired to the court of Arimuri. At a private conference with the king, he intimated his readiness to give up to him the treasures of Joypira, which he represented to be with the invading army; but he at the same time intimated that as the amount and distribution of the money were known to the prince only, it would be neccessary for him, the minister, to have an interview with Joypira, and on some pretence or other elicit from him the required information. The artifice succeeded, and Deva Sarma was admitted into his master's presence. In the interview that followed, the minister urged Joypira to let himself down from the window of his prison and swim across the river to his troops, but the latter declined to make an attempt that must fail on account of the impetuosity of the torrent below. After some further discussion, the minister withdrew to an adjoining chamber, promising soon to return; but as a considerable interval elapsed and he did not reappear, the king went to seek him. He found him lying dead on the floor strangled by means of his own turban. Beside him lay a leaf on which he had scratched some words with his fingernail. In these words the devoted minister instructed Joypira to inflate his dead body and using it as a float to escape with all expedition to the opposite shore. Penetrated with admiration, at this proof of attachment Joypira hastened to obey his friend's counsel, and reached his troops in safety. Eager to wipe off his disgrace, he made a sudden attack upon Arimuri, slew him and left his country a depopulated waste."

Vincent Smith has considered Jayapida's visit to Pundravardhana and his alleged expedition against Arimuri as purely imaginary (1). Kahlan flourished in the eleventh century A. D. while Arimatta was probably ruling somewhere in Assam a century or two later. The identification of Arimuri (Aramudi according to Vincent Smith) with Arimatta seems therefore to be fanciful. In the genealogy of the kings of Kamarupa there is no room for Arimatta towards the close of the eighth or the beginning of the ninth century. There is however mention of Ārath (eldest son of Arathi) the elder brother of Prālambha who flourished about this time and who either succeeded his grandfather as king or was killed in battle before being installed as king. It is not probable that either Arathi or Arath was the same as Arimuri or Arimatta. Local traditions are almost unanimous that the Bhuyans ruled the country not very long after Arimatta who therefore must have flourished in the fourteenth century.* The Kamatā king who gave his daughter Bhajani to the Ahom king Sudangpha and sought his aid to drive out the Muslim invaders was very probably Sukarānka the son of Arimatta.

(1) Early History of India, p 387.

* In the quasi-historical *puthi* known as the *Hara Gauri Sambad* it is stated that after Mriganka's death petty kings ruled over every *mandala* of Kamarupa and that after these the Koch kings and the *Indra Vangshi* Ahom kings arose.

About the second quarter of the fifteenth century, after the death of Mrigānka, the ruling line of the Kamatā kings appears to have been supplanted by what is known as the Khān or Khen dynasty, the first king of which, Niladhvaj by name, occupied the throne of Kamatā probably about 1440 A.D. It is said that he imported Brahmans from Mithila and settled them in his kingdom. He is said to have rebuilt and strengthened the city of Kamatāpur. He was succeeded by his son, Chakradhvaj, who might have been the king who had encountered the general of Sultan Barbak and defeated him near Santosh. On his death his son, Nilambar, succeeded him. This king also appears to have been a powerful prince and his kingdom extended from the Karatoya to the Barnadi. It does not appear that the Ahoms came into conflict with him but he is said to have wrested a part of northern Bengal from the Mussalman rulers (1). It is also stated that he constructed a road from Kamatapur to Ghoraghat and also a fort at Ghoraghat. (2)

According to Buchanan Hamilton a young Brahman, the son of a councillor named Sachi Patra, had intrigues with Nilambar's wife. He was caught and secretly put to death. Nilambar then had a a part of the dead body cooked and invited Sachi Patra to dinner. The Brahman came on invitation and unwittingly ate of his son's flesh. After the repast the king related the whole story. The Brahman said that his son no doubt deserved punishment for his sin, but as he had been made to eat human

(1) Gait's History of Assam. p 44.
(2) Glazier's Report on Rangpur.

flesh, he must retire from the world and become a religious mendicant in other to expiate his sin. The king allowed him to depart from his kingdom. Sachi Patra went straight to Hussein Shah, the Sultan of Gaur, and invited him to attack Nilambar. Hussein Shah then led an armv against Nilambar in 1498 A.D. and invested Kamatapur which was strongly fortified. Nilambar held out for a long time and at length Hussein Shah reduced the capital by resorting to a stratagem. Nilambar escaped and fled towards the hills. After this some local chiefs named Rup Narayan, Ghosal Khan, Mal Kumar, and Lakshmi Narayan, who were probably Bhuyans, came and tendered their submission to Hussein Shah who then returned to Bengal leaving his son, Danial, with a strong force, to hold the conquered country. On his return to Gaur Hussein Shah struck coins in 1502 A.D. in which he is mentioned as "Conqueror of Kamru Kamata." In the meantine, after his departure from Kamata the rains set in. The Raja on getting information of Hussein Shah's departure came out of his hiding place, collected his forces and, attacking the Muslim garrison, put it to the sword.

This is the account given in the Muslim chronicles such as the *Riyaz-us-Salatin* and the *Tarikh-Fate-i-Assam* wherein the defeat and destruction of Danial and his garrison is clearly mentioned. It is possible that during the flight of Nilambar the Muhammadans pushed as far as the eastern limit of the then kingdom of Kamatā, but it is not likely that they came into conflict with the Ahoms as there is no mention in the *Buranjis* of any Muslim invasion into Assam prior to the year 1527 A.D. Although Hussein Shah's invasion of Kamata ultimately proved to be a failure it appears that a colony of Muhammadans remained in the country round about Hajo. A mosque was erected there by one Ghiyasuddin Aulia who subsequently died and was buried near the mosque. This place is still considered as sacred by local Muhammadans who regard it as "Poa Mecca" or "One-fourth of Mecca". After the overthrow of Nilambar the rule of the Kamata kings in Kamarupa came to an end. It is very likely that when Nilambar was overthrown, he fled and was heard of no more. Then the Bhuyan chiefs combined against the common foe and, taking advantage of the rains, attacked Danial's garrison and destroyed it. The Ahoms may have helped the Bhuyans in this enterprise but the Buranjis do not mention it.* As will be stated in a subsequent chapter, the first Koch king, Viswa Singha, ascended the throne adout 1515 A.D. after defeating all the Bhuyan chiefs. Some authorities hold the view that even after Danial's defeat the Muhammadans remained in power in western Kamarupa (1). This is not at all likely for Viswa Singha had not to contest with the Muhammadans, but with the local Bhuyans to secure supremacy

* A writer in the Calcutta Review (1867), vol. XIV stated that Hussein's march into Assam did not extend beyond Tezpur and though he succeeded in demolishing the capital he was ultimately repulsed by the Bara Bhuyans. Danial was called "Dalal Ghazi" in the local Assam chronicles to which reference is made by Buchanan (J.A.S.B. 1874 p 281).

(1) Moghul North East Frontier Policy pp 76-77 (Footnote)

over the whole of Kamarupa. Danial was probably defeated and killed about 1503 A.D.* After that the next Muslim invasion of Kamarupa occured in 1527 A.D. when Viswa Singha was the reigning king of Kamarupa. It appears that this was an expedition along the south bank of the Brahmaputra and the line of march did not lie through northern Kamarupa where Viswa Singha had his capital. This expedition was therefore repulsed by the Ahoms.

It is true that Niladhvaj and his successors are not mentioned either in the *Guru Charitra* or in any of the local contemporary writings now extant in the Assam Valley. Perhaps these kings did not exercise any real authority over the eastern part of Kāmarupa where the Bhuyans were ruling and that accounts for the absence of any mention of them in Assamese chronicles. Buchanan-Hamilton, however, found strong traditions regarding these kings current in Jalpaiguri, Cooch-Behar and Rangpur which formed the western part of Kāmarupa and which constituted Kamatā proper. The accounts of these kings given byGlazier and by Rai Bahadur

* Danial is said to have been succeeded in Kamarupa by Musundar Ghazi who, in his turn, is said to have been succeeded by Sultan Ghiyasuddin. The *Kamarupar Buranji* states that Ghiyasuddin came to Kamarupa as the commander of Hussein Shah with 12 000 horsemen and 13 000 Turkish foot soldiers and that the Bhuyans were then ruling the country. This also supports our view that after the fall of Nilambar the Bhuyans joined and expelled the remnant of Hussain's army of occupation in Kamarupa before Viswa Singha came to power. The Mussalmans therefore occupied the country, round Hajo, only for a few years.

Gunabhiran Barua are no doubt based on Buchanan Hamilton's account. Sir Edward Gait has accepted these accounts as correct. It appears that even the Assamese Buranji known as "*Swarganārāyan Mahārājar Janma charitra*" makes mention of one Nilāmbar, as priest of the Kamatā king, and of a dish of cooked human flesh which the Kamatā king made one of his officers to eat and in consequence of which the disgusted officer went to the Muhammadan Sultan and invited him to invade Kamatā. This mention in the Assamese Buranji rather indirectly supports the truth of the tradition collected by Buchanan-Hamilton. We need not try to find out how Niladhvaj came to occupy the throne of Kamāta. He was no doubt an upstart and adventurer. He usurped the throne when Mrigānka, the last king of the line of Arimatta, died without leaving any issue and assumed the name Niladhvaj. In all probability he was a Kayastha Bhuyan having the surname Khān. We know that several of the Kāmarupi Bhuyans had this surname. One of the Bhuyan chiefs who submitted to Hussein Shah, after the flight of Nilāmbar was Ghosal Khān and a relative of Śrí Śankar Deva was named Buda Khān and another was named Ketai Khān. The chief minister of Hussein Shah himself was a Kayastha named Purandar Khān (1). It seems that the surname Khān was used to indicate a noble lineage.

Kamatāpur which was the captial of the kingdom from the middle of the thirteenth till the first

(1.) Memoirs of Gaur and Pandua, edited by Stapleton p 34.

quarter of the sixteenth century appears to have been a city of considerable size. The following description of the ruins of the city is given in the "Cooch-Behar State" by H. N. Chaudhuri:-

"The remains of the city of Kāmatāpur are gigantic works of human art and bespeak great power and wealth in the Prince or Princes who conceived such an idea of a capital. The city was of a triangular shape, long from east to west, with a perimeter of about 20 miles. The two sides of this triangle met in the west, and were defended by a high rampart, protected by an inner ditch and an outer moat, and covering a length of about 15 miles, while the old Dharla formed the base about 5 miles long and protected in the east from foreign invasion. There were two redoubts, one towards the north-east and the other towards the north-west. The rampart was pierced by four gates of huge proportions, in the north, south and west. The northern gate was called the Hoko-duar. The sides of the rampart here at the gate-way were faced with bricks in mortar, which are still in good condition. The gate in the south was called the Sil-duar or stone-gate, and it cut the rampart in an S curve... It is said that the rampart at this gate-way was lined with stones, and that the gate had a door-way of stone. Several large slabs of granite are still lying in it and a few are yet standing. From this gate issued a high embanked road, which at the time marked the southern boundary of old Kamarupa".*

* A good description of the ruins of Kamatapur is to be found in the Assam Sahitya Sabha Patrika vol II No. 4 pp 209-215. It appears that this city continued to be the abode of learned men. This is proved by the

We may now attempt to prepare a chronological list of the Kamatā kings from the middle of the thirteenth century. We get the names of the kings from Sandhyā to Durlabhnārāyan from the *Guru Charitra* by Ramcharan Thakur. We get the name of Indranārāyan from a contemporary writer Kaviratna Saraswati. After Indranārāyan we get no authentic account of the Kamatā kings. It seems that the throne was occupied by one usurper after another and that one of them, Arimatta, established himself as king and founded a dynasty which ended with Mrigānka. Niladhvaj, who was probably a Bhuyan chief having the surname Khān, then became king. The approximate chronology from Indranārayan to Nilāmbar is shown below:-

Name of king.	*Approximate reign.*
Indranarayan	1350-1365
Arimatta (of the line of Dharmanarayan)	1365-1385
I	
Sukaranka	1385-1400
I	
Sutaranka	1400-1415
I	
Mriganka	1415-1440
Niladhvaj (Khān dynasty)	1440-1460
I	
Chakradhvaj	1460-1480
I	
Nilambar	1480-1498

---

reference to this city by Pitambar Dasa, a poet who according to his own statment wrote in the Saka year *rasa vana veda chandra* i e 1456 Saka equivalent to 1534 A.D. when the first Koch King Viswa Singha must have been ruling in Cooch Behar. Pitambar wrote that it was the *avatar* of the temple of Kamateswara Siva and the poet meant that the god Siva actually lived there.

CHAPTER XI.

THE CHUTIA KINGDOM.

It is believed that the Chutia kingdom was founded towards the end of the thirteenth century when the Kamarupa kings lost their hold over the eastern part of the kingdom and the capital was transfered to Kamatapur. It is further supposed that prior to the rise of this kingdom a Hindu dynasty ruled, probably over a small tract round about Sadiya. This dynasty claimed descent from Bhismak the father of Rukmini, one of the wives of Śri Krishna. It is stated that this kingdom was known as Vidarbha and that the capital was at Kundil standing on the river of the same name. It may have been another small pre-Aryan, possibly Dravidian, kingdom which was, in course of time, wiped out by Mongoloid invaders. Gait supposes that this dynasty collapsed by a process of internal decay and that on the ruins of this old kingdom the Chutia kingdom was subsequently built.

The old ruins round about Sadiya were described by Hannay in 1848. The fortifications found by him were ascribed to Bhismak. Dalton described, in the Calcutta Review, other forifications in a jungle along the banks of the Burai river in the Darrang district. Photographs of these were subsequently published by Edwards and Mann in 1903 (1). Curiously enough, these fortifications are assigned by local tradition to Arimatta who has been referred to in the previous chapter. The fortifications on the banks of the Burai river included two stone walls made of chisseled sand-stone blocks put together with great precision. A large number of these stones were found to contain marks, cut deeply into the sand-stone. Messrs Edwards and Mann took them to be builders' marks, but it is interesting that identical marks were found also in the marked stones found by Hannay in the fort near Sadiya assigned to Bhismak. It is therefore evident that the ruins near Sadiya and those on the banks of the Burai river can be assigned to the same period which cannot be prehistoric, since one set of ruins is connected by tradition with Arimatta. The probability is that these ruins are the traces of a Hindu or Hinduized dynasty of local rulers who ruled over a small kingdom confined to the north bank of the Brahmaputra and extending from the Burai river on the west to Sadiya on the east.

The dynasty is evidently the line of Chutia

(1) J.A.S.B. (1904) pp. 254-261.

kings who assumed the surname Pala, in imitation of the Kamarupa kings of the dynasty of Brahmapala. There are several accounts and chronological lists of these kings. One of them is given in an appendix to Brown's Deori-Chutia grammar and two are published in the *Deodhai Assam Buranji* as miscellaneous historical accounts. Like the Ahom kings and the Koch kings the Chutia kings also claimed divine origin. It is narrated that one Birpal *alias* Birbar who belonged to the line of Bhismak was a petty king ruling at Sonagiri. His queen Rupavati worshipped the Hindu god Kuvera, the God of Wealth, in order to be blessed with a son. One day Kuvera assumed the shape of Birpal and had sexual intercourse with Rupavati. Birpal then had a dream in which the god Kuvera asked him to go to a particular tree where certain articles would be found and which should be treasured and worshipped. According to the directions given in the dream Birpal went to the tree and found underneath it a sword, a shield and a gold cat covered by the shield. In course of time his queen Rupavati give birth to a son, the offspring of Kuvera. This son was named Gaurinarayan. It is stated that subsequently Gaurinarayan succeeded his father and became king in the year 1146 Saka corresponding to 1244 A.D. (1) assuming the name Ratnadhvaj Pala*

(1) *Deodhai Buranji*, p. 182.

* It seems that the words "dhvaj" and "narayan" were favourite appendages to names of princes and nobles of north-eastern India between the thirteenth

The genealogy of the Chutia kings as given by Kellner in the appendix to Brown's book and that published in the *Deodhai Buranji* agree with each other. It is shown below:—

Ratnadhvaj Pāla	*alias*	Gaurinārāyan
Vijayadhvaj Pāla	"	Sivanarayan
Vikramadhvaj Pāla	"	Jagatnārāyan
Garudadhvaj Pāla	"	Pramathnārāyan
Hangshadhvaj Pāla	"	Harinārāyan
Mathuradhvaj Pāla	"	Goloknārāyan
Jayadhvaj Pāla	"	Brajanārāyan
Karmadhvaj Pāla	"	Satyanārāyan
Dharmadhvaj Pāla	"	Dhirnārāyan
Niti Pāla	"	Sadhaknārāyan

It is found from the Ahom Burajnis that Dharmadhvaj *alias* Dhirnarayan was a contemporary of Suhunmung, the Dehingia Raja and that he invaded the Ahom territories in 1513 A.D. (1) We can therefore easily place Ratnadhvaj Pala in the middle of the thirteenth century as stated in the account incorporated in the *Deodhai Buranji*. It is said that after subduing a king named Bhadrasen Ratnadhvaj founded a city and named it

and the sixteenth centuries just as the surname "Pala" was fashionable in the previous age and the surname "Varman" was popular in a still earler age. Singhadhvaj, Pratapadhvaj, Tamradhvaj, Niladhvaj and Chakradhvaj were all Kamata princes between the thirteenth and the fifteenth centuries. Dharmanarayan, Durlabh narayan and Indranarayan were Kamata princes of the fourteenth century and Swargananararayan was the Ahom king towards the end of the fifteenth century. The Chutia kings used all the three surnames "Dhvaj", "Narayan" and "Pala", the last perhaps, in imitation of the defunct Pala rulers of Kamarupa.

(1) Gait's History of Assam.

Ratnapur. Then he received the submission of another local ruler named Nyāyāpala who gave his daughter to him. Ratnadhvaj now became powerful and demanded a daughter from the king of Kamata. The latter having refused the demand Ratnadhvaj prepared for war and marched upon Kamatapur (1). The Raja of Kamata then came to terms and presented a princess to Ratnadhvaj(2). It is stated that after this Ratnadhvaj grew more ambitious and, advancing towards Gaur, sent an envoy to the Bengal Sultan (Gaur Badshah) and established friendship with him. It is stated in one account that Ratnadhvaj sent his minister Vijayasena with presents to the Sultan who in his turn sent his great "uzir" with presents for the Chutia king (3). About this time the Bengal Sultan was Jalaluddin Masud Malik Jani. We do not find any mention of such exchange of presents in the acconnt of the Muslim historians. The accuracy of the statement published in the *Deodhai Buranji* is open to serious doubt since the Sultan is said to have agreed to forward to the Chutia king, regularly, water of the holy Ganges and asked the latter to forward to him regularly water of the Parsuram Kund. Evidently the Sultan did not regard the water of the Parsuram Kund as sacred. The story that Ratnadhvaj and the Sultan of Bengal exchanged presents is perhaps a myth. It is further said that a son of Ratnadhvaj was kept in Bengal with Gaudeswara for study. This prince died in

---

(1) Deodhai Buranji, p 180.
(2) Ibid.
(3) Ibid.

Bengal and Gaudeswara not knowing how the Chutia kings disposed of their dead sent the corpse to Ratnadhvaj who was then building a palace at *Sindhukshetra.* As the corpse was received by him there the city was named Sa-diya (place where the corpse was given (1). It is possible that Ratnadhvaj had hostilities with the Kamata king of the time who was perhaps Sindhu Rai. Ratnadhvaj died at Sadiya and was succeeded by his son Sivanarayan *alias* Vijayadhvaj.

It appeaas that during the first quarter of the fourteenth century the Ahom king fought with the Kamatā king, probably Pratāpadhvaj, but did not dare to attack the Chutia king who was powerful. Towards the middle of that century however the Ahoms came into conflict with the Chutias. At length in 1376 A.D. there was a reconciliation. The Chutia king paid a visit to the Ahom king Sutuphā and invited the latter to witness a boat race. When Sutuphā came to attend the regatta he was treacherously murdered. Sutuphā was succeeded, after an interregnum, by Tyao Khamti who marched against the Chutias and chastised them. After this there was no further hostilities between the Ahoms and the Chutias till the reign of Dharmadhvaj alias Dhirnārāyan who in 1513 A.D. is said to have invaded the Ahom territories with a flotilla of boats but was repulsed by the Ahoms at Dikhoomukh. Warfare continued till 1523 A.D. when the Ahom king Suhunmung, who personally conducted the operations, defeated the Chutias who then sued for peace. Suhunmung

(1) Deodhai Buranji p 182.

demanded the gold cat which was the heirloom of the Chutia kings. As this demand was not complied with hostilities were resumed. The Chutias bravely defended position after position and at length occupied an almost impregnable hill with a precipitous frontage. The Ahoms ascended the hill holding on to creepers and surprised the Chutias who fled and took their last stand at a place called Mathadang. Here a severe engagement took place in which the Chutia king and his eldest son were killed. The principal queen then committed suicide. The youngest son Sādhaknārāyan, who was then an infant, was spared by the Ahoms. The whole of the Chutia country was then annexed to the Ahom kingdom and to administer this tract the Sadiyā khoā Gohāin was appointed. This conquest was regarded as a great triumph and Suhunmung performed the *Rikhvan* ceremony.

The Chutias were originally a tribe of the Bodo race. Their kings being Hinduized accepted the Tantrik faith. Their tutelary goddess was known as *Kesāikhāti* as human sacrifices were offered to her. The deity was known also as *Tāmeswari Mai* as the idol was placed in a building having a roof made of copper-sheets. According to Dalton's note recorded in 1848 A.D, the ruins of the temple existed till that year and the copper roof was then lying on the ground. The building was of stone blocks joined together by iron pins and the interior was only eight feet square. The enclosure of brick walls measured 130 by 200 ft. Dalton wrote that human sacrifices were yearly offered " till a very recent date".

CHAPTER XII.

THE RULE OF THE BHUYANS.

With the death or flight of Nilāmbar ended the line of the kings of Kamatā who ruled over the western part of the old kingdom of Kāmarupa. As a matter of fact these Kamatā kings exercised only nominal authority over the modern districts of Goalpara and Kamrup which now constitute the western part of the Assam Valley. That is the reason for the scantness of the traditions about these kings in the modern Assam Valley. As already stated, probably since the transfer of the capital to Kamatāpur the actual government of eastern Kāmarupa, as far as the Subansiri in the north and the Kapili on the south, was in the hands of petty Bhuyan chiefs who were nominally feudatories of the kings of Kamatā or Kāmarupa but who were actually independent chiefs. As correctly stated by Gait, each chief was "independent of the others within his own domain, but they seem to have been in the habit of joining their forces whenever they were threatened by a common enemy". (1)

As stated by Gait the term "Bhuyān" had nothing to do with caste. It meant the "lord of the land". Śri Śankar Dev himself used the word "Bhowmik" as a synonymn of the term "Bhuyan" (2). The Bhuyans were therefore petty chiefs exercising practically regal authority over small tracts. When the central authority of the kings of Kāmarupa were strong these Bhuyans were feudal lords over *Vishayas* or districts. When this central authority grew weak the Bhuyans became the rulers. Each Bhuyan chief was the administrative and judicial head of a particular tract. Each had a court, called *Karkhana*, a Persian word meaning literally a house for work, where he performed magisterial duties, perhaps assisted by a *Punchayat*. There is every reason to suppose that their rule was just and mild. It is stated that after the Muslims set up their rule in Gaur many Hindus of that area migrated into Kamarupa. The period of the Bhuyan rule in Kāmarupa cannot therefore be regarded as a period of anarchy.

As already stated, these chiefs, though independent of one another, occasionally combined. Usually some of them within a specified area always combined to form a confederacy and the leader of such a confederacy was known as *Gāmathā*, the Kamarupi equivalent of the Persian

---

(1) Gait's History of Assam p. 38.
(2) Bhāgavata, Chapter X by Sri Śankar Deva.

word *gomasta* meaning an agent. When a common enemy, such as a Muslim invader, appeared all the Bhuyan chiefs combined and joined their forces. Durlabhnārāyan, who was a powerful and resourceful ruler, was probably the only king of Kamatā who was acknowledged as the sovereign over all the Bhuyans of the eastern part of Kamarupa. After him Arimatta had to fight against several Bhuyan chiefs or petty kings of eastern Kāmarupa in order to subdue them. The kings of the Khan dynasty, who were actually Bhuyans using the Persian surname "Khan" to denote noble birth, probably exercised no authority over the modern districts of Goalpara and Kamrup and hence they are unknown in the local traditions. When Hussein Shah overthrew the last king of this line he received the submission of the more prominent Bhuyan chiefs but when he left Kāmarupa leaving his son Danial to consolidate the conquered country, the Bhuyan chiefs again combined and drove out the Muslims who had temporarily occupied the country.

It is a mistake to suppose that the Bhuyan chiefs originated with the seven families of Brahmans and the seven families of Kayasthas whom Durlabhnārāyan settled in Kāmarupa with the *Siromoni* Bhuyan Chandidar, as the leader of them all, about the year 1330. It is true that it is stated that the Bhuyans came into existence in 1236 Saka equivalent to 1314 A. D. This is about the time of Durlabhnārāyan's accession to the throne or a few years earlier and therefore the origin of the Bhuyans was dated from the settlement of the Kayastha and Brahman families under the leadership of Chandidar in eastern Kāmarupa. We, however, find, from the Rautkuchi grant of Purusottam Dasa recorded in the year 1329 A. D. that his father Jayadeva and his grandfather Vāsudeva were also feudal lords or Bhuyan chiefs under the kings of Kamatā. It would therefore be more correct to suppose that the Bhuyan chiefs became prominent in Eastern Kāmarupa after the transfer of the Kāmarupa capital from North Gauhati to Kamatāpur about the middle of the thirteenth century. As already stated, the Bhuyans were not confined to Kayasthas and Brahmans. According to the author of the *Darrang Rāj Vansāvali* there were Bhuyan chiefs who were Ganaks by caste and who flourished about the beginning of the sixteenth century before the rise of the Koch king Viswa Singha. We do not find that Durlabhrārāyan settled any Ganak or Daibagna family in Eastern Kāmarupa.

The Bhuyans of the Eastern Assam valley claimed a different origin. They traced their descent from Sāntanu and Sāmanta the two grandsons of Samudra who was the minister of Arimatta. It is said that Sāntanu was a *Vaisnava* while Samanta was a *Sākta.* The descendants of Sāntanu settled in the Nowgong district while the descendants of Sāmanta remained in Lakshimpur which was named after Lakshmi the mother of Sāntanu and Sāmanta. It is said that one of Sāntanu's descendants was Rājdhar, the grandfather of Śri Śankar Deva. This genealogy of Śri Śankar Deva is no doubt incorrect and that given in the *Guru Charitra* is the correct one but it is clear that the Bhuyans cannot be restricted to the descendants of the families of Kayasthas and Brahmans settled by Durlabhnārāyan.

According to the *Guru Charitra* or the life of Śri Śankar Deva the seven Kayasthas settled by Durlabhnārāyan were Śrihari, Śripati, Śridhara, Chidananda, Sadananda, Hari and Chandivara. It is said that five other families of Kayasthas accompanied the seven Kayastha families to eastern Kamarupa. The headmen of these five families were Gandharva Bhuyan, Śripati Datta, Bura Khān, Lohavara and Chanu Giri (1). The seven Brahmans were Krishna Pandit, Raghupati, Rāmavara, Lohara, Bayana, Dharam and Mathurā. According to the *Gamatha Vansavali* quoted in the "Social History of Kamarupa" these Bhuyans were originally in Kanauj. When the Muslims occupied that country and began to kill cows and Brahmans, they migrated to Gaur. There also the Muslims followed them and committed atrocities on the Hindus. The Bhuyans then removed themselves to Kamatā and settled there. There they combined and successfully resisted the Muslims. They elected a Śiromani Bhuyan among themselves and followed his lead in war. Each Bhuyan was a petty king, but the *Gāmatha* was the chief of all. It is also stated that the Bhuyans excelled both in fighting and writing (*Asi mosi ubhaye lāgata*). This migration of leading Hindu families from Gaur into Kamarupa is corroborated from Muslim sources. According to the *Tabaquat-i-Nasiri* when Mahammad, son of Bukhtiyar, first invaded Bengal, a considerable number of Brahmans and other

(1) Social History of Kamarupa vol. II p 8.

Hindus fled into Kamrud, Bang and Sankanat (Jagannath or Orrisa) (1). The actual fact, therefore, was that in order to escape from Muslim persecution many families of Brahmans and Kayasthas from Gaur sought refuge in Kāmarupa when the Kamatā kings were ruling. A number of them were recent settlers in Gaur. They had migrated into Gaur from Kanauj, probably towards the end of the twelfth century. In the beginning of the thirteenth century Gaur was also conquered by the Muslims. Then these immigrants from Kanauj again moved into Kāmarupa where they settled in a place which they named Kanaujpur and which was near Kamatāpur.**

It appears that during Durlabhnārāyan's reign some families of this colony were settled by him in Eastern Kāmarupa where the authority of the Kamatā kings were getting weaker and weaker and where the mountain tribes of Bhutan were incessantly making raids. This is how Chandibor and his associates, mentioned in the *Guru Charitra*, came to be settled within modern Assam in the fourteenth century. The story that they were sent to Kāmarupa by the Gaudeswara at the request of the king of Kāmarupa seems to be a myth.

On the death or overthrow of Indranārāyan, the

(1) *Tabaqat-i-Nasiri vol. I p 557.*

** That the Bhuyans who settled at Kanaujpur had to fight with the Muslims is stated also in the *Guru Charitra* of Ramcharan Thakur. Landa deva the father of Chandibar was one of the Bhuyans who, under orders of the Gaudeswara (title assumed by the Kamata king), fought with the Muslims.

son of Durlabhnārāyan, there was anarchy for some time and during this opportunity the petty Bhuyan chiefs of Eastern Kāmarupa again raised their heads and became independent. At length Arrimatta established his rule in Kamata and toured through eastern Kāmarupa subjugating all petty kings. It is quite possible that, for better administration, he established his capital, at least temporarily, somewhere within modern Assam. That is why there are so many traditions about him in Assam down to this day. When he died his descendants ruled at Kamatāpur and none of them seems to have exercised any real authority over Eastern Assam. When Mrigānka died without any issue the throne was seized by an adventurous Bhuyan chief who had the surname Khān but who on becoming king assumed the name Niladhvaj. He was very likely a Kayastha like Purandar Khan, the Kayastha chief minister of Sultan Alauddin Hussein Shah and Bura Khan, one of the associates of Chandibor, in the previous century. Chakradhvaj the son of Niladhvaj and Nilambar the grandson of Niladhvaj were both powerful and capable monarchs, but these kings also exercised no real authority over Eastern Kāmarupa. Towards the end of the fifteenth century Sultan Alauddin Hussein Shah invaded Kamatā and after encountering stubborn resistance at length overthrew Nilāmbar who fled to the hills and was heard of no more. When a few years later Danial and the Muslim garrison were put to the sword the Bhuyan chiefs, who by combination among themselves had brought about this result, again became independent and ruled the country.

CHAPTER XIII.

THE KOCH KINGDOM.

It seems certain that after the death of Nilambar, the last powerful king of Kamata, about the end of the fifteenth century, a sort of *Matsyanyaya* prevailed in Kamarupa. The country was ruled by a number of petty Bhuyan chiefs. This state of things could not naturally continue for a long time. Ultimately a leader appeared who raised his head above all the other petty chiefs and gradually subjugated them all. This was Bisu, the son of Haria Mandal, who subsequently became king and assumed the name of Viswa Singha.

Bisu had a very humble origin. His father, Haria Mandal, was only the mandal or headman of a village consisting of twelve other Koch families. The leading men of these families were Panbar, Phedela, Phedphedo, Barihana, Kathia, Guabar, Megha, Baisagu, Jagai, Gurikata, Jugbar and Dakharu. Haria married Hira and Jira, the two daughters of one Haju. Bisu was the son of Hira and Sisu was the son of Jira. Bisu was probably a young man when Hussein Shah invaded Kamatapur and put Nilambar to flight. It appears that some years after Nilambar's overthrow Haria Mandal came into conflict with the Bhuyan chief of Phulguri. He was subdued and taken as a captive but was released on his promise to pay tribute. Bisu saw his father humbled and resolved to take revenge. He gathered together a number of followers and attacked the Phulguri Bhuyan but was defeated. This did not however damp his spirits. Subsequently he with some followers again approached Phulguri. This time bidding his followers to remain concealed he himself alone entered the city at night and stole into the apartments of the Bhuyan. There he killed the Bhuyan chief and at once gave a signal to his followers who then rushed in and occupied the city. After this Bisu grew more powerful and collecting more followers challenged and defeated a confederacy of some of the Bhuyan chiefs headed by the Bhuyan of Karnapur. According to the *Darrang Raj Vansavali*, written by Suryakhari, the Bhuyans subdued by Bisu were Bar Bhuyan and Saru Bhuyan who were both Brahmans the Bhuyan of Owguri who was also a Brahman, Chuti Bhuyan who was a Doibogna, Kusum Bhuyan, Dighola Bhuyan, Kolia Bhuyan, Jargoya Bhuyan, Kavilash Bhuyan and the Karnapur Bhuyan. Next he defeated the Bhuyan of Bijni and thereafter came into conflict with Pratap Rai, the Bhuyan of Pandu. Finding Pratap Rai too powerful he avoided an open fight but, lying in ambush, first killed Pratap's brother while the latter was bathing in the Brahmaputra. This sudden assasination unnerved Pratap Rai who, not knowing the strength of Bisu's following, at once fled and took refuge in the Ahom kingdom. Bisu then conquered the whole of the southern portion of Kamrup as far as Gauhati after defeating Charu Bhuyan.

Bisu now turned his attention to the Bhuyans of the north bank. They were the Bhuyans of Bajali, Kshetri and Baushi under the leadership of Narayana Bhuyan who was the Gamatha or head-Bhuyan. These Bhuyans were not in good terms with Charu Bhuyan who had therefore become an ally of Bisu. Bisu with the help of Charu Bhuyan attacked the Bhuyans of northern Kamrup but the resistance was stubborn and determined. Finding no other way of overcoming such strong resistance Bisu had recourse to strategy and opened secret negotiations with the Bhuyans subordinate to Narayana. He succeeded in alienating Gandharva Bhuyan of Baushi from Narayana's cause and ultimately crushed all the Bhuyans one by one.

Having thus cleared all obstacles from his way Bisu now proclaimed himself as King at Kamatapur. According to Gait Bisu was installed as king about 1515 A. D. but Mr. Bhattacharya holds that he could not have ascended the throne before 1529-30. He argues that Narnarayana's earliest coins are dated 1477 Saka equivalent to 1555 A. D. and this was probably the date of his accession (1). As Viswasingha reigned for 25 years his accession may therefore be placed about 1530. This would lengthen the period of the anarchy in Kamarupa for nearly 30 years to render plausible Mr. Bhattacharya's theory that even after the defeat of Danial the Muslims loitered in Kamarupa. His supposition that Naranarayan struck coins on the year of his accession is however open to serious doubts. The

(1) Moghul North-East frontier Policy, p. 77.

minting of coins was introduced by him first and it is hardly possible that he struck coins as soon as he occupied the throne. We would therefore accept Gait's chronology and place Viswasingha's accession about 1515. A. D. and that of Narnarayan about 1540. A. D.

It appears from the Behula Upakhyan that on becoming king Bisu was called Lord of Kamata or Kamateswar. He assumed the name Viswa Singha and subsequently removed his capital to Koch Bihar where he built a fine city. Brahman courtiers now thronged round him and extolled him as a Kshatriya. A powerful king must have a Kshatriya origin and so they invented the origin in this wise:- "There was a powerful king of the lunar dynasty called Sahasrarjuna who went out hunting one day with a contingent of soldiers and in the evening became the guest of Jamadagni Rishi, the father of of Parasurama. The Rishi with the help of Kamadhenu, the fabulous cow that could grant any prayer, gave the monarch a royal reception befitting his dignity. Sahasrarjuna asked Jamadagni for Kamadhenu, saying that such a cow was more suited for a royal palace than a Rishi's hermitage. Jamadagni having refused to part with the cow the king took it by force and Parasuram who was then away from home, having on return learnt the discomfiture of his father, went to Sahasrarjuna and fought with him and returned home triumphantly with the cow, after having beheaded the king. The sons of Sahasrarjuna, with a view to retaliate for their father's death, came surreptitiously and cut off the head of Jamadagni when he was absorbed in deep meditation, taking advantage of Parasurama's absence from home on a pilgrimmage. Parasuram, on his return, heard the death of his father and took a vow to make the world bereft of all Kshattriyas. He led a crusade against all Kshattriyas in general and the sons of Sahasrarjuna in particular and massacred all the sons of that king except twelve who saved themselves by taking refuge in the jungles of Assam concealing their identity by adopting Mech manners and customs and by marrying Mech girls"(1). The Kshatriya origin of Bisu was thus established, but that was not enough. A king must have also a divine origin. The ancient kings of Kamarupa were descended from the Primeval Boar, an incarnation of Vishnu. For the Ahom kings, who had then established themselves in eastern Assam, a descent from Indra had been invented. There was the God Śiva handy enough to be turned into the progenitor of Bisu. It was then narrated that one day while Haria Mandal was working on his field his wife Hira was carrying food for him. Śiva, enamoured of her beauty, then took the form of her husband and had sexual intercourse with her, the result of the union being Bisu. He was named Bisu as he was born on the Bihu day (*Visuva Sankranti*).

Viswa Singha was very generous towards the Brahmans who thus obliged him. He rebuilt the temple of Kamateswari which the Mussalmans had demolished. He imported several families of Brahmans from Kanauj and other places of northern

(2) Darrang Raj Vansavali by Pundit Hem Chandra Goswami in the Annual Report of the Kamarupa Anusandhan Samiti (1920).

India and sent his sons Malla Deva and Sukladhvaj for study in Benares. He also organized his army appointing military officers of various grades. He attempted to invade Saumara, the Ahom kingdom, but his attempt failed owing to bad communications and the difficulty of obtaining supplies. During his reign in 1527 A.D. the Mussalmans invaded Assam, but this invasion was, as already stated, resisted by the Ahoms. The theory that the Muslim attack was organized by some local Muhammadan chiefs is untenable as Viswa Singha had then thoroughly consolidated his power over entire Kamarupa. There is hardly any doubt that the invasion proceeded from eastern Bengal, probably from the direction of Mymensingh. The Muslim commander was known as the Uzir. Mr. Bhattacharya indentifies him with Rukunudin Ruku Khan who was the Wazir and general of Hussein Shah(1). It appears that the Muslims had advanced far into Ahom territory where the Ahoms attacked them both in front and on both flanks and defeated them. According to Wade's account the Uzir, after his defeat, returned to Bengal. It appears that after his defeat Uzir first fell back on the Burai river, the Ahoms capturing forty horses and twenty guns (2). The Ahom king then despatched another force to capture Uzir who on getting this information fled to Bengal (3). The Bengal Sultan then despatched his general Mit Manik, also called Bit Manik, with an army of one thousand horse and ten thousand foot to assist Uzir. It appears that Uzir

(1) Moghul North-Est Frontier Policy, p 86.
(2) Deodhai Assam Buranji p 21.
(3) Ibid p 22.

advanced by boats up the Brahmaputra while Bit Manik marched by road and both attacked the forces of the Barpatra Gohain (1). The Muslim forces having advanced the Ahoms met them at Temani where a great battle was fought. Mit Manik who was riding an elephant, was wounded and fell to the ground and was taken prisoner*. The Uzir fled on horse back. It is stated in Wade's account that 1060 Muslim soldiers and 20 horses were killed while only 100 Ahom soldiers were killed. The Muslim troops fled precipitously. According to Wade, the Saleng Barua while according to the Buranji Shenlung (the Barpatra Gohain) pursued the fugitives and captured a large booty including some firearms. In 1532 A. D. the Muhammadans under Turbak again invaded Assam reaching the Ahom fort at Singri. This expedition also appears to have proceeded along the bank of the Brahmaputra. At first the Muhammadans who were using guns and cannons were successful because these weapons were till then almost unknown to the Ahoms. In the first encounter the Ahoms lost about 1300 soldiers killed in battle including Prusengmung Gohain. According to Wade's account the widow of this Gohain, on receiving news that her husband had fallen, came herself to fight and fell fighting in the thick of the battle. The Ahoms then retreated to Sala. There also they were defeated and their elephants thrown

(1) Deodhai Assam Buranji p 27.

* It is stated in the Ahom Buranji translated by Rai Sahib G. C. Barua that the Barpatra Gohain killed Meet Manik or Bit Malik with his sword.

into confusion by the Muslim artillery. In 1533 however the Ahoms gained a decisive naval victory at Duimunisila, the invaders sustaining heavy losses. Then Turbak was re-inforced by Hussein Khan but the Ahoms again defeated them in a series of engagements. The last battle was fought near the Bharali river where Turbak was slain. The Muslim troops then fled being hotly pursued by the Ahoms. During the pursuit Hussein Khan was also killed. The Ahoms under the Barpatra Gohain pursued the Muhammadans as far as the Karatoya evidently through the Koch kingdom, but Viswa Singha wisely did not interfere in the pursuit. If he had embroiled himself in the war, perhaps he would have weakened himself and his army and it would not have been possible for his sons Malladev and Chilarai to attain to the military greatness which they did after his death. He died about 1540 A.D. leaving as many as eighteen sons. It is stated in the *Darrang Raj Vansavali* that as the result of a Brahman's curse Viswasingha developed fever after which *Barkhasu* or big erruptions appeared on his body and subsequently he died. There is hardly any doubt that he contracted small-pox to which his son, Chilarai, also succumbed. In the Guru Charitra also we find mention of *Barkhasu* or small-pox. It was evidently a dreadful pestilence in Assam in the old days. Two of the sons of Vyaskalai Bapoo, a Brahman follower of Śankar Dev, died of *Barkhasu*. When his second son contracted the disease the Brahman, to save his son, secretly worshipped the Goddess, Śitala. On knowing this Śankar Dev turned out the Brahman from his camp.

At the time of Viswa Singha's death the heir-apparent, Malladeva and his brother Sukladhvaj were studying in Benares. It appears that taking advantage of their absence the third brother Nara Singha occupied the throne. On getting this information Malladeva and Sukladhvaj hastened from Benares. Either they fought with Nara Singha and defeated him or on their approach Nara Singha fled towards Bhutan and was heard of no more. It is said that he ruled over a part of Bhutan but this is not probable.

On ascending the throne Malladeva assumed the name of Narnārāyan and appointed his brother, Sukladhvaj, as his prime minister and commander-in-chief. After having ruled for about five years he decided upon the conquest of Saumara. It is stated in the Ahom Buranji, translated by Rai Sahib G.C. Barua, that in Lakni Khulsi i.e. 1546 A.D. the Koch army invaded the Ahom territories. Both the *Darrang Raj Vansavali* and Wade's account say that the army was led by both Narnārāyan and his brother, Sukladhvaj. It is also stated that Narnārāyan's other brother, named Gohain Kamala, preceded the forces and constructed the road which is still known as the Gohain Kamala Ali. The march was along the north bank of the Brahmaputra river. After having traversed the present districts of Goalpara and Kamrup Narnārāyan collected all the Mongloid people living between the Bhutan hills and the Gohain Kamala Ali and ordered that they could follow their tribal customs and eat pork and beef but that in the country between the Gohain Kamala Ali and the Brahmaputra the Brahmanic rites must be observed. The

Koch army then reached Singri where a halt was made. After this the Bhairabi river was reached. Sukladhvaj crossed the river on horse back though the river was not fordable and for this act he was nicknamed Chila Rai or the Kite-king. The Koch army advanced further east. At length the Ahoms resisted the invasion near the Dikrai or the Dehing river, according to Wade's account. The fight continued for seven days but the Koches at last won the battle and the Ahoms fled. The Ahom king and the nobles fled to Charai Khorang and both Narnārāyan and Chila Rai occupied Garhgaon, the Ahom capital.

The Ahom Buranji gives a different version according to which the Ahoms engaged the Koches near Dikrai on the north bank of the Brahmaputra. At first the Ahoms were defeated and they fell back on Koliabor on the south bank of the Brahmaputra. Next the Ahoms concentrated at Sala where a great battle was fought in which the Koches suffered a defeat and again crossing to the north bank of the Brahmaputra proceeded to Narainpur where a fort was erected in Lakni Rungshen (1547 A.D.). Near about this place another battle was fought in which the Koches being defeated retreated. They made no further attempt to invade the Ahom territories before Lakni Mungrao (1563 A.D.) when the Ahom king Chaopha Sukhram alias Khora Raja was ruling. This time the Koches advanced up the Brahmaputra and encamped near the mouth of the Dikhow river. From this base the Koches began to devastate the surrounding country. The Ahoms then sued for peace sending Katakis. The Koch king accepted the peace terms and withdrew. Shortly afterwards the Koch army again advanced as far as the Dehing river. The Ahoms retreated and the Ahom king with his nobles fled and took refuge in theNaga Hills. Peace overtures were again made and Chao Ikhak was sent to meet the Koch king who was then at Majuli. Ikhak came and met the Koch king who said "you better tell the king of the east that he must send your son, the son of Thaomunlung, the sons of Shengdang and the son of Khamshong to me and I shall go back to my country leaving all here."(1). This was reported to the Ahom king who ordered that the hostages demanded should be sent. Thao-munglung's wife, named Nāngbakla gābharu who was the Ahom king's aunt, however refused to part with her son saying "I will not allow my son to be sent to the Koch country. Tell the king what he and the ministers are for when they have yielded to the enemies? Why should he reign when he is unable to save his subjects from the enemies"?" (2). Then addressing her husband she said "Let me have your head-dress, girdle, belt and sword. Though I am a female, I shall fight with the Koch king and let him know how a female can fight with the male." On her husband replying that he would give up his son for the good of the country the lady replied haughtily, "who can give my son ? If the course of the Dikhow river can be diverted upwards to the hill

(1) Ahom Buranji translated by G.C.Barua, p. 87.
(2) Ibid.

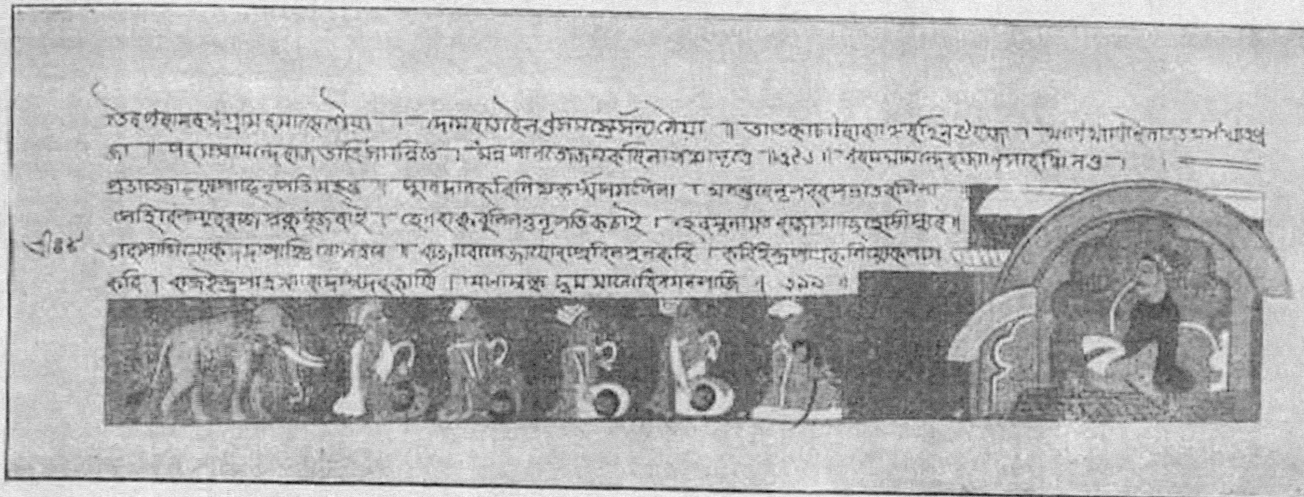

Narnārāyan seated on throne.

(From painting in the Darrang Raj Vamsavali.)

by putting a dam across there, my son may be taken" (1). The king then sent his own brother Chao Sungam *alias* Sundar Gohain in place of Thaomunglang's son. (2) He also paid tribute to the Koch king who returned to his country.

The Koch accounts represent Narnārāyan and his brother reducing all the independent kingdoms in an all-conquering tour but according to the Ahom accounts the first Koch invasion along the north bank resulted only in the construction of the 350 miles long road from Koch Bihar to Narainpur. The next invasion was undertaken som 15 or 16 years after and this time the Ahoms were defeated near the Dikhow river. This defeat led to the submission of the Ahom king. We consider the Ahom account more reliable. The Ahom power was not so weak as to be overthrown at the first attempt.

After reducing the Ahoms the Koches turned their attention to the Kachari kingdom on the south. Narnārāyan sent his brother, Chila Rai, accompanied by Kavindra Pātra,* Rājendra Pātra, Damodar Kārji and Meghā Mukundum to conquer the Kachari Raja. They easily succeeded because on their approach the Kachari king submitted giving presents and agreeing to pay an annual tribute of 70,000 silver coins, 1000 gold coins and 60 elephants.

Then, on the advice of Chila Rai, messengers

(1) Ahom Buranji translated by G.C. Barua, p 87.
(2) Deodhai Buranji p 44.
* The present Raja of Gauripur, in Dhubri Subdivision is descended from Kavindra Patra.

were sent to the king of Manipur demanding his submission. The messengers returned with the king of Manipur who performed obeisance and presented Narnārāyan with 40 elephants, 1000 gold coins and 20,000 silver coins and agreed to pay an annual tribute of 10 elephants, 300 gold mohurs and 20,000 rupees.

The kingdom of Jaintia was next attacked. In the fight the king was slain and Narnārāyan installed on the throne the king's son who presented 100 horses, 1000 gold mohurs, 10.000 rupees and 100 swords known as *Nakoi dao*. He also promised to pay an annual tribute of 70 horses, ten thousand rupees and three hundred swords.

Chila Rai then invaded the Tippera kingdom with 40, cco troops. There was a stiff fight in which the Raja of Tippera was killed. The Raja's brother then submitted to Chila Rai presenting 30 horses, 100 gold mohurs and 10,000 rupees. After this the Raja of Khairam came and voluntarily offered his submission. The Koches then retraced their steps and, on their way back, attacked the Raja of Dimorua who was captured and produced before Narnārāyan. He was released on his promise to pay an annual tribute of 7000 rupees.

According to the *Vamsavali* it was after the submisson of the Raja of Dimorua and the straightening of the course of the Brahmaputra near Pandu that an expedition was sent against the Padshah of Sirath (Sylhet) which lay to the south-west of Jaintia. Gait holds that this campaign lacks confirmation. It is not clear why Sylhet was not attacked when Jaintia and Tippera were subjugated and why an expedition against Sylhet was decided upon after the return of the army all the way from Tippera and Jaintia through an extremely difficult country. It can therefore be surmised that the invasion of Sylhet was a myth.

After the conclusion of these conquests Narnārāyan and Chila Rai proceeded to visit the shrine of Kamakshya. They found the temple in ruins, and decided that it should be rebuilt but the work had to be postponed as the king was then under the influence of evil stars. The two brothers then decided to invade Bengal. According to the Koch accounts Narnārāyan took the aggressive and invaded Bengal. This led to very sanguinary conflicts and at length the Koch army was defeated and Chila Rai was taken prisoner. It is stated that while Chila Rai was in prison the mother of the Sultan of Bengal was bitten by a snake. Chila Rai cured her of the snakebite and the Sultan being pleased released Chila Rai. A different version is given by the Muslim historians who say that Suleiman Kararani, the Sultan of Bengal took the offensive and invaded the Koch kingdom because Narnārāyan ignored him. The renegade Kala Pahar was then the general of the Sultan. The Muslims defeated the Koch army and reached the eastern limits of the kingdom. All the Hindu temples on their line of march, including those at Kamakshya and Hajo, were desecrated and destroyed. Unfortunately the valorous Bhuyan chiefs of the previous generation who had combined to resist such invasions were no longer in existence. They had been uprooted by Viswa Singha and many of them had escaped to the Ahom territories. On the defeat of Chila Rai therefore there was none to check the vandalism of the iconoclast Kala Pahar. The Muslims however did not tarry long in Kamarupa but hastened back to Bengal as, it is said, there was an insurrection in Orissa. Perhaps the real reason of their hasty withdrawal was that the Koch king had collected his forces and was ready for reprisals and had perhaps also invited the Ahoms to his assistance. The Muslim historians make no mention of the. capture and imprisonment of Chila Rai. The Muslim invasion and the sack of Kamakshya took place about 1564 A.D. for in the next year Narnārā-yan rebuilt the Kamakshya temple. The same Kala Pahar as a general of Suleiman Kararani sacked the temple of Jagannath in Puri about 1568 A.D.

After the withdrawal of the Muslims Narnārāyan first released the Ahom hostages. This was prompted perhaps by a desire to remain on friendly terms with the Ahom king in order to be able to count on his assistance in case of another Muslim invasion. It may also have been due to the prompt response of the Ahom King to his call for assistance which compelled the Muslims to evacuate his territories hurriedly. The next thing to be done was the reconstruction of the Kamakhsya temple. Megha Mukudum was deputed for this work which took six months to complete. When the building was completed both Narnārāyan and Chila Rai came to dedicate it ceremonially. It is stated in the *Vamsavali* that one lakh sacrifices were offered consisting of buffaloes, goats, deer, pigeons, tortoises and fishes. In this account there is no mention of any human sacrifice but Gait states that on this occasion no less than 140 human beings were sacrificed and their heads offered to the Goddess on copper salvers. Evidently Gait has made this astounding statement misunderstanding the meaning of the couplet in the *Vamsavali* which states that the king offered three lakhs of *hom* and one lakh sacrifices and dedicated to the temple the families of 140 *paiks*, for service in the temple, by means of a copper-plate grant. It is clearly mentioned that besides giving lands, fisheries, musical instruments, utensils of gold, silver, copper and bell-metal, mace, throne and white chameri the king gave as *shebaits* or *paiks* families of Brahmans Ganaks, Nats, Bhats, Tantis, Malis, Kamars, Kahars, Barhoi (carpenters), washermen, oil pressers, sweat-meat makers, goldsmiths, potters, leather-workers, fiishermen and scavangers. Evidently these constituted the 140 families of *paiks*. Narnārāyan also caused two statues, one of himself and the other of his brother Chila Rai, erected inside the temple. An inscription was also recorded on a stone tablet. The inscription runs thus:—

"Glory to the king Malla Deva, who by virtue of his mercy, is kind to the people, who in archery is like Arjuna, and in charity like Dadhichi and Karna; he is like an ocean of all goodness, and he is versed in many *S'astras*; his character is excellent; in beauty he is as bright as Kandarpa, he is a worshipper of Kamakshya. His younger brother, Sukladeva, built this temple of bright stones on the Nila hillock, for the worship of the Goddess Durga in 1487 Saka. His beloved brother, Sukladhvaj, again, with universal fame, the crown of the greatest heroes, who, like the fabulous Kalpataru, gave all that was devoutly asked of him, the chief of all devotees of the Goddess, constructed this beautiful temple with heaps of stones on the Nila hill in 1487 Saka" (Translation from Gait's History of Assam, page 57).

It will appear from the above that Chila Rai was so beloved of his brother, the king, that the entire credit for reconstruction of the temple and for endowment is given to him by this inscription evidently under orders of the king. Narnārāyan is stated to have been merely a "worshipper of Kamakvhsa" but the fact that his brother built the temple is repeated. It may be that Narnārāyan was till then under the influence of evil stars and hence it was found necessary to emphasize that the temple was rebuilt by his brother.

About this time great political changes were taking place in Bengal. Suleiman Kararani died and was succeeded by his son, Daud. The Mughul Emperor Akbar, resolved to conquerBengal and crush Daud. Narnārāyan who had been humbled by Daud's father and who was in dread of the growing Ahom power on the east seized this oppurtunity to establish friendly relations with the Moghul Emperor. In 1574 he refused asylum to certain Afghan rebels who had been driven by the Moghul officers from Ghotaghat. In 1576 the Moghuls defeated Daud at the battle of Akmahal. Daud was captured and beheaded. According to the *Vamsavali* Chila Rai actively assisted the Moghuls in this war on the conclusion of which a part of the Afghan Sultan's kingdom was given to Narnārāyan. The Muslim chronicles however make no mention of such military assistance. It is however a fact recorded in the Akbarnamah that in 1578 A. D. Narnarayan sent an envoy with presents to Akbar. This mission led to a mutual understanding between the Moghuls and the Koch king. Evidently Akbar prized this professed friendship because though Daud was overthrown the numerous Afghan rebels had not been uprooted and the aid of the Koch king who was powerful and who at this time, according to the Ain-i-Akbari, commanded 1000 horse and 100,000 foot soldiers, was almost indispensable. Chila Rai now became an able ally of the Mughuls. In 1583 he appears to have cooperated with the Mughuls in the fight with Masum Kabuli on the banks of the Ganges. Here he contracted small-pox and died.

His death was a great blow to his loving brother in his old age. The loss of such an able and faithful co-adjutor was indeed irreparable. Other miseries were also in store for Narnā-āyan. On the death of Chila Rai his son, Raghu Deb, rebelled and established his seat at Barnagar within the present district of Kamrup. All attempts of Narnārāyan to pacify his nephew failed and at length instead of reducing by force of arms the son of his beloved brother he divided the kingdom, keeping to himself the portion west of the Sonkosh and giving up to his nephew the territories to the east of the river. Narnārāyan did not long survive this disruption of the powerful kingdom originated by his father and extended by him with the help of Chila Rai. Alter a very eventful reign of about 50 years he died unhappy at an old age. His death occured about 1586 A.D.

During Narnārāyan's reign the Koch power reached its zenith. His kingdom included practically the whole of the old kingdom of Kamarupa of the kings of Brahmapala's dynasty with the exception of the eastern portion known as Saumara which formed the Ahom kingdom. Towards the west the kingdom appears to have extended beyond the Karatoya for according to Abul Fazl, the author of the Akbarnamah, the western boundary of the Koch kingdom was Tirhut. On the south-west the kingdom included the Rungpur district and part of Mymensingh to the east of the river Brahmaputra which then flowed through that district. We find that till the beginning of the seventeenth century the Raja of Soosung in Mymensingh was a vassal-chief under the Koch Raja (1). On the south-east the kingdom included the whole of the Dakhinkul or south bank of the Brahmaputra as far as Mayang and Dimorua including modern Gauhati and its neighbourhood.

On the death of Narnārāyan the Koch kingdom fell to pieces. The two branches of the royal family subsequently engaged in fratricidal war calling for the intervention of the Moghuls as well as the Ahoms. In course of time the Moghuls and the Ahoms fought for the possession of the kingdom. During this opportunity the local chieftains again raised their heads. We find that in the early part of the next century the Moghuls had to contend

(1) Raghunath, the Raja of Soosang was a vassal of Parikshit Narayan who imprisoned his whole family. Raghunath then appealed to the Moghul Viceroy. (*Padishanama and Baharisthan-i-Ghaibi*).

not with the degenerate Koch rajas but with local chieftains such as Sanatan of Dhamdhama, on the north bank, Shumaroad Kyeth (Samudra Kayastha) of Rangjuli, Parsuram of Solmari, Mamu Govinda of Beltala and the petty rajas of Rani, Luki, Burdwar, Owguri, Moirapur, Pantan, Dimorua, Bongaon and Mayung on the south bank (1).

An English traveller named Ralph Fitch visited Kamarupa towards the end of Narnārāyan's reign when his brother, Sukladhvaj, was living. According to Fitch Sukladhvaj was then the king as he was really the *defacto* ruler. After a journey of 25 days from the Bengal capital Fitch reached the Koch capital. He found that the king and his subjects were all Hindus. By this time, under the benign auspices of Narnārāyan, the new Vaisnava tenet of Sankar Dev had been propagated so wide that Fitch found the people averse to the killing of animals. He found veterinary hospitals established for all domesticated animals and asylums for all old and disabled cattle. The kingdom was a large one and it was not far from Cochin China for he was told that from that quarter the people obtained pepper. The people used to erect fences made of pointed bamboos or cane. They could, by damming the streams, inundate the country when necessary making it impossible for men or horses to traverse it. When war broke out they used to poison the water-supply in order to kill the invaders. Fitch found a good deal of musk and both silk and cotton fabrics manufactured in the country.

---

(1) *Baharisthan-i-Ghaibi* quoted in "Moghul North East Frontier Policy."

CHAPTER XIV.

THE VAISNAVA REFORMATION.

It has been already said that a very debased form of later Buddhism known as the Vajrayana system or the Sahajia cult was prevalent in Kamarupa for some centuries. It is said that Kamakshya in the very centre of Kamarupa, Lanka, which can perhaps be identified with the locality of the same name in the Kopili valley and Sri Hatta (Sylhet) which was then under the Jaintia or Tippera kings became the reputed centres of this system of religion. The excesses which were indulged in the name of religion under this system are too revolting to be enumerated. The *Rātikhoā* or *Purnadhariā* sect of Assam, which continued till recent times, had its origin undoubtedly in this system which was evidently a mixture of Tantrik Buddhism and tribal customs. The adherents of this sect were known as night-worshippers.* It is said that a neophyte had to resist his temptations in the midst of meat, drink and a naked young woman. The ordinary common people may not have been the votaries of such a cult. They were, it is stated by Dwija Ramananda, one of the biographers of Śri Sankardeva, worshippers of demons, *Bhairabs*, the shades, trees and stones. It is stated that goats, buffaloes, tortoises and pigeons were sacrificed in order to propitiate these deities, but no mention is made of human sacrifices. Gait refers to the statements of certain Muslim writers to the effect that about this time there was a class of persons in Kāmarupa called *Bhogis* (enjoyers) who voluntarily offered themselves as victims for sacrifice before the Goddess Durgā in return for the privilege to indulge in all manner of licenses for a whole year previous to their immolation. It is hardly possible to believe such exaggerated stories wholesale. There is, however, no doubt that previous to the propagation of the new Vaisnava tenet of Sri Śankar Deva, a gross form of Tāntrikism prevailed in the country and it is quite possible that human sacrifices, so extolled in the Kālika Purana, were also resorted to.

Śri Śankar Deva was the descendant of the

A full desciption of this sect is to be found in the paper read by Mr S.C. Gowami B A in the meeting of the Kamarupa Anusandhan Samiti and publishedin the first report of that Society (1920). According to this writer the sect was founded by one Gopal a contemporary of Sri Sankar Deva but very probably the cult was much more ancient and an offshoot of Buddhism of the degraded type.

of his family priest. It is said that both of them could cross the Brahmaputra by swimming, a feat which the other youths of the locality could not perform. On attaining manhood Śankar married and settled down to domestic life. A daughter was born to him and when she reached the proper age he gave her in marriage to one Hari. Then his wife died.

Śankar, who had always religious leanings, now felt inclined to renounce the world and devote himself to religious exercises. One day he quietly set out on a pilgrimage to the holy places of India. All the different countries of India actually visited by him, during his long pilgrimage of 12 years, have not been mentioned but we find from his biographies that during this period he met the well-known saint Kabir, with whom he contracted friendship. He also visited the temple at Puri and possibly travelled further south, for it appears that he accepted as his faith the system of qualified monism or *vishistādwaitabāda* taught by the celebrated South Indian reformer Rāmanuja Swami. At the end of his travels, in course of which he must have met and associated with many learned pundits, *sādhus* and religious teachers, he returned home convinced that in order to elevate oneself spiritually and at the same time be of service to humanity one need not renounce the world. As a matter of fact he himself re-married on his return from the pilgrimage. He then began to preach his tenet which was derived from the teachings of the *Gitā* and the *Bhāgavata*.

As already stated Śankar's creed was qualified

monism as expounded by Rāmanuja. It differed from the absolute monism of Śankarāchārya on the one hand and the dualism of Maddvāeharya on the other hand. The tenet of dualism was adopted in Bengal by Adwaitācharya and latterly by Chaitanya. The tenet of Chaitanya therefore was different from that of Śankar Deva fundamentally. Śankār could not have been a follower of Chaitanya or even of Adwaitācharya for the following reasons:-

(1) Śankar was born in 1449 A. D. whereas Chaitanya was born in 1486 A. D. The latter was perhaps not born when Śankar set out on his pilgrimage. Further Chaitanya did not renounce the world and turn out a preacher until he was 24 years old or about 1510 A. D. On the other hand Śankar began to preach his tenet much earlier before the end of the fifteenth century.

(2) Śankar could not have met Chaitanya during his first pilgrimage but during his second pilgrimage from Barpeta he actually met Chaitanya about 1530 A. D. at Puri. At this time Śankar was an old man of about 81 years of age.

(3) As already stated Adwaitācharya was a believer in pure dualism while Śankar's creed was monism of the qnalified type. Śankar could not therefore have been a disciple of Adwaitācharya.

It was the neo-vaisnavism with its allegiance to one supreme God, its abhorence of animal sacrifices, its freedom from esoteric rites and its simple ceremonial consisting only of hymns and prayers which strongly appealed to Śankar. This phase of Hinduism was first presented by Rāmanuja, the great commentator of the *Vedanta sutras* and the *Bhāgavat Gitā*, who flourished in the twelfth century A. D. As an exponent of the Vedanta he differed from his predecessor, the great Śankarāāharya, in interpreting the texts. He held that by unity with *Brahman* the scriptures meant nothing but dependance on God. According to him therefore the finite self is dependant on and cannot exist without the infinite self. The finite self is like the ray of the sun. There can be no ray without the sun and each ray is a part of the sun and proceeds from the same fountain source, but a ray is not the sun itself. Though implying unity with the Infinite, Rāmanuja recognized and laid great stress on the difference between the finite soul and the *Brahman*. The result is a reconcilation between the opposite schools of monism and dualism. There is room for faith and devotion (*bhakti*) in this philosophy whereas absolute monism presents the Infinite Self as an absolute cosmic principle pervading all matter, which is beyond the conception of most men and which is hardly distinguishable from the nothingness of the Buddhist doctrines which Śankaracharya tried to extirpate. The school of qualified monism, at the same time, rejected dualism which presents the finite self as something fundamentally different from the Divine Self. The relationship between God and man, as that between father and son or between master and servant, is possible in qualified monism. The relationship between husband and wife, which presupposes equality to some extent as well as fundamental distinction between *Jiva* and *Brahman*, is however possible in the philosophy of dualism. The *Dāsya bhāb* or relationship of master and servant was the idea adopted by

Śankar Deva who, almost on every page of his writings, describes himself as the "servant of Śri krishna." On the other hand the *Modhur* or the *Sringār bhāb* (idea of cohabitation) was the peculiarity of Chaitanya. According to Śankar Deva, therefore the *Brahman* though impersonal and attributeless can be attained only through devotion to a personal God who is endowed with all the best attributes. His follower Mādhava Deva referred to Śankar in the following paradoxical way:- "Śankar made known the attributes of Śri Krishna who is attributeless." The meaning is that though God is above all attributes conceived by man (*nirguna*) still for the sake of the devotees He is presented as a personal God. In the *Gitā* this personal God assured Arjuna saying "Leaving aside all other religions, Oh Arjuna, be dependant on Me only and worship Me only. I will save you from all sins, do not fear." In the *Bhagavata* also the same personal God gives a similar assurance to Uddhava. Śankar's creed was therefore based on the *Gitā* and the *Bhāgavata*.

Śankar began preaching this creed to the people of his locality. The Brahmans first repudiated his claim to preach but on the occasion of a ceremony in the house of one of his relatives he vanquished the assembled pundits in a disputation and since then the Brahmans did not boldly and openly oppose him. Ratnākara Kandali and Byāh Kalai were among his early Brahman followers besides his old friend Rāmrāma. Mādhava Deva's brother-in-law Gayāpāni became a disciple of Śankar and it was Gayāpani who introduced

Mādhava to Śankar. When the two met a long controversy followed as Mādhava himself was a scholar, well-versed in the Śāstras and who being by faith a Sākta had already bought a goat for the purpose of a sacrifice. Śankar argued with him in order to desist him from offering the sacrifice. He at length recited a *sloka* the meaning of which is as follows:-

"Pouring of water at the root of a tree causes the branches leaves and flowers to thrive, but if you pour water on the leaves and the branches no part of the tree will thrive. To sustain and nourish the limbs and organs of the body you have got to satisfy your hunger by eating but if you fast and wear ornaments on every limb you feel no satisfaction. In the same way, he who worships the supreme deity appeases the minor deities also but if he worships any one of the minor deities he pleases none."

Mādhava was vanquished and he at once gave up the idea of offering the sacrifice and became an ardent follower of Śankar. The joint efforts of Śankar and Madhav led to quick promulgation of the new tenet. The Brahmans then became alarmed and reported to the Ahom king that Śankar was subverting religion by advising the people to refrain from performance of ordinary religious rites such as the *srāddha* enjoined by Hindu Sāstras. Śankar was summoned before the Ahom king who enquired what *Srāddha* meant. It was explained to him that when a man died his relatives offered *pinda* and other gifts consisting of cloths, utensils, ornaments etc. through a Brahman priest and that these presents were actually taken by the priest. The king was surprised that the people were so credulous and could be so easily influenced by the priests. He at once held that Śankar did nothing wrong and allowed him to depart. The Brahmans however continued to misrepresent him and ultimately he found it impossible to remain within the Ahom kingdom any longer. The renown of the Koch king as a mild and accomplished ruler had already reached him. He therefore, together with his followers, removed to the Koch kingdom about 1537 A. D. when Naranārāyan had not perhaps ascended the throne. In any case Śankar was quite old when he settled down at Pātbousi after stopping for short periods at Kāpla, Sunporā bheti and Kumārkuchi. It was at Pātbousi that his famous Brahman co-worker Dāmodar Deva joined him. While he was there the Brahmans conspired against him and reported to the Koch king Naranārāyan. Śankar went to the court of the Koch king and defeated the assembled Brahman Pandits in controversy. Naranārāyan was so pleased that he appointed Śankar as the *gomasta* or magistrate of Tāntikuchi in Barpeta. This office he soon resigned and set out again on his second pilgrimage, accompanied by Madhav Deva. He attempted to find out his old friend Kabir but learnt that he was dead. He went to Puri and there met Chaitanya who was then observing silence. There was no conversation between the two reformers but by pouring water from his *Kamandalu* Chaitanya indicated that devotion to

God, continuous and directed to one channel only, like the flow of running water, was his creed Śankar did not long survive after his return from the second pilgrimage. He died in Koch Bihar in the year 1568 A. D. after having attained a very long life of 118 years. Both Mādhav Deva and Dāmodar Deva outlived him and spread his tenet far and wide. When the English traveller Ralph Fitch visited Koch Bihar his teachings had already taken a firm root in the country.

Both Mādhav Deva and Dāmodar Deva promulgated the new creed by appointing preachers and founding *sattras*. Those originating from Mādhav Deva and the teachers appointed by him are known as the *Māhāpurushia sattras* while those originating from Dāmodar Deva and his immediate disciples are known as *Dāmodaria sattras*. These constitute the most important religious institutions in Assam even at the present day. With the spread of the new creed was also introduced the institution known as *nāmghars* meant for congregational prayers. Every Hindu village in the Assam Valley now has its *nāmghar*.

As already stated, Śankar Deva was a prolific writer. Besides metrical versions of the *Bhāgavata* he wrote several dramas in Assamese. Mādhav Deva wrote two important books viz. the *Nām ghosā* and the *Bhakti Ratnāvali*. It is not known whether Dāmodar Deva was the author of any work but his favourite disciple Bhatta Deva translated the *Gita* into Assamese prose and this work is believed to be the first literary production in Assamese prose. Both Śankar and Mādhav were musicians and both of them composed a large number of devotional songs known as *bar geet.*

The special feature of the new tenet was its uncompromising hostility to the worship of minor Gods and Goddesses and animal sacrifices. It was explained, on the basis of the Upanishads, that God was the only eternal, changeless Spirit, the individual soul or *Atman* was a part of it, but all the rest was matter and therefore subject to change and decay. People who worshipped matter, being oblivous of the everlasting Spirit, were fools. Śankar Deva was so particular in this respect that he spurned his own faithful follower Byāhkalai as soon as he came to know that the latter, in order to save his son from the clutches of small-pox, had offered *puja* to the Goddess *S'italā.* On the other hand, Chaitanya, it appears, did not ban worship of the numerous deities and is said to have himself worshipped Śiva though he was a Vaisnava.

Animal sacrifices were no doubt strictly forbidden but killing of animals for food was not prohibited. Even now the Assamese Vaisnavas eat meat and fish. The description of Ralph Fitch in this respect seems to be overdrawn. Probably he meant that the people did not kill animals to offer sacrifice before Gods and Goddesses.

In his History of Orissa the late Mr. R. D. Banerji stated that the decline of the power and prestige of Orissa was solely due to the national adoption of the sublime *Bhakti-mārga* of Chaitanya (1). This seems to be an astounding statement but

1) History of Orissa pages 330-333

Mr. Banerji points out that when Rāmānanda Rai, governor of an important province under Pratāpa Rudra, accepted the teachings of Chaitanya he retired from the important position and became a religious man. Pratāpa Rudra, thus lost the services of a capable administrator and military commander at a time when the Mussalmans were trying their level best to conquer Orissa. Chaitanya had a powerful hold over Pratāpa Rudra and succeeded in dissuading him from invading Bengal though such an invasion was necessary for the proper security of his kingdom.* We can say without hesitation that similar baneful political results did not follow from the promulgation of the neo-vaisnavism of Śankar Deva. For one thing, Śankar Deva gave a wide berth to kings, nobles and other high personages. He was busy with the common folk and tried to make them religious. There is a *fokora* or cryptic saying in Assamese:-

Bāra hāt jalor tera hāt phatā

---

* Another fact worth mentioning here is that the two brothers Rup and Sanatan were both ministers of Sultan Alauddin Hussein Shah under the chief minister Purandar Khan. Both Rup and Sanatan were favourites of Hussein Shah. The former was given the title Dabir Khas and the latter was styled Shakir Malik. Towards the end of Hussein Shah's reign Chaitanya visited Gaur and there Rup and Sanatan visited him. After Chaitanya's departure from Gaur both Rup and Sanatan resigned their high posts. The Sultan was so vexed that he put Sanatan into prison. Sanatan effected his escape by heavily bribing the jailer. Subsequently both Rup and Sanatan, as devout disciples of Chaitanya, became *Sanyisais* and spent the rest of their lives in Brindaban. (Memoris of Gaur and Pandua, edited by H.E. Stapleton pp 34-35).

Bhāl mārile bāpor betā
Row borāli soroki gol
Puthi Kholihanā roi roi gol.

The above may be translated thus:-

"The net is twelve cubits in length but it is a torn net, the rents being altogether thirteen cubits long. Such a net was thrown by that worthy son of a worthy father. The bigger fishes like *row* and *borali* escaped but the small fishes like *puthi* and *khalihana* were caught."

Stripped of metaphor the meaning of the saying is that the net of the new religion, based on the twelve chapters of the *Bhāgavata* with its thirteen hundred *slokas* was spread by Śankar Deva. He could not catch the big men but caught shoals of the common folk. As a matter of fact the king and the nobles, who naturally loved elaborate and pompous ceremonies involving *puja, hom* and sacrifices and accompanied by gifts to Brahmans and the poor, were not fit for the simple tenet of Śankar Deva which therefore largely appealed to the masses. It is said that Śankar refused to initiate Narnārāyan although the latter pressed him. He knew that a king, of all persons, could not stick to the simple observations enjoined by him. During the seventeenth century his tenet was adopted as the national religion of the Assamese people throughout Kamrup and the Upper Assam districts, but this period synchronized with, what Gait calls, the climacteric of the Ahom rule. The Ahom power reached its zenith during this period. It was not the national adoption of the faith but the religious organizations called *Sattras* which no doubt sapped, to some extent, the authority of the Ahom kings of the eighteenth century.

These *Sattras* came into existence after the demise of Śankar Deva. They were really modelled on the Buddhist *Viharas*. In most of these *Sattras* the spiritual head or *adhikāra* is usually a celibate and the *bhakats* residing in the *Sattra* are also celibate monks who go about begging like the Bauddha *Bhikshus* of old. Monasticism is a peculiar point in Buddha's religion. Between the seventh and the ninth centuries Brahman revivalists adopted it in imitation of the Buddhists and the Vaisnava preachers of Kāmarupa also did the same after the death of Śankar Deva. Thus it would appear that Buddhist teachings and customs, which must have been widely prevalent in Kāmarupa prior to the sixteenth century, persisted even after Śankar's creed had been widely diffused. Even up till this day the portion of an Assamese Vaisnava *nāmghar* (hall for congregational prayers) which is covered by a rounded roof is called *Tūp*, perhaps to perpetuate the memory of the ancient Buddhist *stupa*. The word used to denote initiation of a neophyte in the Assamese Vaisnava tenet is "*S'aran*". We find the word *S'aran* used in the initiation of a Buddhist, *Buddham śaranam gachhāmi*. Instances may be multiplied to show the wide prevalence of some form of Buddhism in Kāmarupa before the rise of Śankar Deva.

CHAPTER XV.

THE GROWTH OF LITERATURE.

As already stated, Yuan Chwang, in the seventh century A. D. found that the dialect of Kamarupa differed only a little from that of Magadha or mid-India. The Kamarupi dialect was originally a variety of eastern Maithili and it was no doubt the spoken Aryan language throughout the kingdom which then included the whole of the Assam valley and the whole of northern Bengal with the addition of the Purnea district of Bihar. It is not therefore at all strange that the language of the Buddhist *dohās*, composed in Kamarupa during the tenth and the eleventh centuries, should be a mixed Maithili-Kamarupi language bearing close resemblance to modern Assamese, the direct offspring of the old Kamarupi dialect. Perhaps these *dohās* were composed in a language which could be easily understood throughout Eastern India.

The earliest Kamarupi literature was unwritten and consisted of nursery songs, pastoral ballads sung by cowherds, songs of boatmen, songs describing the twelve months, songs for propitiation of the goddess of small-pox (*S'itala*) and wedding songs. Naturally the composition and language of these songs and ballads differed somewhat from district to district. Those collected and published by the University of Calcutta in the first volume of the work known as "*Asamiyā Sāhityar Chāneki*" were not necessarily the ones current throughout the kingdom of Kamarupa. Some years ago Grierson published, in the Journal of the Asiatic Society of Bengal, a version of the "*Kanyā Bāromāhi geet*" current in northern Bengal towards the end of the last century. This very song is still current in Assam in a somewhat varied form. It is quite possible that when northern Bengal was a part of Kamarupa the same version of the song was current throughout Kamrup, Goalpara and Rangpur. The *mantras* or incantations uttered to exorcise ghosts, to cure snake-bites or to perform feats of sorcery as well as the wise sayings or aphorisms ascribed to Dāka Purusha belong to this category of unwritten literature. The late Pundit Hem Chandra Goswami thought that the aphorisms of Dāk were first reduced to writing about 800 A.D. We have already mentioned that some of these aphorisms refer to trading on the Arracan coast when the sea stretched from the southern slopes of the Garo Hills. We can therefore easily assign Daka to a very early period. He belonged to the village of

Lehi-Dangara in the Barpeta suddivision of the Kamrup district.

The earliest written *puthis* in the Kamarupi language date from about the second quarter of the fourteenth century when Durlabhnarayan was the king of Kamata and Kamarupa. During his reign flourished two poets, viz, Hema Saraswati and Haribar Bipra. Both of them make mention of of Durlabhnarayan as the ruling king. Hema Saraswati composed the "*Prahlād Charitra*" based on the *Vāmana Purāna* while Haribar Bipra translated the *Aswamedha Parva* of the Mahabharata. Kaviratna Saraswati, whose father Chakrapani Kayastha was a petty revenue officer under king Durlabhnarayan, was a contemporary of Indranarayan, the son and successor of Durlabhnarayan. Kaviratna was the author of the "*Jayadratha Vadha*". His home was at Sila, a village within the Barpeta suvdivision. The writings of all these three poets are still extant. To a somewhat later period belonged Mādhava Kandali and Rudra Kandali. The former versified portions of the Ramayana and the latter composed, in Kamarupi verse, portions of the Mahabharata. Śankar Deva who was born in 1449 A. D. refers to Mādhava Kandali as one of the reputed poets belonging to an earlier age We may therefore place both Mādhava Kandali and Rudra Kandali towards the end of the fourteenth century. In his Ramayana, Mādhava Kandali himself states that his other name was Kaviraj-Kandali and that though he could easily compose verses in Sanskrit he composed the Ramayana in Assamese verse for the benefit of the people at large, at the request of Śri Mahā Mānikya, the *Varāhi Raja*.* Mādhava Kandali wrote also another poem entitled "Devajit."

The reigns of Viswa Singha and Narnarayan, which covered the greater part of the sixteenth century, witnessed a great development of the vernacular literature of Kamarupa. The *Yogini Tantra*, a well-known Sanskrit work which gives the boundaries of the kingdom of Kamarupa as it existed during the rule of the Pāla kings but which also mentions the Kamarupa kings Jalpeswar *alias* Prithu and Viswa Singha, was very probably written in Kamarupa during the first part of the sixteenth century when Viswa Singha was ruling. To this period we must also assign the compilation of the *Behulā Upākhyāna* by Durgabar Kayastha, a native of Kamakshya. Durgabar addresses his salutation to Viswa Singha as the king of Kamata:-

* The late Pandit Hem Chandra Goswami stated that Maha Manikya was a king of the Barahi Kacharis and that he ruled about the middle of the fourteenth century at Dimapur. In an old Ahom Buranji seven generations of the Barahi kings are given. The last of these kings Dersong Phā, great-great-grandson of Maha Manikya was the contemporary of the Ahom king Suhunmung *alias* Dehingia Raja, (Banhi Vol. XVIII No.5.).

These Barahi kings were, it seems, rulers, at one time, over the Kapili valley. The antiquities discovered in this area include an inscription on a stone tablet now deposited in the museum of the Kamarupa Anusandhan Samiti. This inscription is much obliterated. With much difficulty the word "Mani[illegible]ya" has been deciphered in it. It is no doubt the surname used after the name of the king.

"*Kamatā iswara bando Visua Singha nripabar*
Athchallis mahishi bando othara Koar."

The story of Behula and Chand Sadagar appears to be common to both Bengal and Kamarupa. The ballads connected with this story must have been current in western Kamarupa and the rest of northern Bengal long before the verses were reduced to writing by Sukavi Nārāyan probably in the thirteenth century and by Durgabar in the early part of the sixteenth century. The ballads of Sukavi Nārāyan's composition are still sung in Kamrup and they are known as *Sūk-Nānis* or Suk-Nārāyanis to this day. Sukavi Nārāyan was very likely a poet of Kamarupa who described the sea-voyages of a Kamarupi trader named Chand Sadagar whose home was in Chaygaon in modern Kamrup, on the south bank ot the Brahmaputra but, strangely enough, both Sukavi Nārāyan and Chand Sadagar have been claimed as natives of Bengal(1). The songs of Durgabar are still known as Durgābari.

Narnārāyan was a ruler of mild disposition, religiously inclined and a patron of learning. Under his auspices the great Pandit Siddhanta-vagisha compiled in Sanskrit, the eighteen volumes of a work on *smriti* known as the *Kaumudi.* Another Pandit wrote a more authoritative work on *smriti* known as *Smriti-Sāgara* in four volumes. The famous Bengali *smārta* Pundit Raghunandan mentioned this work as the "*Kamaruvi nibandha*". Unfortunately this valuable work has now

(1) **A History of Indian Shipping by R.K. Mookerji.p.158**

disappeared. Sridhara compiled a treatise on astronomy while Purusottama Vidyavagish compiled a Sanskrit grammar known as *Ratnamālā* which is still regarded as a standard work. Narnārāyan's reign was really the Elizabethan period of the vernacular literature of Kamarupa. In his court were gathered a galaxy of the poets of the sixteenth century. They all belonged to what is now known as the Vaisnava period of Assamese literature. Among the reputed writers of this period were Śankar Deva, Mādhava Deva, Rāma Saraswati, Ananta Kandali, Chandra Bhārati, Sridhara Kandali, Pitāmbar Dvija, Gopāla Misra, Chandrachura Aditya, Vishnu Bhārati, Rāmcharan Thakur, Krishnānanda Dvija, Dāmodara Dasa, Ratnākara Misra, Rāmānanda Dvija, Bhusana Dvija, Norottama Thakur, Gopinath Pāthak, Rāmrāi Dasa, and Śrirām Jadumani.

Nearly all of the abovenamed writers composed verses but Bhatta Deva wrote in prose. His "*Kathā Bhāgavata*" and the "*Kathā Geetā*" constitute perhaps the earliest vernacular prose composition in Kamarupa. Śankar Deva was a prolifc writer in Assamese verse and a poet of high order. His most popular works were the "*Kirtan*" and the *Daśam* meant to popularize his own tenet. Śankar Deva also wrote a Sanskrit work entitled *Bhakti-Ratnākara*. The two most important works of Mādhava Deva were the *Nām-Ghoshā* and the *Bhakti-Ratnāvali*.

There is much controversy as to the authorship and date of a work known as *Dipikā Chanda*. Internal evidence points to the compilation of the work after the death of Śankar Deva. The author is said to have been a king called Purusottama Gajapati. Several Assamese writers have attempted to locate him somewhere in Assam but all have failed to notice the fact that Purusottama Gajapati was a well-known powerful king of Orissa who ruled from 1476 to 1497 A. D. and whose kingdom, or rather empire, extended from the Hugli district in modern Bengal as far as the Guntur district of the Madras Presidency. He was the son of Kapilendra Gajapati and the father of Pratapa Rudra, the last powerful Gajapati who ruled from 1497 to 1541 A. D. and who was a contemporary of Śri Chaitanya. Purusottama Gajapati was a devout Vaisnava and he may have written the work known as *Dipikā Chanda* in order to ridicule the later Buddhist cult and the Tantrik system.* There was close connection between Kamarupa and Orissa in the sixteenth century on account of the existence, in the latter country, of the famous temple of Jagannatha at Puri. It is possible that an Assamese Vaisnava came across the book and translated it into Assames verse. The title *Gajapati* could not have been assumed by an ordinary king. It was assumed by Kapilendra, the father af Purusottama, who possessed, according to the Muslim account *Burhan-i-maasir*, two hundred thousand war-

* We now know that the Orissa king Purusottama Gajapati was the author of another work known as *Nama-Malika* in Sanskrit. Sri Sankar Deva brought a copy of this work to Assam and Madhava Deva translated it into Assamese verse. (Descriptive Catalogue of Assamese Manuscripts pp 50-51).

elephants (2).

The late M. M. Pandit Haraprasad Śastri was presented by the staff of the Nepal Durbar Library with copies of two works one of which was the Dākārnava. Pandit Śastri says that this work, though almost entirely written in Sanskrit, contains some verses in a curious form of Prākrit. He writes:-

"I was anxious to get a copy of the work because in Bengal there are numerous agricultural sayings known as *Dākar Vachana* in an old form of language. I am enquiring all my life as to who this Dāka was, without getting any satisfactory explanation from any quarter. This work may give a clue to the meaning. It says Dāka is Vireswara and is the masculine of Dākini, mischievous imp, much dreaded by the credulous people of Bengal. Now we know that Vira is a votary of the left-handed worship. So this Dāka of our proverbs was probably a saint of the left-handed form of worship. I have examined the verses in the curious dialect in the work but it will require a more careful examination than I can give at present". (Report on the search of Sanskrit Manuscripts 1895 to 1900).

It is rather strange that a well-informed scholar like Pandit H. P. Sastri could not find out that Dāka was a native of Kamarupa and that the "old form of language" met with by him was nothing else than old Assamese. As a matter of fact however, the Dākarnava, which we have not seen, may have nothing to do with Dāka Purusha the

(2) Banerji's History of Orissa, vol. 1 p 202.

famous author of the proverbs. It is probably a Tantrik work dealing with the propitiation of Dāks and Dākinis (male and female evil spirit).

The Assam Government collection of Sanskrit and Assamese manuscripts now deposited in the library of the *Kamarupa Anusandhan Samiti*, includes quite a good number of works belonging to the pre-Narnārāyan period. These are mostly works on astronomy, astrology, mathematics, proverbs, riddles, *mantras*, medicine, history or traditions and also *tantras*. Among the Sanskrit works the most note-worthy are *Adbhuta Sāra* a book dealing with the propitiatory rites for ascertaining mischief likely to be caused by the occurence of strange events, the *Apaduddhāra mantra*, a tantrik work, the *Astabargi dasā*, an astrological work, the *Graha Vija Jnāna*. an astronomical work, *Grahana Aryā*, a treatise on eclipses, the *Graha Puja Vidhi*, the *Graha Stava* and the *Graha Snāna Mantra*, all works on planetary worship and the *Hastamuktāvali*. a treatise on the art of dancing. The author of the last named book was one Subhankara Kavi. A copy of this work was recovered by Pandit H. P. Sastri from Nepal and another was found in Mithila. This also indicates close cultural intercourse between the adjacent kingdoms of Kamarupa, Mithila and Nepal in the old days. The *Yuddha Jayārnava Dasā*, *Jyotisha Chakra*, *Jātaka Chandrika*, *Kerali*, *Jyotisha Darpan*, *Jyotisha Ratnamālā* and the *Jyotisha Muktāvali* are all astrological works pertaining to preparation of horoscopes. The *Mantra Prākasa* and the *Mandalādhyāya* are Tantrik works. The *Samudrika* is a treatise on palmistry.

The *Shatachakra* by Purnananda Paramahamsa is also a Tantrik work dealing with astral physiology. Besides the above there are numerous works on Hindu religion and religious rites based upon the *Smriti Sastras*. Of the works in the vernacular language of Kamarupa the most important are *Bhāswati*, an astrological work by Kaviraja Chakravarti, the *Ghora Nidana*, a treatise on horses and treatment of equine diseases, *Gu-Karati*, a collection of *mantras* to ward off charms practised by Tantrik Buddhists who defy the authority of the Vedas, the *Hara-Gauri Sambāda*, an important book which, like the *Yogini Tantra*, gives, in the guise of prophesies, the history of ancient Kamarupa, the *Jyotisha Churamoni* by Churamani Kayastha, a work on Arithemetic and land-surveying, the *Kamaratna Tantra*,** an Assamese translation of a Tantrik work of that name ascribed to Gorakshanath, a celebrated Buddhist *Siddha* who flourished in the fourteenth century and the *Kitābata Manjari* by Bakul Kayastha written in Saka 1356 equivalent to 1434 A. D. This last named work is a poetical treatise on arithmetic, Surveying and book-keeping. The book teaches how accounts are to be kept under different heads and how stores belonging to the royal treasury are to be classified and entered into a stock-book. The *bhāndāragā-radhikāra* of the Kamarupa kings mentioned in the

** This book was published by the Govt. of Assam in 1928. It is a curious collection of Tantrik *mantras* and recipes for various purposes some of which are too obscene to be mentioned.

Nidhanpur inscription and the *Bārbhandāra Baruas* of the Ahom kings were generally Kayasthas who were trained in book-keeping and accounts. Bakul Kayastha was the greatest mathematician of his time in Kamarupa. Suryakhari Doibogna, the author of the *Darrang Raj Vamsavali*, wrongly placed him a century later making him a contemporary of Naranārāyan and the translator of the famous arithmetical work of Lilavati, the well-known lady mathematician. Another remarkable work on erotics is a collection of *mantras* used to secure the love of young damsels. There are several books containing *mantras* for the cure of fever, snake-bite, small-pox etc. In the domain of history the important work is *Swarganārāyan Mahārājar Akshyāna* written in 1526 A. D. which is a historical account of the Ahom kings from Sukaphā to Suhunmung. The *Swapnadyāya* is a book on dreams and their interpretation.

It will appear from the above that the manuscripts collected represent literary activities covering a very wide range of subjects. Works dealing with astronomy and astrology are numerous. The conclusion that can be drawn is that Prāgjyotisha, as its name implies, was, from the ancient times, a noted seat of learning in these two subjects and that the temple of the nine planets on the Navagraha hill near Gauhati was meant not merely for planetary worship but also, perhaps, as an observatory. The Tantrik works collected support the fact that Kamarupa was a stronghold of Tantrik Buddhism between the eighth and the fifteenth centuries. In Bengal and Bihar the

Muslim conquerors, shocked by the debased practices of the *Sahajia panthis*, killed a good number of Kāpālikas and burnt their books found in Odantapuri. Many of them escaped to Nepal and Tibet. In Kamarupa they continued to practise their rites undisturbed till the rise of Śrí Śankar Deva in the fifteenth century who roused public opinion in Assam against Tantrikism to such an extent that the followers of the cult were compelled to abandon most of their revolting rites previously practised openly. The small number of Tantrik works collected is due to the fact that the Tantriks scrupulously observed the injunction of their preceptors to conceal their books, "*Kula Pustakāni gopāyet*". It was with a great deal of persuasion that the owner of the manuscript entitled *Kāmaratna Tantra*, mentioned above, was induced to hand it over to the Government collector. Further, after the spread of the Vaisnava cult of Śri Śankarā Deva far and wide, Tantrikism fell into disrepute and Tantrik works were therefore probably destroyed in large numbers. A Tantrik work called *Deva Dāmara* was found by Pandit H. P. Śastri in Mymensing (1). The *mantras* of this work, meant to propitiate the 24 classes of demigods, are in Assamese. This is not strange as Mymensing was always within Kamarupa.

---

(1) Report on the Search of Sanskrit Manuscripts 1895-1900.

APPENDIX II.

COPPER-PLATE INSCRIPTION OF HARJARAVARMAN.

Translation in English.

(Note-The translation below is of the middle plate of the inscription which consisted of three plates. The first and the third plates are now missing. The first page of the plate found cannot be deciphered in places. The translation follows the decipherment made by Pandit Padmanath Bhattacharya Vidyavinod. The undeciphered portions are marked by asterisks.)

* * * All powerful and high spirited. * * *

Oh Parthiva (1) your future descendants will, for this reason, be called) *mlechhas**

* * * * of king Bhagadatta * * * *

After this slayer of enemies, Salastambha became the ruler of the earth.

When that tiger-like king died his son, the powerful Vijaya, who subdued all his enemies, became the powerful king of the earth.

That king having died the rulers (palaka) (2) Palaka,

(1) Son of *Prithivi* or Earth or king.

* As Salastambha is mentioned afterwards it seems that his predecessors were also called *mlechhas*, according to the writer of this inscription. On the other hand, according to the Ratnapala inscription, Salastambha founded the mlechha dynasty.

(2) Note the pun on the word *palaka*.

Carving on black schist, Bamuni Hill.

Kumara and Vajradeva successively became kings and disappeared from the earth, After them he who bore the famous name Harshavarma became king. He was possessed of great virtues and he loved his subjects like his own children and never oppressed them.

When that monarch ascended the heavens his powerful son Balavarma became king and subsequently died.

Alas, in that family, which was pure like the moon and and white like milk, there were born two princes named Chakra and Arathi who were both ill-tempered and who disregardel the advice of their religious preceptors. The sovereigaty was therefore exercised by the son of the younger brother. (1)

In this world she alone is blessed and is the abode of fortune and wealth by whom * * * * .

She whose pure fame is still proclaimed in the world that Jivadevi * * * * * *

As Yudhisthira was born from the womb of Kunti and Abhimanyu from the womb of Subhadra, in the same way Harjara Deva, who was the future king of the world and powerful like a lion, was born from the womb of Jivadevi (2).

The kings anxious to conquer territories, having fought against one another in sub-montane tracts, accepted him as the mediator; he is possessed of all the virtues in equal proportion and though constantly engaged in work pertaining to the welfare of his subjects he is always untired and accessible to all.

That prosperous Harjara Deva ascended the throne being surrounded by the vassal rulers as Indra is surrounded by the Devas. He was anointed, during his coronation with the water of all sacred places, contained

(1) Here Pralambha, the son of Arathi is referred to. In the inscription of Vanamala it is stated that Prâlambha's brother was Arath (son of Arathi).

(2) Jivadevi was the queen of Pralambha and mother of Harjaravarman. In the Vanamala inscription she is named. Jivada.

in a silver pitcher, by the princes of noble birth.

At the Hāruppeswara camp (skandhāvāra) Parama Parameswara Parama Bhattaraka Parama Maheswara Sriman Harjaradeva, who meditates at the feet of his parents, is prospering. There his queen Mangalasri, (1) like Lakshmi, is shedding her beauty and her qualifications. Born of her womb, Prince, Vanamāla, who is bright like the full moon, without blemish, having the light of his sun-like father shed upon him and who is possessed of numerous virtues hereby commands: Let it be known to all of you-Maha-Sainyapati (Commander-in-Chief) Srigana, Maha-Dwaradhipati (Chief of the gate-keepers) Sri Jayadeva, Maha-Pratihara (Chief Usher) Janardan, Maha-Amatya (Chief Counsellor) Sri Govinda and Madhusudana, Brahmanadhikara (probably chief priest) Bhatta Srikantha * * * *

(1) In the Vanamala inscription she is named Sri Mattara which is evidently a mis-reading by Pandit Kamalakanta.

APPENDIX III

FIRST COPPER-PLATE INSCRIPTION OF DHARMAPALA VARMA DEVA.

Translation in English.

(Note-This translation is based on the decipherment of the plates by Pandit Padmanath Bhattacharya Vidyavinod.)

Salutation to the primeval *Deva, Ardha juvatiswara*, one side of whose neck is adorned by the blue lotus and the other side by the hooded snake; on one side of whose body is the raised breast of the woman and the other side is covered by ash; who is therefore the embodiment of both the *Sringāra* and the *Raudra rasas*.

There was a king named Naraka who was the son of Nārāyana in his Boar incarnation by the Prithivi (Earth). He ruled in the city of Prāgjyotisha for a long time after subduing all the lords of the various directions.

He had a powerful son named Bhagadatta whose feet were rubbed by the crowns of numerous kings and after fighting with whom even the the most powerful Bhima lost his consciousness.

In that dynasty of kings was born Sri Brahmapala who was like Indra and who was feared by his enemies and praised by those who knew the worth of virtues.

From him was born the gem of a son who was rightly named Sri Ratnapala, who was the conqueror of kings and from whose feet, adorned by the head-garlands of numerous kings, *rāja lakshmi* took her birth.

He had a son named Purandara Pāla who died as *juvarāja* after having produced a valiant, handsome and well-mannered son named Indrapāla.

That king Indrapāla ruled the Earth for a long time. He by his own power overcame all his enemies and satisfied Indra by performing numerous *yajnas*. He was the foremost among all who performed religious ceremonies. He was like the god Kāmadeva (Cupid) to to all women.

He had a son named Gopāla who was very powerful and was like the lamp of his family. During his life time he was the foremost of all valiant, virtuous, learned and liberal men.

From him was born Harshapala who was praised by all virtuous men and who was the favourite of the goddesses of learning and wealth.

The enemy elephants killed by him in battle appeased the thirst of the *Rākshasas* who drank the warm blood of the slain in the battle field.

That king had a queen of noble birth named Ratnā

who was pure and pious as if she was part and parcel of the moon.

Their son is Dharmapāla, the king of the world, bounded by the oceans, and the ornament of the three worlds. Although named Dharmapāla (defender of the faith) he is also at proper time the defender of both *Kāma* and *artha.* He is victorious in the battle field adorned by the garland made of the pearls strewn from the heads of the elephants killed in battle. Victory to that king named Dharmapāla who is the paramount king of the earth, the protector of all who have sought his protection, who is the conqueror of all enemeies and whose fame is known throughout the world.

This inscription of king Sri Dharmapāla has been composed by the poet Prasthāna Kalasa who is expert in both prose and verse composition.

He who is famous by his sovereignty over the kingdom of Pragjyotisha, whose rule is unquestioned and subduer of all enemy parties, that *Vāraha Parameswara Parama Bhattāraka* Mahārājadhirāja Srimat Dharmapāla Deva who meditates at the feet of Parameswara Parama Bhattāraka Mahārājādhirājā Srimat Harshapāla Varma Deva.

The king sends his respectful greetings and commands to all and several living in the locality known as Subhankara Pātaka Kanjia bhiti, viz. the district revenue officers, lawyers, as well as to the Rājas, Rājnis, Rānakas, Rāja-putras, Rāja Vallabhas and all who live there now and in future. Be it known to all that this land together with homestead lands, water, mines, cattle pastures, etc. and freed from all worries due to fastening of elephants and boats, searching for thieves, inflicting of punishments, pasturing of elephants, cattle, buffaloes, camels, goats, etc. have been donated as set forth in this charter.

In Sravasti there is a village named Krosanja which is free from the sins of the Kali age as it is full of smoke caused by the performance of *Yajnas.*

In that village was born Rāmadeva who was the chief among the Brahmans who were learned in the vedas.

He had a son named Bharat who was like Sakya (Buddha) self-controlled, who was the foremost among the learned and virtuous and who was skilled in all the six *karmas* enjoined for Brahmans.

His wife was Pāuka who like Rohini to Chandra and Pārvati to Mahādeva was of very good character and possessed of many virtues.

Their beloved son is Himānga who is expert in archery and a charioteer who can pierce the formation of the opposing army and accomplish other difficult tasks.

To him the king, in the third year of his reign, hereby gives the lands, known as Subhankara Pātaka included in Olinda an Kanjiā bhit, which may produce 6000 dons of paddy.

To his brother Trilochan the king donates lands sufficient to produce 2000 dons of paddy out of the same area.

(Here follow the boundaries of the two areas given to the two brothers.)

Seal

Swasti Prāgjyotishadhipati Mahārājadhirāja Sri Dharmapala Varma Deva.

APPENDIX IV.

SECOND COPPER-PLATE INSCRIPTION OF DHARMAPALA

Translation in English.

(Note-This translation is based on the decipherment of the plates by the late Pandit Hem Chandra Gossain).

Victory to the God Vishnu who assumed the shape

of a boar, by whose tusk, while the earth was lifted, the mountains were thrown into the air, whose hoofs pugged the mire of the nether world (Pātāla), whose breath put even the severe gale of the time of the destruction of the world to shade and drained the waters of the four oceans and again replenished them.

There was a king named Naraka who was the son of Vishnu by the Goddess of Earth. From him was born Bhagadatta whose feet were kissed by the vassal-kings.

In that great dynasty – the repository of high politics – were born Brahmapāla and other great kings. Who can fully describe their great virtues? Our tongue is only one and not a thousand, to find suitable words our intellect also fails.

In that family was born a virtuous king named Sri Gopāla. The fire of his power burned the forests of enemies. His virtues like the *amrita* of heaven caused the froth and foam of the heavenly river Mandakini.

That famous and powerful king had a queen named Nayanā. Their son was Sri Harshapāla who was the lamp of the Pāla family and well-known in the three worlds.

His son is Dharmapāla. His charming virtues are known throughout the world and his heart is dedicated only to *Dharma.* In his mouth always resided both Bhagavati and Saraswati.

Oh future kings, listen to this prayer of Dharmapāla. The glory of sovereignty is uncertain like the flash of lightning and is therefore to be shunned but *Dharma*, the root of eternal bliss is never to be given up.

Raja Sri Dharmapāla, the sun of the Pāla dynasty, the chief of the circle of poets and the mine of all the gems of virtues has composed this charter.

Swasti. Sri Vārāha Parameswara Parmaa bhattāraka Mahārājadhirāja Srimat Dharmapāla varma Deva, who is famous by his sovereignty over Pragjyotisha.

(Here follows the usual proclamation in the charter

addressed to all residents in or in the vicinity of the donated land.)

There is a village named Khyātipali which is like a religious temple, and which is ornamented by good Brahmans.

In that village, where the smoke arising from the numerous *homs* performed overcast the sky, the peacocks, mistaking the smoke for clouds, in the rainy season, began to dance. The sound caused by the reading of the four Vedas by the Brahmans in that village is like the sound of ripples in the junction of the Ganga and the Yamuna.

(Here follows the genealogy of Madhusudan, the donee, a resident of Khyātipali.)

Dharmapāla is a properly named king reigning in Kamarupanagar. Raja Sri Dharmapāla has by this charter granted lands in Digdol Guheswar, sufficient to produce ten thousand dons of paddy, to the virtuous Madhusudan. This portion of the charter has been composed by Sri Aniruddha who is anxious to earn merit by recounting the virtues of the highborn men. The copper-plates have been incised by the engraver Sri Vinita.

(Here follows the boundaries of the donated land).

ADDENDA AND CORRIGENDA.

ADDENDA.

Page 27 lines 18-20.

According to tradition Ghatakasur had his capital on or near the Sarania hill close to Gauhati town. When the top of this hill was cleared in 1917-18, two big stone-slabs, with lotuses cut in each, were found besides scattered broken bricks and a figure of Ganeśa on all sides of which are mystic diagrams cut into the rock.

To the north-east of the hill is the site of an ancient ruined city, about a square mile in area which seems to have been inlaid throughout with bricks about 3 ft deep. The Archaeological Deparment, in 1918-19, expressed inability to undertake exploration of the site "within visible time". It is needless to state that till now (1933) no exploration has been undertaken.

Page 50 and footnote.

The five Damodarpur inscriptions edited by Mr. R.G Basak in the *Epigraphia Indica* vol xv would indicate that Gupta rule over Pundravardhana continued till the first half of the sixth century but such sovereignty was really nominal and Mr. Basak admits that the overthrow of the Gupta power was completed by the invasion of Yasodharman. It seems that after Yasodharman had crushed the Gupta power in eastern India the Kamarupa king of the time, very probably Mahābhutavarman who reigned till about 540 A.D., brought the whole or at least the northern half of the Pundravardhana *bhukti* within Kamarupa. The last of the Damodarpur plates is dated 533-34A.D. The Chandrapuri *Vishaya*, which extended as far as the Kosi river, was evidently within the northern half of Pundravardhana. That explains how Mahābhutavarman could grant lands within this *vishaya* about the second quarter of the sixth century.

Page 51-

It appears that Dr. Bhandarkar in his latest contribution on the subject of the Nagar Brahmans (Indian Antiquary, Vol. LXI, 1932) has accepted the suggestion that the lands granted by Mahābhutavarman were situated within the modern district of Sylhet, because the Nidhanpur plates were found in that district. The Brahmans and Kayasthas of Sylhet claim their origin from Mithila. It is from Mithila-Kamarupa that they originally immigrated into Tippera and Sylhet. When

Mahābhutavarman made his grant the donees were living in the eastern part of Mithila, on the banks of the Kosi, which was then within Kamarupa It is very probable that subsequently the descendants of some of these donees migrated to Sylhet and took the copper-plates with them as these were, not doubt, treasured as heir-looms. Dr. Bhandarkar has gone further and assumed that the temple of "Hātaka Sulin" repaired or re-built by Vanamālavarman in the ninth century A.D. was the temple of Hātakeswara Siva in Sylhet. His supposition that Sylhet continued to be within Kāmarupa from the sixth till the ninth century may be correct, but he appears to be somewhat inconsistent. He regards Sylhet as "a part of old Bengal" and at the same time assumes that it was within Kāmarupa for at least 400 years and that a temple in that district was repaired by a king of Kāmarupa who had his capital in modern Tezpur. The very mention of the Sapādalaksha Brahmans in the *Karatoyā māhātmya*, as pointed out by he learned doctor himself, indicates that the country to the west of the Karatoyā i.e. between the Kausika and the Karatoyā (Mithila-Kamarupa) was the place of the original settlement of the Nagar Brahmans in eastern India.

Page 68 lines 18-20.

Mr. Prabhash Chandra Sen in his monograph on "Mahāsthan and its environs" writes that Vārendra or Bengal to the north of the Ganges was annexed to Kāmarupa after Bhāskaravarman's victory over Saśānka.

Page 72, lines 3-5-

Mr. Bhattasali has attempted to identify Deva varman, mentioned by the Korean priest, with a king of Samatata but his arguments do not seem to be convincing.

Page 93, lines 27-28-

Dr. Bhandarkar's theory that the Bengali Kayasthas

were originally Nagar Brahmans, who in Guzerat have been degraded to the caste known as *Bania*, has been contested by Bengali scholars, particularly by Babu Nagendranath Basu.

Page 113, lines 15-20.

R.D.Banerji in his "Palas of Bengal" writes that Sri Harahavarman must have held Bengal sufficiently long so as to enable him to pass through that country and conquer Orissa, Kalinga and Kośala.

Page 114, lines 13-15.

On this point reference may by made to Sylvain Levi's contribution "King Subhakara of Orissa" published in Epigraphia India Vol. XV pages 363-64.

Page 158, line 8.

There are at present many Siva temples within the modern district of Kamrup. These can be broadly divided into two classes, viz., (1) those where the *bhog* or daily offering to the God is *nirâmish* i.e. cooked victuals consisting of rice and vegetables and (2) those in which the *bhog* is *âmish* i.e. victuals consisting of meat and fish. Now the presiding deity of the Siva temple where *âmish bhog* is offered is invariably the *Ardha-Nâriswara* Siva whose worship is conducted according to Tantrik rites. The first copper-plate inscription of Dharmapāla, recorded in the third year of his reign, begins with the adoration of the *Adi Deva* (primeval deity) *Ardha Juvatiswara* (*Ardha Nâriswara*). The story of the origin of *Ardha-Nâriswara* is given in the Kalika Purana which was probably compiled in Kāmarupa about this time. This is another indication of the fact that Dharmapāla and his predecessors of the dynasty of Brahmapāla were the votaries of Tantrikism. It is very probable that the temples of *Ardha-Nâriswara* Siva were founded by these kings and that the Siva temples where *nirâmahis bhog* is still given are of older orgin.

Page 173, lines 11-14.

It is to be noted that the first batch of British officers administering the province of Assam, in the early part of the last century, were struck by the abundance of the architectural remains then existing. Some of them, particularly Westmacott, Hannay and Dalton described these ruins in the Journal of the Asiatic Society of Bengal. As photography was then unknown these officers laboriously executed drawings of some of these remains and published them. The "Description of Ancient Temples and Ruins at Chardwar" by Capt. Westmacott published in the J.A.S.B. for 1835, "Brief Notice of the Silsako or Stone Bridge in Zillah Kamrup" by Major Hannay published in the J.A.S.B. for 1851 and "Notes on Assam Temple Ruins" by Capt. Dalton published in the J.A.S.B. for 1855 are worthy of mention in this connection.

Page 193, lines 6-11.

Dharmapāla, by his first inscription, donated lands to two Brahmans of Krosanja within Sravasti. Pandit Vidyavinod locates this Sravasti in the extreme western part of Kāmarupa. Himanga, one of the two donees, appears to have been a prominent military commander under Dharmapāla. It would therefore appear that during the reign of Dharmapāla the extreme western part of Kāmarupa was within his kingdom. Vidyavinod's theory that Dharmapāla ruled over the eastern part of Kāmarupa simultaneously with Tingyadeva and Vaidyadeva who ruled over western Kāmarupa is therefore untenable.

Pag 198, lines 18-21.

Our conjecture is supported by Mr. N.G. Majumdar in his "Inscriptions of Bengal" vol. III page 109 wherein he states that the mention in the plate of Vallabhadeva probably referred to the conflict with Vijayasena as related in his Deopara inscription.

Page.	Line.	Incorrect.	Correct.
33	4	mangnificent	magnificent
47	31	Chadrapuri	Chandrapuri.
61	19	Rājavardhana	Rājyavardhana.
96	24	an	are
144	6	prabably	probably
166	5 (of footnote)	shool	school
173	16	authoriry	authority
196	14	1250 A.D.	1150 A.D.
236	5	pespatched	despatched.
256	18	Sācharuchand	Suchāruchand

INDEX.

C.

D.

W..

Y.

Z.